D0364174

Running for Their Lives

Running for Their Lives

The Extraordinary Story of Britain's Greatest Distance Runners

Mark Whitaker

YELLOW JERSEY PRESS
LONDON

Published by Yellow Jersey Press 2012

2 4 6 8 10 9 7 5 3 1

First published in Great Britain in 2012 by
Yellow Jersey Press
Random House, 20 Vauxhall Bridge Road,
London SW1V 2SA

www.rbooks.co.uk

Addresses for companies within The Random House Group Limited can be found at:
www.randomhouse.co.uk/offices.htm

The Random House Group Limited Reg. No. 954009

A CIP catalogue record for this book
is available from the British Library

ISBN 9780224082587

The Random House Group Limited supports The Forest Stewardship Council
(FSC®), the leading international forest certification organisation. Our books
carrying the FSC label are printed on FSC® certified paper. FSC is the only forest
certification scheme endorsed by the leading environmental organisations, including
Greenpeace. Our paper procurement policy can be found at
www.randomhouse.co.uk/environment

Typeset in Minion by Palimpsest Book Production Limited,
Falkirk, Stirlingshire
Printed and bound by
CPI Group (UK) Ltd, Croydon, CR0 4YY

for Lynn
and for Gabriel, Jonah and Leah

Contents

List of Illustrations

Plate 1

Prologue: Los Angeles, 1928

It is mid-February 1928, at an Art Deco speedway stadium on the eastern edge of Los Angeles, and it is raining. In the centre of the track are several large marquees. The flags of various countries and of different US states fly over them. From early in the morning groups of men – mostly in their twenties and thirties, th'ough some are middle-aged and a handful are still in their teens – run slowly and relentlessly around the cinder track, lap after lap after lap. A casual visitor observing the daily routine of these men might have thought they were the inmates of some kind of punitive camp. They all got up at 6 a.m. They ran until lunch was provided at noon. Then they ran again. Dinner was at six. Lights out at nine.

But if these men were prisoners, it was only of their own obsessions or their desperate need. They had come from every corner of the United States and Canada. They had come from Australia, England, South Africa, France, Russia, Finland, Germany, Hungary, Estonia . . . all responding to an advertisement that had appeared in newspapers across the world the previous autumn. This is what it offered: 'International

Transcontinental Foot Race. Open to any physically fit male athlete in the world. Route of the race will be over US Highway 66 between Los Angeles and Chicago. Route between Chicago and New York will be announced later.' The winner, the advertisement specified, would get $25,000; second place would be worth $10,000, and considerably smaller prizes were on offer to runners who finished in the first fifteen. For the rest, nothing.

The men who responded to this bizarre and unprecedented offer had to pay a $25 entry fee, and they had to agree to arrive in Los Angeles three weeks before the race was due to start on 4th March – so that a medical team could assess whether they were up to what the event's promoters fetchingly called 'the long grind'. What was facing these men, once they crossed the starting line in LA, was the prospect of running an average of more than forty miles a day, *every* day, for nearly three months. They would have to cross mountains and deserts, to run in snow, in rain, in sandstorms and in blistering heat. Those who made it to New York would have covered nearly 3,500 miles.

The medics on hand at the speedway stadium were not optimistic that many would. After the race was over, they went public with the assessment they had made of the 199 competitors before it began:

In the entire group not over forty appeared capable of withstanding strenuous athletic competition. Six runners were found to be suffering from acute respiratory infections, nine had gastrointestinal symptoms. One runner had signs of active pleurisy, four had chronic bronchitis, eleven had moderate emphysema. Approximately 50% of all competitors were underdeveloped physically and could scarcely be compared with long distance runners usually seen in universities or athletic clubs.

They could not be compared, that is, with the gilded amateur elite who ran for Harvard, Yale or Stanford – the sort of men who had represented the USA at the Paris Olympics of 1924 and who were, in the early spring of 1928, preparing to do so again at the forthcoming Amsterdam Games.

The men at the speedway stadium were already, or were about to become, professional runners. They were doing it – as, ironically, the original Greek Olympians had done it – for the money; not for any privileged notion that sport was an ennobling human activity. There was a handful of serious, and seriously good, runners. Some had taken part in Olympic marathons, some held amateur or professional world road-running records at distances from 50 to 1,000 miles. But the very idea of a non-stop transcontinental run was so extra-ordinary, somehow so unconnected to the normal expectations of athletics, that no one seemed sure what qualities might be needed to succeed in it. Stamina certainly, but perhaps above all a capacity to withstand both pain and boredom. The official race programme provides a clue to the bizarre pool of experi-ence and fantasy that was collected together during that uncommonly wet and cold Los Angeles February. There was Golden Calkin, 'a cowboy from Oklahoma who has received many hard knocks in "bronco-busting" and has a good past on the football and baseball fields; this is his first try at distance running'. There was Charles Gallena from Miami Beach in Florida, who 'possesses the remarkable feat of skipping 11,000 times standing in one place'. There was the German Fred

Kamler, who 'has many great swimming records, and this will be his first start on land'. There was fifty-two-year-old William Nagel, 'a rural letter carrier from Alabama who thinks he knows how to cover the ground', while another German, George Rehayn, was introduced succinctly as 'a good bicycle rider and a vegetarian'. But alongside these were the likes of the Estonian Juri Lossman, the silver medallist from the 1924 Olympic marathon, and the Californian Eugene Estoppey, who held the world record over 1,000 miles.

The largest national group – other than Americans – came from Finland. Many of the contingent were resident in the US, and there was a thriving Finnish-American Running Association. One of its members on the starting line for the Transcontinental was Arne Souminen, a doctor based in Detroit; and he gave a disarming answer when asked by a journalist why so many of his countrymen were there. 'We're a queer lot, we Finns. We run because we don't know any better. There's nothing else to do in our country. If we ever started thinking, we'd quit running. A man with too much imagination can't stand punishment.' The Finns shared a tent with the Scandinavians. There were separate ones for the Germans, the French and the Italians. And it says much about the possible political significance of the race that there were also tents for what would now be called Native American and African American competitors. In 1928 terminology they were, of course, 'Indians' and 'Negroes'. But while they slept and ate separately, they competed on equal terms. The 'Indians' had already established something of a national reputation for ultra-distance running, and Nick Quamawahu – from the Hopi tribe in Arizona – was one of the pre-race favourites. The 'Negroes' were largely an unknown quantity. They were to be lionised when the caravan passed through black neighbourhoods on the long road east; and they were to be spat at and physically threatened in Texas by Ku Klux Klan gangs, who awaited them on lonely stretches of highway.

The English entrants found themselves thrown in with the Canadians and Australians, and it was in this British imperial atmosphere that a fateful meeting took place between two of the Transcontinental competitors. One of them – both to himself and to everybody else – was the overwhelming favourite to collect the winner's cheque, even though he was one of the oldest men there. He was of medium height, thin, straight-backed and sporting a neatly clipped moustache. With his round, thin-framed spectacles and his ever-present pipe, he looked more like a bookish and rather strict schoolmaster than a long-distance runner. Arthur Newton had entered the race under the joint colours of Natal and Rhodesia, but these colonial territories were seemingly too obscure for the organisers, and the official programme had him down as representing South Africa. Otherwise it described him accurately enough: 'the holder of every amateur running record from 29 to 100 miles, he is 44 years old and was passed up for the last two Olympic Games because the 26 mile Marathon is too short for him'.

The extraordinary thing about Arthur Newton was that all his records, which he had set in South Africa, in Rhodesia and in England, had been achieved in the previous four years – that's to say, since his fortieth birthday. Before that he was unknown to the athletic world. He had been born in Weston-super-Mare, the fifth of eight children, and then brought up in Brighton. His father was a Nonconformist minister, and the family, though not rich, was sufficiently well off for Arthur

5

and his brothers to be educated privately. He was sent, briefly, to Bedford and then to the smaller Banham School in Norfolk. He became a competent pianist and developed a taste for both literature and philosophy. He also enjoyed cross-country running, and had an obvious talent for it. But he was somehow unfocused and lacking in ambition, and when he left school he had no clear idea of what he wanted to do in life. His two elder brothers had both gone off to South Africa and in 1902, when the rootless Arthur was nineteen and the Second Boer War had just been concluded, his father arranged for him to follow them. By the time he left Africa in November 1927, less than three months before his arrival in Los Angeles, Arthur Newton had become both famous and infamous. Famous because of his running; infamous because of why he had taken it up and pursued it so single-mindedly. He was undoubtedly the only entrant in the Transcontinental race who had started running to make a political point.

His fateful encounter in that Los Angeles marquee was with a small, slight, dark-haired man who moved with the grace of a dancer. He was, at just twenty-two, half Newton's age, and his surname suggested that he should really be bedding down with the Italians. But Peter Gavuzzi was as English as the south London twang to his speech. He'd been born in Folkestone to an immigrant Italian father and a French mother. The former was a sought-after chef, and he'd met his chamber-maid wife while cooking at an upmarket Mayfair hotel. The surname is rare even in Italy. The country's telephone directories list only forty-one Gavuzzis, with twenty-five of them being found in Turin, the capital of Piedmont. The name originated in the early Middle Ages in a small cluster of villages to the south-east of Turin – Monticello, Alba and Santa

Vittoria. The villages are in the valley of the River Tanaro, where the low hills are covered in vines and groves of hazelnut. The vermouth Cinzano is a local product. That there are virtually no Gavuzzis now living in the valley says much about the hardships of nineteenth-century life on the land and the consequent flight to the city.

Peter Gavuzzi's father, Battista, grew up in Monticello and it was from there, in the late 1890s, that he and his brother Pietro took the brave and (within the extended family) unprecedented step of emigrating to England. Whether they had contacts there we do not know, but they certainly had a skill that was in demand and they had little difficulty in establishing themselves in London. Pietro set up his own West End restaurant, and it is indicative of the nature of its clientele that in 1904 he was asked to become the chef at one of the Empire's most prestigious hotels: the Grand in Bulawayo. When he returned to London he found that his brother Battista had married and had become the chef at a famous Folkestone hotel. It was there in 1905 that Battista's second son, also called Pietro, was born. Not long afterwards the family moved back to London, where there was a vibrant Italian community of more than 10,000 centred on Clerkenwell. It was soon to spill over into Soho, where it continued its domination of the West End's restaurant trade. At some stage in his childhood the young Pietro anglicised his name, and it was as a teenaged Peter Gavuzzi that he pursued his first ambition of becoming a jockey. But he grew too tall and followed his parents into the hospitality industry, getting a job as a steward on transatlantic liners. It was in killing his boredom on the seas by running round and round the decks of grand White Star boats that Gavuzzi first discovered his remarkable skill; and his love of the solitude of running.

When Newton and Gavuzzi were first introduced to each other in Los Angeles in February 1928 the older man addressed the younger by his first name. This was natural enough; even in those more formal times there was a natural camaraderie among runners. But when Gavuzzi responded in kind, perhaps saying something like 'It's an honour to meet you, Arthur', he was firmly put in his place. As far as Newton was concerned, both his age and his class made such familiarity impossible. He told Gavuzzi in no uncertain terms that he must always address him as 'Mr Newton'. And throughout their long subsequent partnership, and a friendship that lasted until Newton's death, Peter Gavuzzi honoured this. For years his conversation, his letters and his diaries were to be full of references to 'my friend Mr Newton'.

Newton and Gavuzzi were to get to know and admire one another, as runners and as men, on that endless painful slog across America in the spring and early summer of 1928. They were to team up the following year when the Transcontinental was staged again, from east coast to west. They were then to establish a uniquely successful professional partnership in both the USA and Canada. They were to run in ultra-distance relays, in twenty-four-hour and six-day events; they were to run against teams of horses in American arenas, and in snow-shoes across the frozen wastes of Canada. They were to become briefly so famous that they were put on stage in both North America and Europe to run on treadmills and talk about their exploits. And years later – after the Second World War had separated them – they were to live not far from each other in suburban Middlesex, where 'Mr Newton's' bachelor home became a mecca for anyone in the world who was serious about running over seriously long distances. Their advice was never sought by the upper-class amateurs who controlled British athletics. But runners themselves knew better.

The story of Newton and Gavuzzi is one of an unlikely partnership set against the obsessions of an interwar culture that found endless fascination in things to do with distance and endurance. It is also the story of two very remarkable athletes – perhaps the greatest long-distance runners Britain has ever produced – whose professionalism at a time when amateurism ruled the roost has condemned them to an unjust obscurity. Their partnership and friendship crossed barriers of age, class and education: Arthur Newton was rarely without a dog-eared volume of Shakespeare, while Peter Gavuzzi's favourite reading was the racing press. Newton never married or had other close emotional ties with women, while Gavuzzi did marry (unhappily) and had other, if brief, sexual relationships. Yet for thirty years they expressed a deep affection and respect for each other, which was rooted in their shared experience of ultra-long-distance running. It was as though they both recognised in the other something that very few people had – an ability to feel fully alive only when they were running, and running, and running.

1

'A Chap Called Newton'

Running and Politics in South Africa

I

On 20th May 1956 a frail, almost blind Arthur Newton was the guest of honour at a small civic ceremony in the town of Harding in the South African province of Natal. It was his seventy-third birthday, and he had been asked to plant a tree in the Town Gardens. When he died just over three years later a commemorative stone was placed next to the tree. It carried the following inscription: 'This tree was planted by Mr Arthur F.H. Newton (Montabeni) on 20/5/56. He was a resident farmer of the District from 1910 to 1925.'

'Montabeni' was the name local Zulus had given to Newton. It translates roughly as 'Master of the Mountains'. The old runner, who had long been settled in the London suburbs, had dreamed for decades of an eventual return to South Africa. Yet, when the country's Marathon Runners' Club formally asked him to come out, entirely at their expense, Newton was reluctant to accept. By then he thought the time for South Africa had passed. He felt old and tired, and in any case he had never been entirely comfortable when he was the centre of attention. He had liked winning races, but had disliked the fuss made of him when he did. South Africa, though, was where he had made his closest friends, and where for a time he had got as near as he ever did to putting down some roots. So eventually he replied to the invitation to say that yes, he would go.

Newton's old friend Bill Payne had written to him spelling out what was being planned for his visit:

> You will be welcomed at the Harding Town Hall by the Chairman of the reception committee and many other residents of your acquaintance, after which we would like you to say a few words to the gathering of school children, who will be awaiting you in the Town Hall. A Luncheon will be held at the Southern Cross Hotel, where you will be the guest of the Harding Town Board, and possibly a few of your intimate Harding friends will be present. In the afternoon we hope to take you on a tour of the various sporting bodies, and in the evening there will be a social gathering at the Harding Town Hall. On Sunday we feel that you would prefer to be with your old acquaintances when you could perhaps visit farmer friends in the district.

No wonder Arthur Newton had been nervous about the trip. This was just the sort of hullabaloo he dreaded. It seemed that the whole of Harding's population, both old and young, was involved in welcoming him back; but just in case there were residents for whom the name Arthur Newton meant little or nothing, a local weekly, *Outspan*, had asked the elderly runner to write a piece for them explaining how he had first come to live in the area.

He explained that he had left school at eighteen and had had no particular career in mind, though teaching seemed a possibility. But this, for some reason, was not accepted by his clergyman father, who decided his son needed a taste of the Empire. 'He sent me out in January 1902 to South Africa to join my two elder brothers in Durban. On their advice I stuck to clerical work for a year or two but finally got fed up with it and turned to teaching, first at Hilton College and then at a school on Town Hill, Maritzburg.' This was Blenheim College, which – along with Hilton in Durban – was one of a handful of establishments in Natal that were attempting to replicate a British public-school education for the sons of the colonial elite. Whether Newton was employed on anything other than a temporary or part-time basis is unclear, but in any case his father was still intent on persuading him away from the classroom. 'In 1909 my father sent for me, saying that he could find me a good opening as an assistant tea planter in Ceylon. So back to England I went. But while on the water the offer fell through and on my arrival my father said that if I would wait a month or so he would get me a similar position.' Newton was now twenty-six years old, and any prospect of financial security must have been tempting, even if it meant accepting what his father wanted for him. But the attractions of Kingston-upon-Thames soon palled. 'Several weeks at home just idling around proved too much, and I told my father that I wanted to get back to South Africa. He said he had guessed as much, and perhaps I had better go. So back to Natal I was sent, and accepted a position as tutor on a farm near Harding.'

Two years later Newton became a farmer himself. The decision was an extraordinary gamble. He had no experience; he was on his own; and purchasing the land put him deeply in debt. His aim, he says in *Running in Three Continents*, the memoir he published in 1940, was simply 'to settle down for good and all'. 'I took up 1,350 acres of Crown Lands from the Union Government in 1911 and set to work to learn something entirely new to me. Farming is anything but an easy game for the recruit and I had a desperate struggle to make both ends meet. Assistance from home helped me to tide over the worst and at last there came a time when I had learnt enough to be able to get along on my own, with every prospect of complete success.'

Arthur Newton had a definite gift for friendship, but it could never match his passion for solitude. Someone who did not have what amounted to an addiction to being on his own could not have devoted so much of his life to ultra-distance running. So the isolation of his farm at Ihluku, near Harding, would have suited him down to the ground. The work was back-breaking, but he still found time, somewhat surprisingly, for playing the piano – particularly Beethoven's Sonatas – and reading deeply in philosophy. We know this from his neighbour and close friend, Bill Payne, with whom Newton also fought in the First World War. In May 1956, during the athlete's final valedictory tour of South Africa, Payne gave a speech in his honour before an audience of their old military comrades. 'I met Arthur Newton in 1910 when he was teaching in the Harding district . . . At our first meeting I realised that he was a man of my own peculiar wave-length, for not only was he an avid reader of books, a useful musician and a philosopher, but he was a cross-country runner and was possessed of a crisp and brittle sense of humour.' When Newton acquired his own farm, Payne mentioned, he also revealed that he was no mean hand at imaginative DIY. 'He had made himself a windmill from four gum-tree poles, a lot of sheets of corrugated iron, lengths of fencing wire and odds and ends of ironmongery.' But home-grown feats of engineering were not the most important reason why Bill Payne went to considerable trouble to seek out Arthur Newton's company: 'When Tom was Laird of Lovat, his farm in that wild but beautiful area on the southern heights of the Umzimkulu River, I used to visit him. In those far-off days there was no nonsense about visits: there was no getting into a car and being driven there. No Sir! I used to pack a ruck-sack, put it on my shoulders and walk from our farm, Burnside, and slog along the 25 miles that lay between us. And how well worth was the effort! For at the end of the trek there was always Arthur Newton with his kindness and hospitality and philosophic talk.' Payne was the only person outside Newton's immediate family to be allowed to use the nickname 'Tom'.

But then, in September 1914, Newton was obliged to put his farm work on indefinite hold. 'Germany saw fit to interrupt my designs' was how he described the outbreak of the First World War, and his immediate decision to join up:

I turned up at Pietermaritzburg and signed on as a trouper in the Natal Light Horse. I offered to take my motorcycle at my own expense, as I realised I was far more likely to be useful as a despatch rider than anything else, being a competent and experienced motor-cyclist. As there was no corps of this description yet formed, I had to engage for the ordinary three shillings a day and take my chance of being transferred to the proper department later on. Six months afterwards, when we returned from the Orange River, I joined the Motor Despatch Riders.

That is all his memoir says about his experience of the war. But his mention of the Orange River is significant in relation to his later political troubles in Natal – because it means that he was involved in the suppression of the 'Maritz Rebellion', in which South African troops from the Boer community sided with Germany in their desire to rid their country of British rule. Their rebellion took place near the border with German South-West Africa (present-day Namibia) and was quickly suppressed in October 1914. A decisive battle the following March at a ford over the Orange River led to the rapid conquest of all German-occupied territory in the south-west. Newton and his colleagues in the Natal Light Horse would then have headed north and east, in what was to turn out to be a long and ultimately futile attempt to defeat the German East African army.*

---

* The Natal Light Horse was commanded by one of the colony's more colourful characters, Lt Col J.R. Royston, known throughout Natal as 'Galloping Jack'. The historian of the South-West African Campaign, Gerald L'Ange, describes him as 'typical of what might be called the irregular officers produced by the British Empire in its colonies, and who had a penchant for raising their own units in time of war and naming them after themselves'. 'Natal Light Horse' was the name insisted on by General Smuts, the Commander-in-Chief of South African forces. The unit's leader had wanted it called 'Royston's Horse'.

II

Newton's return to his land in 1918 did not mean the end of fighting for the thirty-five-year-old farmer. It just meant the exchange of one enemy for another, as he returned to a situation that was tailor-made for misunderstanding and conflict. Like the majority of white settlers in Natal, Newton shared his land with a certain number of indigenous Zulus. The latter traditionally kept cattle, which of course required land on which to graze; and by the time Newton arrived in the Harding area it had been established in law that while Zulu cattle herders could not be expelled from the land, they *were* required to pay an annual rent. We know nothing about Newton's dealings with his resident Zulus before 1914, but it is important to recognise that he had only been on the land for three years at the most before going off to war, and he returned determined to convert a large part of his acreage from grazing to arable. He had become convinced that the best way for him to make money reasonably quickly was by cultivating cotton and tobacco; and for this he needed a labour force. No problem, he thought, for he had a resident one. But it did not seem to cross his mind that his Zulu tenants might object to changing the lifestyle of centuries, to substituting wage-labour in the fields for the age-old rhythms of cattle herding.

It is probably anachronistic to condemn Arthur Newton as a racist – after all, one of his closest friends and most admired rivals in later life was the black Canadian runner Philip Granville. But he simply could not comprehend that his Zulu tenants had no culture of 'work'; and he fell all too easily into using the white-settler cliché of condemning the South African black as 'lazy'. The cultural gulf between them was immense, and it was expressed most starkly in the way the two communities regarded land. For the Zulus, land was to be lived on; for white farmers like Arthur Newton it was to be grappled with and transformed. 'Only kafirs [Kaffirs, or black Africans] are content to live on a place without improving it, and I happened to be a white man,' he insisted in his 1940 memoir. He went on, 'If the white man wanted to be useful to the country he lived in, that was his concern, not theirs: his mere presence enabled them to live securely and indulge in an unending series of beer-drinks, and they asked for no more. The white man's work could go to Timbuktu before they would turn out and help.'

Nothing expressed the land's transformation as sharply and as noisily as the building of roads; and from Newton's descriptions, one can easily understand how his Zulu neighbours would have experienced it as an act of violence against them. The farm Newton bought outside Harding was ten miles from the nearest road, its only link to the outside world a handful of what he called 'dangerous' footpaths. But not for long:

Soon there were ten miles of good motor road to the main highway, and another four on the farm itself. This had been made with a road machine and gelignite, for many long escarpments had to be cut out of the sides of mountains. There had been the usual trouble of course: the kafirs objected to the road where it touched their farms and could not be made to realise that it enhanced the value of their land. Consequently the work was stopped more than once and it was only with the authority of the court that I was able to continue.

But it was over the question of cattle that the incompatibility between Arthur Newton and his Zulu tenants became most clear. It led to a crisis in relations between them that was in turn to lead to a stand-off between Newton – the English colonial – and the Union government in Pretoria, a government led by the Afrikaner descendants of Dutch settlers. The irony is inescapable in post-apartheid times, but Newton came to be convinced that a government of Boers put the interest of South African blacks before those of English settlers; and it was to publicise this that he decided, not far short of his fortieth year, to become an athlete. It was for reasons of politics that an obscure, if philosophically minded farmer in southern Natal transformed himself into the world's greatest distance runner.

East Coast Cattle Fever, known as 'Tick', was endemic in Natal, and a particularly bad epidemic of the disease was ravaging herds around Harding at the time that Newton began his farming adventure. The fever, potentially the most disastrous cattle disease in Central and East Africa, is caused by a parasite that is transmitted to cattle by three different varieties of tick; and it is estimated that even today one million cattle die from the disease each year in Africa. Nothing can be done to eradicate the ticks, so the question is how to protect the cattle. Vaccines are now undergoing trials, but until they become available – and affordable – the best method of control is, as it was in the 1910s, immersing the cattle in a chemical dip. Newton wrote that when he first took over the farm there were 123 head of 'kafir cattle' on his land, but that at the end of his first year there the number had been reduced by East Coast Fever to no more than a dozen. He decided to invest in a dipping tank: 'and therewith started trouble with the kafirs, trouble that would go on for all the rest of my time in the district'. The Zulus initially refused point-blank to bring their cattle for dipping, believing, according to Newton, 'that the white man was only trying to kill what stock they had left'. Then it struck him that he could use his ability to keep their cattle alive as a way of persuading his Zulu tenants to provide him with the thing he needed more than anything else – labour. Without people to work in the fields his ambitious plans for cotton and tobacco production would never get off the ground. He had tried the obvious route, offering to forgo any rent in exchange for the Zulus working for him for six months of the year, a strategy he thought would 'educate them to the value of decent labour'; but, hardly surprisingly, the Zulu herdsmen mistrusted anything that would change their relationship with the land, and they refused to become wage-labourers. Newton's next offer was more successful. 'There was one way to make sure of regular dipping that would at the same time supply the labour I required: I would cleanse their cattle only on a basis of labour in exchange. On this basis things now worked in very much better style and there wasn't half the trouble . . . each week I had about thirty women and children turning out for a day's work in the fields.' The men, needless to say, while accepting the benefits of having their cattle dipped, still regarded manual labour as beneath their dignity.

Newton began to speculate that the Harding area would soon see a vibrant and expanding economy based on both cotton and tobacco; and he suggested publicly that former soldiers who had fought for the Empire in southern Africa during the war should be given preferential access to government loans, so that they too could start clearing and planting on the Crown Lands that surrounded Ihluku. But larger political forces were at work in the Union of South Africa, and they would quickly put an end to any such optimism that

Newton might have had – forces that had decided that the land surrounding his farm was to become home to an increasing number of blacks rather than whites. The first inkling Newton himself had of this, he insisted, was when a new tank for dipping cattle suddenly appeared not far from his boundary fence. It had been put there and paid for, he soon found out, by the Department of Native Affairs; and its impact on Newton's hard-won deal with his Zulu tenants was, it seems, immediate and disastrous. If he wasn't going to dip their cattle any longer they were not going to provide him with any labour:

> Work on the farm had been going on as usual when I got pulled up with a sudden jolt: dipping day arrived and not a single animal turned up. From enquiries I learned that all cattle, private farms and Crown Lands alike (kafirs only, of course) were now supposed to be using the new tank, the charge being five shillings per kraal per annum whether they sent one beast or a hundred. So without a moment's notice the whole of my labour negotiations were wrecked.

It did not take Newton long to realise that the expense of a new dipping tank could not be justified if it were only to be used for the handful of cattle that his own Zulu tenants possessed. There was only one conclusion that he could come to: 'All the way through I seem to have been kept as much in the dark as possible lest I should give an untimely exposure to the designs of the officials who, without authority from Parliament, were going to make a "black area", a place where only kafirs might own land or reside.'

One can date the first beginnings of what soon became known in much of South Africa as 'the Newton Case' to a letter that the owner of Ihluku farm sent to the *Times of Natal* at the end of September 1922. It was published under the heading 'Native Areas'. Newton said he was going to use the example of a particular 'improved' freehold farm of some 1,400 acres to expose why the 'proposed Native Areas' were 'responsible for a very sorry state of affairs'. 'A few years ago 50 acres of cotton were grown annually on this farm: today there is not one acre. Kraals from Cape Colony and elsewhere are arriving and settling on the surrounding Crown Lands, and all kafir stock are allowed free grazing all the year round. These kafirs consequently have no need to work for a living, and labour is as a result almost unobtainable. So cotton culture, which is dependent on labour, has ceased.' He said that as a result his farm, despite all the work he had put into it, had become worthless, 'as no European wishes to live with a belt of five miles of "black area" all around him'.

Two months later, the *Natal Witness* reported on a meeting of the Dundee District Farmers' Association, where a discussion had been triggered by its receipt of a letter from Arthur Newton, 'pointing out the ruination of his farm'. A Mr Stein complained that 'natives from other provinces were steadily being squeezed in, and Natal was being made a black province'. This is quite clearly what Newton himself believed. He was convinced there was a larger politics in the new Union of South Africa that was intentionally undermining his attempt to become a successful cotton farmer in the deep south of Natal. It was this conviction that led to his bizarre decision to become an athlete.

III

In July 1915 General Jan Smuts was in command of imperial forces that conquered German South-West Africa. He described it as 'the first achievement of a united South African nation, in which the races have combined all their best and most virile characteristics.' By 'the races' he did not mean white and black; he meant English and Boer. The two decades that Arthur Newton spent trying to establish himself in South Africa were decades in which an Afrikaner-dominated country tried to come to terms with the fact that Britain had won the Boer War of 1899–1902. The formerly independent Afrikaner republics had become part of the British Empire – and this was something that many an Afrikaans-speaker found hard to stomach. But British rule was problematic in that there were precious few Britons actually living in South Africa, and it was only in the relatively small Cape Colony and in the province of Natal that English-speaking white immigrants outnumbered the Dutch. So for the British government in London there was an urgent need to try and populate the vast spaces of the veldt with as many settlers as possible. Sir Alfred Milner had been High Commissioner in South Africa at the end of the Boer War, and he had regarded the encouragement of British immigration there as one of his most urgent responsibilities. Milner, according to the historian Leonard Thompson, 'planned to rule the former republics autocratically, without popular participation, until he had denationalised the Afrikaner and swamped them with British settlers . . . He planned the anglicised former republics should join the Cape Colony and Natal in a self-governing dominion that would be a source of economic as well as political strength to Britain.' Immediately after the end of the war a scheme was announced that offered generous subsidies to British people who wanted to settle in South Africa. The uptake was paltry, but – though he never mentioned it – it seems likely that one of those who did accept the financial help was nineteen-year-old Arthur Newton.

The Natal that Newton arrived in was a complex and uneasy place. The single most important thing that distinguished it as a province – and set it apart from its majority-Afrikaner neighbours – was the ratio of white to black in the population. Whereas in South Africa as a whole there were approximately four blacks to each white, in Natal the ratio was ten to one. This led to a distinct atmosphere of white paranoia. There was also, especially in Durban, a steadily growing Indian community – but the whites tended to regard them more with disdain than fear. Natal's English population felt vulnerable, and isolated: and they knew they could not bank on help from the Boers of the Orange Free State or the Transvaal. Shula Marks, Britain's leading expert on the province in the early twentieth century, believes that 'the tightly knit nature of white Natal, the free mingling of officials and settlers, of farmers, shopkeepers and artisans led to a high degree of uniformity and conformity of opinion on most issues; and to stereotypes being formed of the other racial groups'. The stereotype of the black African was of his violence. Marks has also written of the 'pathetically small white population of Natal [whose] psychological security depended on the unquestioning acceptance of their superiority by the Africans'. But a sure sign that they felt they could not depend on that came in 1903, the year after Newton's arrival in Durban, when Natal's government passed a new Militia Act, introducing compulsory conscription for white males. And it was not long before the Militia Act was put to the test. In September 1905 a new Poll Tax was introduced, and it was as rigorously collected as it was deeply resented by Natal's Africans. Rumours of possible black uprisings intensified; so too did white paranoia.

Then on 9th February the next year a party of around thirty armed Africans attacked and killed two policemen near the town of Richmond. The response from the provincial capital of Maritzburg was immediate and brutal. Martial law was declared, and the Natal Militia was deployed in central and southern districts of the province. This is how Shula Marks describes the militia's behaviour: 'For the next six weeks the troops marched through the lands of Africans reported to be defiant or restless, burning crops and kraals, confiscating cattle, and deposing chiefs. On March 31 twelve of the participants in the Richmond affray with the police were shot by drumhead court martial.' It was, it seems fair to say, a questionably appropriate or wise response; and the Colonial Office in London communicated its unease at the severity of the crackdown. They were probably right to do so, for during the spring and early summer of 1906 the conflict in Natal spread and escalated. In the western hills a force raised by the prominent Zulu leader Chief Bambatha continually exposed the white militiamen's lack of expertise in that difficult terrain – so much so that in June their commanding officer, Colonel Duncan MacKenzie, mounted a full-frontal assault on Bambatha's stronghold. The chief was killed and beheaded. The rebellion, it seemed, had been crushed – at an estimated cost of twenty-four white lives and more than 3,500 African ones. Although he never specifically mentions the events of 1906, it is clear that Arthur Newton was actively involved in them. Looking back, years later, on his dispute with the South African government, he says he had expected better treatment as someone who had 'on two occasions' fought for his country. Obviously one was the First World War; the other can only have been in the suppression of the Natal uprising of 1906.*

However, the death of Chief Bambatha, and the subsequent lifting of martial law in September, did not stop the violence. African anger went too deep; so did a white desire for retribution and revenge. It became clear during 1907 – when another important chief, Dinizulu, was accused of fermenting rebellion – that Natal's minority white population had come to the conclusion that their militia was inadequate in itself to protect their interests and, most importantly, their land. What can only be called a systematic attempt to terrorise Natal's Africans into quiescent deference was embarked upon. Its most important weapon was the whip – that everyday tool of racial degradation in so many parts of the British Empire. While in all the other South African provinces any sentences handed down that involved flogging had to be referred to a Supreme Court judge, that was not the case in Natal: and even the white press in the province was appalled at the tidal wave of flogging that spread across the province. The *Times of Natal* reported that during the disturbances of 1906–7 a total of 4,700 sentences of flogging had been carried out, and calculated that 700 Africans had had their backs 'lashed to ribbons'.

But this reign of what has been called 'legalised brutality'

---

* Another participant, in a very different capacity, was an Indian lawyer from Durban by the name of M.K. Gandhi. With the rank of Sergeant-Major, he led a team of twenty-five stretcher-bearers gathering the dead and wounded from the battlefields. The cost of the unit was covered by the Natal Indian Congress, and it was Gandhi himself who had made the offer of assistance to the governor of the province.

was ultimately self-defeating for the English elite of Natal. It revealed (both to the Colonial Office in London and to South Africa's Afrikaner leaders) that if they could only maintain control of their province through fear and intimidation, then they risked inciting a black backlash that could threaten the position of the white man in South Africa as a whole, both English and Dutch. Indeed in 1907 the leaders of the Transvaal offered assistance to their counterparts in Natal to help maintain 'the unity of the white races'. As Leonard Thompson has put it: 'The result was that whites in Natal were unsure of their capacity to control a distinct state, whereas whites in other colonies feared the consequences if Natal was left to its own devices.' It was a political logic that led in 1910 to the creation of the Union of South Africa, and to the dilution of English Natal in a larger polity in which the majority of whites were Afrikaners. This meant that when Arthur Newton came to feel victimised by government, it was to Pretoria and not to Maritzburg that he would have to turn for redress.

Newton's decision to try his hand at farming coincided precisely with the formation of the Union – and questions of land ownership were inevitably at the heart of the new government's commitment to establishing a strict separation between black and white. This was essential, the argument went, for white Englishmen and white Boers to feel that what they had in common was more important than what separated them. South Africa was in a truly bizarre political situation. It was subservient to the needs and requirements of the British Empire, yet – as the imperial historian Robert Holland has written – it was 'a society in which Britain had recently been at war with a large part of the European population'. And it seems fair to say that the Colonial Office in London quickly realised that it would only be able to rely on *Afrikaner* loyalty if the Union was premised on *Afrikaner* ideas about the necessary separation of black and white. So the first really significant piece of legislation of the new Union government was the Native Land Act of 1913. In setting out its stall, as it were, it was finally putting into practice the recommendations of the landmark Native Affairs Commission, which had concluded in 1905 that 'it will be far more difficult to preserve the absolutely necessary political and social distinctions if the growth of a mixed rural population of landowners is not discouraged'.

The Act established Native Areas, outside which blacks could neither buy nor rent land; equally, whites were barred from selling to blacks in their areas. The black enclaves amounted to roughly twenty-two million acres – 7 per cent of South Africa's land for 75 per cent of its population; and the expectation was that by starving Africans of land they would have no choice but to offer themselves as farm labour to white settlers – a chronic shortage of labour being the single biggest impediment to the development of South African agriculture. Government officials toured the countryside telling white farmers to expel their black tenants. They did so. Francis Wilson, the historian of South African farming, has described the immediate effect of the 1913 Act as being 'to uproot hundreds of black South Africans from white-owned farms and to send them wandering round the roads of the country seeking a new place to live'. The real zealot in the government for separating white from black was the Minister for Native Affairs, J.B.M. Hertzog, the man who, as Prime Minister in the mid-1920s, was to become Arthur Newton's sworn enemy. Hertzog had joined the Union government reluctantly, such was his gut antagonism to the British Empire and all things English; and it was his response to the expectation that white South Africans – Dutch as much as English – would fight for the Empire in the First World War that revealed how stark was the ethnic fault-line running through European South Africa. Just before war broke out in 1914 Hertzog had founded a new National Party, whose stated purpose was the protection of the economic interests of Afrikaners and the celebration of their distinct culture.

Where the complex Jan Smuts – a philosopher as much as a soldier or a politician – agonised over how to fashion a self-governing white nation in South Africa within the framework of the British Empire, Hertzog took a simpler and more confrontational position. To him, South Africa was an Afrikaner country that happened to be going through a period in which its destiny was regrettably tied up with that of the British Empire. That would pass. In the meantime, in so far as this was possible in time of war, the country should be ruled in the interests of the (white) Afrikaner majority. English settlers, especially in Natal, were dismissed by Hertzog as 'fortune-seekers'. They were interlopers. In a 1912 article he had spelt this out: 'Only one person has the right to be "boss" in South Africa, namely the Afrikaner. The people have become conscious of themselves as a nation. They feel their own power, they have reached nation manhood and they feel that Afrikaners and not strangers should rule the country.' 'Strangers' of course was code for the English – men like Arthur Newton, who in 1914 found himself, as a member of the Natal Light Horse, fighting to push the Germans out of South-West Africa, while Hertzog was involved in Boer efforts to undermine the imperial war effort.

The war made Smuts into an international figure. He was put in command of the Empire's forces in East Africa; he served on the Imperial War Cabinet in London; and after the end of hostilities he was asked to go to Versailles for the discussions that led to the formation of the League of Nations. This left the field of South African politics to Hertzog, and it was an opportunity that he seized with both hands. He knew he could build a new sort of nationalist Afrikaner political movement simply by identifying with popular Boer anger; he did not need to take the risk of actually instigating anti-British action, he just had to sympathise with it when it occurred – which it did, both in the mines and in the army.

Furthering Afrikaner economic interests was not just a question of land reform in favour of farmers; there was also a Boer working class, concentrated in the mines of the Witwatersrand. And here, in the years leading up to the outbreak of war, it became clear that the ethnic division within South Africa's European population was also a class division. The men who worked deep underground to bring out coal, or in search of diamonds, were Boers; the mines they worked in were owned and managed by the English. In one sense, of course, the Boer War had been a struggle for control over South Africa's mineral riches; and the victors were not going to have their profits undermined by an obstructive or too-well-paid workforce. White miners were paid on average fifteen times what their black counterparts received, so the incentive was obviously there to replace the former with the latter. But this was a symbolic and explosive issue. The first white miners' strike over black competition for jobs took place in 1907; it was followed by other, more serious and more confrontational stoppages in 1913 and 1914. These laid the groundwork for an unlikely political alliance between Hertzog's Nationalists and a nascent South African Labour Party – right and left brought together by a shared hatred of the English, whether they were in Kimberley, Durban or London.

If lining the coffers of British mining companies was one thing, being actively engaged in fighting for the Empire was another. Yet that is what was expected of Afrikaner troops, under Smuts, in 1914–15. Some, as we have seen, refused and attempted to join forces with German units in South-West Africa. The rebellion put J.B.M. Hertzog in a difficult position. He was personally pro-German, but could not afford to openly advocate what might be seen as a traitorous position. So while he came out against the decision of Boer soldiers to take up arms against the British, he refused to condemn them when they did so. It was good politics, and at the general election later that year the Nationalists increased their number of parliamentary seats from seven to twenty-six. Five years later they became the largest party, but Smuts was able to continue as Prime Minister with support from the Unionists. Hertzog finally became PM himself in 1924, when the Nationalists negotiated a coalition with Labour; and what assured this were the bloody events on the Witwatersrand in 1922. A strike by Afrikaner miners – against the proposed use of black labour in skilled jobs – spilled over into civil violence. Afrikaner commando units took over the streets of Johannesburg, and Smuts responded by calling out the Defence Force. In a week of vicious fighting more than 200 lives were lost: those of white South Africans, killed by other white South Africans. Yet again Jan Smuts had used force on behalf of the British, and it was the effective end of his career as a South African politician. It was in that same transforming year of 1922 that Arthur Newton made his first foray into public controversy by claiming in a letter to the press that he was being discriminated against because he was a British settler. But by then he had already made the extraordinary decision to achieve fame as a runner, so that people would respect him and listen to him.

IV

By 1921 Arthur Newton had no option but to accept that his farming days at Ihluku were over. As an English settler in Natal, he had come up against what he experienced as a brick wall of Afrikaner dislike, disinterest and distrust. Newton was at times a naïve man, whose instinct, many said, was to look for good in others. So it must have been difficult for him to grasp that he represented everything that Hertzog set out to fight against in his attempt to ethnically cleanse white South Africa. The government would argue that Newton should have known what he was getting into by choosing to farm near Harding; and the Department of Native Affairs was not particularly keen to see him farming elsewhere in Natal. If they were intent on encouraging blacks to move to the 'English province', then they needed as much 'native' land as possible. So when Newton asked if they would exchange his farm for another in a 'white area', the Department refused. They also refused to purchase Newton's farm. As he put it later, '[they] were determined to ignore the matter, and probably felt all the safer because I was quite unknown and therefore likely to be helpless'.

Newton agreed. He *was* helpless as long as he remained simply an isolated farmer in a remote corner of the province.

So he resolved to make his name. 'I should then be in a position to show my fellow citizens how settlers should be safeguarded.' But how? By doing what? He had to find something that he had a chance of becoming very good at, within a reasonable amount of time; and, just as importantly, it had to be something that would make him admired by the English community in Natal. It was not enough to become well known; he had to become well known at an activity that exhibited and represented a certain moral high ground, a certain rectitude; one that in and by itself was a character reference for him. He chose to become a runner, and the way he explains the decision says much about the culture of Natal's white elite in the early part of the twentieth century. 'Genuine amateur athletics were about as wholesome as anything on this earth; any man who made a really notable name at such would always be given a hearing by the public.' Or, as he put it more humorously to a Canadian journalist in the early 1930s, 'there were two things I could do, either crime or athletics. I was no Al Capone, so I chose athletics.'

It was to become part of the myth of Newton – encouraged in no little part by himself – that before 1922 he had never even put on a pair of running shoes, let alone taken part in competitive athletics. That, of course, was untrue. He had undoubtedly taken part in school cross-country running, and back in England in 1909 he had joined, and competed successfully with, the Thames Hare and Hounds Club. It has been suggested that he taught athletics while working at Hilton College in Durban before he became a farmer. Newton also realised, at a relatively young age, that the fitter he was, the happier he felt. (This, as we shall see, he was to develop into a whole philosophy of life.) Not long before he died Newton told an interviewer, 'At the age of twenty I had been reading heavily in philosophy and metaphysics and after a time decided that if I wanted to be really healthy I should take regular physical exercise.' But the fact that he was not an athletic virgin in 1921 does nothing to minimise or qualify the courage, audacity and strangeness of his decision. 'I took up long-distance running solely with the object of focussing public attention on the treatment to which I had been subjected,' he told the *Natal Advertiser* in 1924. Or, as he put it more succinctly in the opening paragraph of his final book, *Races and Training* (1949), 'I took up running seriously with the object of obtaining publicity for a farmer's cause.' It was a strategy that met with the approval of the South African writer William Bolitho, who was to reflect on Newton's decision in 1924. 'There are only three fames in a colony,' he wrote, 'riches (hard nowadays and long), military (but the war is over), and best, most dazzling and enduring of all, sport.'

Newton said that he only made up his mind about running after 'careful and protracted deliberation'. He was too old, he knew, for distances that required speed or explosive strength, so he concluded that the longer the race, the better. He also decided, so that his training could be minutely tailored, to focus from the outset on a particular event: a fifty-four-mile road race from Durban to Maritzburg that had been run for the first time in May 1921. The race was known as the Comrades Marathon, and was the brainchild of a Durban train driver by the name of Vic Clapham. Clapham had been born in London in 1886 and was still a boy when his family emigrated to South Africa. In 1914 he had signed up with the 8th South African Infantry, and survived the dire hardships of the long

East African campaign, when the brilliant German general Paul von Lettow-Vorbeck (later to be the last President of the Weimar Republic) had played cat-and-mouse with tens of thousands of imperial troops, leading them on a relentless and exhausting chase from German into Portuguese territory. After 1918 Clapham had joined the Natal division of the 'League of Comrades of the Great War', one of several organisations that had sprung up to publicise and protect the interests of former servicemen, or their widows, and which were eventually to merge to form the Royal British Legion. Vic Clapham wanted to create a living memorial for the friends and colleagues that he had lost, and he wanted it to reflect the defining characteristic of the campaign they had fought – the daily slog of marching mile after mile across savannah and veldt. So he thought a very long road race would be an appropriate memorial, with the fifty-four miles from Durban to Maritzburg being the proposed route. But initially neither the League of Comrades nor the local athletic authorities were at all keen, fearful that the distance was too great for the well-being of the competitors. Clapham's applications to stage the race in both 1919 and 1920 were turned down.

But public pressure, both in Britain and across the Empire, for something to be done to help former servicemen increased during the years after the end of the war, and finally in 1921 Clapham was given permission for his marathon. This was an era when the most common source of sponsorship for sport came from the press, and the *Natal Mercury* stepped in, as did the main brewery in Maritzburg. Only thirty-four runners entered, but the fact that it was to take place on 24th May, Empire Day, gave the event immediate cachet, and for a proud former soldier down on his farm near Harding who had decided to seek fame through running, the 'Comrades' seemed tailor-made: it was amateur, it was British, it was charitable, and it was going to be well publicised. So to take part in that year's race became Arthur Newton's New Year's resolution for 1922, and on 1st January he started training.

After Newton had indeed become famous through running, the initial training regime that he imposed on his middle-aged body became the subject of myth and colourful exaggeration. In August 1930 (at the height of his own and Peter Gavuzzi's professional success in Canada) Newton was profiled by *Time* magazine:

> [He] had never done any running. He was 40 – already past the age for marathoners – yet the plan he decided on was to become the greatest runner in the world. One day he began to run around his farm. Round the fence he went, twice a day for as long as he could keep it up, in the morning and at night. The Kaffirs who had been allowed too near started at the thin sweating man running clumsily in his farm clothes under the glaring sun. He sent to Durban for shoes and shorts. He wore leather socks next his skin. Every hour he drank a half pint glass of lemonade containing eight teaspoons of sugar, half a teaspoon of salt and cracked ice.

When the article was brought to Newton's attention a year after its publication he wrote to thank *Time*'s sports editor for 'a really glorious column of fiction'. 'I never ran round the farm,' he elaborated, 'roads suited me better. I never ran in farm clothes; athletes would not do so. I did not wear leather socks. I did not drink the mixture stated – sometimes I drank ordinary tea. Oh well!'

Newton also claimed in the letter that he 'used science and a trained mind to accomplish my ends'; and he was later to write that 'being fully aware that mentality counted for a great deal more than mere physical strength, I relied chiefly on this to bring me to the top'. As we shall see, he was eventually to devote a good proportion of his time to writing about how athletes should train for long-distance events, and what can best be called his 'philosophy of running' would be both praised and ridiculed. But it had its beginnings, he always insisted, in an insight that he had within weeks of starting to prepare for the Comrades Marathon in 1922 – that common sense was a better guide to training than any existing textbook orthodoxy.

The received wisdom of the day placed speed at the centre of the process – with everything focused on taking progressively less and less time to cover a particular distance – and Newton was soon convinced that an initial attempt to train in this way almost cost him his life. He started on New Year's Day with a two-mile run on his farm track; but 'before I had gone a mile I was obliged to stop for want of wind'. A few days later he was attempting four miles, and within five weeks he was completing a ten-mile run. He knew he had less than five months to get ready to run the fifty-four miles of the Comrades, so early in March he decided to test himself in the context of a 'race' over the sort of mountainous terrain that he would meet on the Durban to Maritzburg road. His opponent was a train, on the narrow-gauge railway that connected Harding with the coast at Port Shepstone. He set out to race it for the first twenty-six miles of its journey, and all went well until he

came to a long and steep hill about two miles from his destination. This is how he described what happened, in *Races and
Training*:

> All went well till I got to a hundred feet from the top –
> the steepest bit of the lot – and then something mighty
> near tragedy occurred. I was actually forcing myself to
> run up a gradient of about 1 in 6 when quite suddenly I
> was pulled up with an abominable ache around my heart,
> so distressing an experience that I knew, without any
> expert advice, that I had in some way damaged the organ.
> Even walking was out of the question for a time and I
> sat down on a rock and waited in the hope that I might
> recover.

He eventually managed to stagger to the crest of the hill,
and then walked in slow stages down to the railway hotel
where friends were waiting for him. Newton was frightened
by what had happened to him; and too frightened to mention
it to a doctor, who would undoubtedly tell him to stop running.
That he could not do; nor, he realised, could he go on with
his present training regime. This was the moment of insight
that was to make him a unique runner – both in achievement
and in style. 'From then on I dropped all "speed trials" and
never attempted to run to time: I travelled ever so casually
and quietly, training for distance only and leaving speed
entirely out of it. At the end of a single month of this the
improvement was so marked that I knew I had struck the
right sort of preparation for a man of my age.' He had also
stumbled on what would remain for him the key to successful
long-distance running – the absence of mental stress. Arthur

Newton, it seems fair to say, became in middle age the world's best distance runner for the simple reason that running produced in him a state of contentment that it became impossible for him to live without. He needed to break records for the sake of his political campaign. But he was able to break records because doing so was a by-product of the fact that running made him happy. As he put it in *Races and Training*: 'When your physique is about as near perfection as Nature can make it, all your abilities become greatly enhanced: you can work better, think more clearly and play more actively and intensely than before. A welcome result is that you get a lot more enjoyment out of life, which is what we look for: we only do things because we consider the result will bring us pleasure in one way or another, even if it is only indirectly.'

Not that he had yet worked this out on 24th May 1922. At six o'clock on a cold winter's morning he was among eighty-eight starters for the second Comrades Marathon. It was to be run on the more challenging 'up' course from Durban on the coast to Maritzburg in the foothills of the Drakensberg Mountains. Public interest was considerable, especially as both the winner and the runner-up from the previous year were competing again. An old friend of Arthur Newton's who lived in Durban was also running, but apart from that it is unlikely that anyone involved with the event knew who Newton was. He had – for a novice racer – an extraordinary confidence in the running strategy he had worked out on the lonely tracks around Harding. Regardless of whether he was going uphill or down, he would maintain a steady unvarying pace, and would try to clear his mind of any thoughts of his rivals. This meant that for the first few miles, which were on the flat, he formed (as he later put it) 'a stately procession of one, well to the rear of the rest of the field'. But, as climb followed climb, he passed runner after runner and at the halfway mark, a mile further than the classic marathon distance of twenty-six miles, he was told there were only four men in front of him, including the winner from 1921, Harry Phillips. Vic Clapham was overseeing the race, and years later he wrote of the general amazement at Newton's run. 'Halfway through I was told that Harry Phillips was in a fight with another runner. Someone said it was no. 77. There was a scramble for programmes to see who this no. 77 was. It turned out to be a chap called Newton, from Ihluku. All I could say about him was that he was a farmer.'

The 'chap called Newton' plodded on, intent on not stopping even for a moment. At the top of the hardest climb, the Inchanga Bank, he came across another of the favourites prone on the ground being massaged, and realised that he was now in the lead. But there was still – four miles before the finish – one agonisingly long final hill; and it almost broke Newton. 'It got so bad that when it came to the steepest part I stopped dead in a single stride, convinced at the moment that it was worse than absolute idiocy to attempt to carry on.' But carry on he did, downhill to a victory that he found perhaps the most painful aspect of the whole day. He wanted fame, but for a reason; and – certainly in the very early days of his career – he found personal adulation almost unbearable. As he approached Maritzburg a procession of cars and motorcycles formed behind him, sending a huge cloud of dust into the clear African sky. Then into the city: 'The moment I was sighted I saw people beginning to run, and in less than half a minute there was a dense crowd – so dense that the police on duty at the spot had considerable difficulty in keeping open a lane for me to get through.' Finally Newton had to run a valedictory lap around the track at the Maritzburg Show-grounds, in front of a crowd of thousands. 'Tired as I was I was still able to feel acutely embarrassed. But I ambled round somehow, and pulled up after breaking the tape to shake hands with the Mayor. Believe me, I got away from there as quickly as ever I could.' At the age of thirty-nine he had won what many regarded as the hardest road race anywhere in the world. He had won it by more than half an hour. He had never raced seriously before.

But remarkable as his victory was, the Comrades was only one race, and Arthur Newton was under no illusions that he was yet sufficiently well known for the general public to rally to his cause in his conflict with the Union government. As he wrote later, he decided that 'more work, even harder work, had to be the order of the day'; and, despite what Vic Clapham had read in the 1922 race programme, work for Newton no longer meant farming. It meant training and lobbying. Everything he did was now focused on putting pressure on the government to admit that their policy on Native Areas had made it impossible for him to make a living as a farmer, and to embarrass them into buying him out. His land at Ihluku reverted to scrub; his plans for a 'proper' farmhouse were shelved. We know also, from a letter he wrote to a friend in March 1926, that he paid an obviously devastating human price for having to renounce his farming dream. A copy of the letter is in Newton's papers, with the addressee identified simply by the initials H.B.K. and it provides the only clue Arthur Newton left as to having led an emotional or sexual life. He mentions that at a certain point – it is unclear when – he was 'prepared to start building a decent house'; and he goes on to explain why. 'I was, after many years of waiting, at last fortunate enough to become engaged to be married. No sooner had I got this far than the trouble started and, like a wise man, I proposed to wait a bit to see what the outcome was going to be. This went on for a couple of years or more, while things steadily got worse.' Most obviously they got worse financially, and Newton came from a culture where men only married when they were in a position to 'support' their wives. 'My sense of honour eventually compelled me to break off my engagement and it will be a considerable time before I can think of any such happy and natural conditions again.' Newton was forty-two years old when he wrote this letter, and, as far as we know, those 'happy conditions' never occurred again. In his autobiographical writings he makes no mention of this engagement; nor does he mention any subsequent love affair. In any emotional sense, women, it would appear, simply ceased to exist for him.

So the Arthur Newton who returned to Harding to run and run was not just angry: he was lonely too. He knew that, given his age, he did not have all that much time in which to become sufficiently famous; so he had to go into full-time training. This meant that he could not afford to have a job, and he mortgaged his farm to the government Land Bank, raising enough money to see him through the next year or so. In athletic terms, his immediate aim was the next Comrades Marathon; in political terms, it was to drum up support for his case among Natal's ruling elite. Newton had gone public with his grievance against the government in late September 1922 with the letter to the *Times of Natal* that has already been mentioned; and he gained an early ally in his local MP, J.S. Marwick, who wrote to him three weeks later to say that he was about to go to Pretoria to discuss provincial financial matters and that while there he would 'certainly make a point of seeing' the Minister of Lands to discuss Newton's case. But, as we have seen, English-speaking politicians from Natal were hardly the most effective lobbyists in Afrikaner corridors of power, and Marwick was told there was no point in his pursuing the issue. Arthur Newton was to get neither new land nor compensation.

But the following May he was to set another record – this time for the 'down' Comrades route from Maritzburg to Durban – and his supremacy over the rest of the field was even more pronounced than the previous year. By halfway Newton was in the lead; and he reached the Indian Ocean sooner than any of the race officials thought possible, so his reception was – to him – gratifyingly low-key. '[They] were quite unprepared. One man, however, happened to spot me shortly before I reached the Sports Grounds and, diving through a broken fence as a short cut, was able to gather another man inside and arrive at the finishing post just in time to hold up the tape and read the watches. It was a close shave.' Newton refused to accept the offered prize, a clock, on the grounds that he was temporarily in the privileged position of being able to train full-time and so had an unfair advantage over most of his competitors. He asked the Mayor of Durban to present the prize to the man who came second, but he would not do so. Finally Newton was able to persuade the people of Harding to take the clock off his hands and keep it as a memento in the Town Hall. But this was not simply a magnanimous gesture. Newton felt somehow tainted by the receipt of prizes, and it is a central irony of his bizarre and unique life that a man who took such pride in being an amateur, and who had chosen amateur athletics as a moral high ground from which to mount his political campaign, should eventually achieve notoriety as a great professional. His amateurism was something he felt it necessary to emphasise in a newspaper article that he published a few months after the 1923 Comrades race. 'In middle age and living on capital I have become an athlete solely that I might be able to focus public attention on the injustice of which I am a victim. Yet, with all this, athleticism remains for me just genuine sport, and although it seems to have become hopelessly mixed in my affairs, I am and always will be an out-and-out amateur.'

Over the next two years Arthur Newton was to extend his fame to England as well as throughout southern Africa: he was to break long-standing world records, yet he was to end up broke – and broken himself. He needed, most importantly, to keep himself in the public eye, and the ease with which he had won the 1923 Comrades suggested the world fifty-mile record as an initial target. So he asked the Amateur Athletic authorities in Maritzburg if they could organise an attempt on the record for him, and they agreed to put it on as part of the city's annual Royal Agricultural Show at the end of June. This meant marking out a twenty-five-mile distance on the road to Durban, as Newton said he could not face running round a track 'because the monotony would be too awful'. He knew the road, and knew what pace to maintain, but he did not have all that much confidence in the accuracy with which the distance had been calculated. (With good reason, it seems fair to say; the position of the twenty-five-mile marker was calculated by taking an average of what various car speedometers estimated the distance to be.) Wanting to make sure that no one could challenge his time on the grounds of his having run something less than the full fifty miles, Newton did a typically Newtonian thing: 'When I came to the turning point I went on for another hundred yards followed by shouts and protests, and then, just as they were hurrying after me, circled round in the road and began the return journey.' At the age of forty, and over a mountainous route, he broke both the amateur and professional world track records by more than twenty minutes. That autumn, armed with his new status as world-record holder, he intensified his anti-government campaign in the press. He knew it was not enough for him simply to try and elicit a wave of moral outrage against the way he felt he had been treated; so he added a more strategic argument about the damage his case could do to South Africa's international reputation.

This mattered because the Union was desperate for European immigrants; and the Colonial Office in London was desperate to make sure that as many as possible of them were British. But, in comparison with other available colonial destinations, South Africa was extremely unpopular among those wishing to leave the UK. This was shown clearly in the response to a scheme that ran from 1919 to 1924 offering free passage to imperial destinations for ex-servicemen and their families. While more than 37,000 chose Australia, and Canada welcomed just under 27,000, only 6,004 went to South Africa and Rhodesia. Even more startling are the figures for the overall number of emigrants given assisted passages after the Empire Settlement Act was passed in 1922. Canada came top of the list, attracting more than 185,000, with Australia not far behind with 172,000; South Africa and Rhodesia attracted a paltry 1,226. Arthur Newton – who was always to claim a great love for the country – set out nevertheless to dissuade possible

English settlers from getting on the boat to Cape Town or Durban. South Africa was not, he wanted to show, a country where British people could expect fair treatment. It was also a country that he himself, he threatened, would have to leave.

On 14th November 1923 a correspondent of the *Natal Witness* reported on a 'long chat' he had had with Newton. The athlete/ farmer, he wrote, 'takes a very philosophical view of his position, his chief regret being that he must sacrifice his two years' hard training and also leave the country'. This, the reporter continued, would be a 'serious loss at the present time of propaganda for South Africa'. He mentioned that both the Olympic Games and the British Empire Exhibition were due in 1924 and asked: 'can we afford to let probably the greatest athlete of them all, probably the greatest at his distance who ever put on a shoe, leave this country and break his training at this juncture, simply because it suited our policy to surround his farm with natives and not compensate him properly?' He finished by suggesting that a 'general subscription list' be opened in sports centres around the country to raise enough money to keep Arthur Newton in South Africa. Three days later another Natal paper carried the headline, 'TO SAVE NEWTON'. Despite the fact that the runner himself (knowing that twenty-six miles was too short a distance for him) never indicated such a desire, the article confidently claimed that 'Mr Newton would like to represent South Africa at the Olympic Games.' But this would not happen, because the athlete, 'after a residence of 22 years, is being driven out of the country by one of the grossest examples of administrative injustice ever perpetrated, and the country appears doomed to lose a desirable settler and a first-rate sportsman'. Newton had told the reporter that immediately after he had broken

the fifty-mile record he had received an offer from the government to exchange farms, but that 'as I was now wholly ruined,
I could no longer accept an exchange of land only, but found
it necessary to ask for compensation for the twelve years' work
of development carried out by me, never dreaming that Natives
would be settled on the land around me'. He went on, somewhat disingenuously: 'Had the public known the circumstances, I need never have considered athletics, but I dislike
talking or writing of things, and prefer to do them. It struck
me that the path to public opinion via athletics was a quick
and sure one, and one also that was above all reproach, only
proving that I wished to be a worthy and hard-working citizen.'

It was on 9th May 1924 – just a fortnight before the annual
Comrades Marathon – that Arthur Newton received what
seemed like a final rejection from the Department of Native
Affairs. He was informed that the Minister, Mr Roos, had
decided there was 'no possibility of making use of the buildings on the farm' and that therefore he was 'unable to recommend the purchase of the property by the Government'.
Newton passed on the letter to the *Natal Advertiser*, which
printed it word for word in an editorial. The case, the paper
concluded, was a symptom of disturbing political develop-
ments: 'How easy it is to see what may happen to a great many
settlers in this country if and when a native segregation policy
and Nationalist antipathy to English-speaking immigrants give
General Hertzog and Mr Roos all the opportunity for the
British depopulation they desire.'

Newton's strategy seemed to have failed; and Empire Day
1924 saw what he must have felt would be his last appearance
in a South African race. He won, of course – his third consecutive victory in the Comrades – but he had made up his mind

to return to England once the race was out of the way. He wrote later that this was partly 'to make an even wider reputation as an athlete'; and partly 'to do what I could through the medium of journalism to warn prospective settlers of what was likely to be a serious outlook for them'. He had not been back to England for fifteen years, and was by his own admission 'completely ruined', so he must have hoped that his athletic success would somehow make it easier for him to go cap in hand to his now very elderly father, who had retired to Devon. There was pride involved too: elements in the British sporting press had openly questioned the status of his fifty-mile world record, and he wanted to silence them in the best possible way – by setting a new one on British soil. Since the early nineteenth century the road from London to Brighton had established itself as a classic fifty-mile route, so there could be no quibbling over the distance and there was an acknowledged record. In the space of six weeks, running each time on his own, Arthur Newton was to beat it twice.

He had long realised that the key to his particular training regime was consistency and regularity. He had to do a certain number of steady miles every day – even on a Union Castle liner. 'Training aboard ship is not so easy,' Newton recalled in an article he wrote for the *Cape Times* three years later:

> especially when the accommodation is fully booked up. The only exercise I could make certain of was walking, and, of course, this had to be done when the decks were not crowded. So I turned in at about seven every evening and got up shortly after midnight, putting in some 20 miles round and round the promenade deck until 6 a.m. There was no fun at all in it; certainly no holiday such

as people look forward to on a long voyage. I know I was glad enough to leave the ship and welcome solid ground again, if only to be in a position to enjoy more natural hours.

But at least during the early part of the voyage there would have been a certain spring in Newton's nocturnal step as he circled round and round the deck. Just days before his departure on 16th June he had finally had a meeting in Durban with General Smuts, the South African Prime Minister and the only man who could overturn the decision of the Department of Native Affairs over Newton's claim for compensation. The meeting had been arranged by J.S. Marwick, Newton's MP, who had led the athlete to believe that Smuts would be well aware of the details of his case. He was not, and the Prime Minister had to be told the whole sequence of events. His response was to offer Newton a deal. At this moment the runner had no intention of ever returning to South Africa; he had no money, no job and no workable land. Smuts (according to Newton) said that he would 'undo the wrong' Newton had suffered as long as he promised to return to the colony. 'He said he was always delighted to meet an industrious South African citizen and was only too aware that the country could not afford to lose such.' Newton duly promised that he would come back as soon as he could; and Smuts gave immediate instructions for Newton's farm to be valued, with a view to the state buying him out. Newton then sailed for England. But by the time he arrived Smuts was out of office. The South African election of 1924 took place against the backdrop of conflict in the mines of Witwatersrand; and Smuts was punished for his seemingly pro-British, pro-mine-owner stance when Labour joined electoral forces with J.B.M. Hertzog's Nationalists. The new Prime Minister of the Union had devoted his political career to furthering the interests of the Boers at the expense of the English; and Hertzog rushed through a deeply symbolic piece of legislation – a constitutional amendment replacing Dutch with Afrikaans as an official language of the country.

V

What was at stake in the Brighton runs was Newton's credibility in British eyes. He knew that doubts had been raised as to the veracity of his South African times, and this hurt him deeply. The runs were also a test of his unconventional approach to training and preparation. When he first tried to spell these out on paper, in a series of articles for the *Cape Times* in February 1926, he looked back on the way he had felt as he prepared for the first Brighton run in October 1924:

> Three years of training without a stop, and on a scale that as yet no athlete had attempted, and in a few days I was to see what it was all really worth. I was considered at least ten years too old for world's records. I had almost wholly disregarded diet; had managed entirely without massage, cold baths, rub downs, coaches etc. and moreover had a brand new and aggressively unorthodox theory of practice and training. Would this run prove them worthy, or should I be let down?

He was certainly not let down by his preparation or by his theories, though he felt he had come close to letting himself down in the first run on 3rd October. He had had a sleepless night in a central London hotel, and had not been provided with the breakfast he had asked for. So he started the run feeling grumpy and out of sorts. He developed cramp and suffered from a bad stomach; and at one point in south London he had to wait while a train crossed the road. But, as he reflected later, he thought better of complaining too much when he arrived in Brighton. 'Seeing that I was twenty minutes ahead of the professional and three quarters of an hour better than the amateur record, I could hardly tell the officials that I had made a compete hash of the affair.' The press were fascinated. *The Times*, making much of the fact that Newton was 'in his 42nd year', described him as 'a tall loosely-built athlete, who runs with a low-action style which he himself has evolved'. Newton had organised the run with the help of the Thames Hare and Hounds Club, with which he had run fifteen years previously, and of Joe Binks, a former champion miler who was the chief athletics correspondent of the *News of the World*. It was the first time of course that Binks had seen the man from South Africa in action. 'I watched Newton closely all the way,' he wrote, 'and he impressed me as the most perfect running machine for distance I have ever seen.' But Newton regarded his run as far from perfect, and decided immediately that he wanted to do it again. On 13th November, in appalling weather, he sliced a further thirteen minutes off his own record time for the distance.

Two days later he was in the BBC's London Station Studio, 2LO in Savoy Hill House, describing his run to the listening public. The Corporation had accepted a script from him after the first Brighton run in October – a rather bland pep-talk on long-distance running – and had asked him back. This time Newton was more personal and engaging. Overnight rain had left deep puddles on the side of the road that he could not avoid, and he described how wet and cold he soon became: 'At twenty miles I found it was getting actually painful to put each foot on the ground. I had by this time lost all control of my fingers and began to feel really uncomfortable.' Earlier than planned, he called for a thermos of tea, only to find that 'the flask had lost its memory and had forgotten to keep the tea hot'. Despite the discomfort he said that he had never felt pressed for time, and was always in control of what he referred to as a 'little stunt'. 'There was no need to hurry over the last mile or two, and I'm quite glad I didn't. As a result I finished up quite happy and contented and have not suffered in any way as a result of the race. I am not stiff anywhere, I've not lost my appetite, and I've been running again this afternoon.' He ended by thanking all those who had helped him, and by saying that he was due to return to Natal within a fortnight.*

Perhaps the first person to understand the true idiosyncrasy of Arthur Newton was the then-fashionable journalist and essayist William Bolitho (the nom de plume of Charles William Ryall). He was the star columnist for *The World*, and was known as much for his aphorisms as for his perceptive reporting on, for example, the rise of Mussolini in Italy. In

---

* In an article in 1944 – one of the first he published in England – he took a more polemical stance: 'In 1924 a runner came over from South Africa to test the result of training methods which completely upset many of the most cherished rules of modern textbooks . . . It is quite possible that most athletes considered that either the times were more or less a fluke or that the runner himself was a freak: the fact remains that training in England continued as it always had been and that no effort was made by anyone to try out the new methods.'

October 1924, not long after Newton had beaten the London to Brighton record, Bolitho wrote a long piece about him, which began with the suggestion that the athlete deserved more attention than a few column inches on the sports page – he was far more interesting than that. Bolitho explained the bare bones of Newton's life in South Africa and of his grievance against the Union government. Then he hazarded an explanation as to why Newton had started *running* at the age of forty:

> In the normal course Newton would only have sulked. But there are natures that cannot work off their bitter conviction of injustice in neighbourly grumbling. They demonstrate, by killing, rioting, or speech-making, until they complete their ruin or get a commission to inquire. Newton is one of that respectable, fearful, strange class. He also made a discovery. It was partly because he was no talker. On the farm he was driven into himself, and found out a secret, just as he might have tripped over a gold reef. To win his case he must be well known, notorious, famous. At forty, for a backwoods farmer in Natal, that is not easy. But the very simplicity of his education and his milieu gave him the clue at once, and by preserving him from vain doubts made its use possible.

What Bolitho understands here is that Newton, in all his strangeness, provides a perfect example of something entirely mainstream: the cachet and meaning of sporting excellence in imperial culture. He also recognises Newton's genius in lighting on a sort of sport that not just allowed, but required him to maintain his solitary existence. Bolitho wanted his readers to understand that there had never been a sportsman like Arthur Newton:

> One mile, two miles, ten miles, round and round the fence of his farm, sun and shade, shuffling along in his farm boots, blistering his feet, cracking his chest, in every weather, heedless of the glare or dust: sustained not by any athletic art, of which he had never heard, but simply by his devouring obstinacy to be revenged. It went better than he had imagined. Every day he increased his distance. He sent to Durban, a week away, for shoes and shorts. And in the evenings his black neighbours, squatting around their fire, around the pot of maize meal, could notice with superstitious fear this white man, who hated them, running against them silently lap after lap around his farm, until his breath sobbed and his legs gave out. It was an incantation he was putting on them – modern magic, the untiring fierce running of the thin white figure behind his fence.

Bolitho was wrong about one thing. Newton regarded his black neighbours with disdain, frustration and annoyance; he did not hate them. His hatred was reserved for the likes of Prime Minister Hertzog; and it was to confront him that Newton decided to return to South Africa at the end of 1924. Amateur athletic records do not pay; so his father had to come up with the fare.

2

From Amateur to Professional

Arthur Newton in Rhodesia

I

The first six months of 1925 can only have been deeply humiliating for Arthur Newton. He had returned to South Africa solely to test whether Hertzog's government would honour the promise he believed General Smuts had made to him the previous year; and he was desperately short of money. The Land Bank, with which he had mortgaged his farm, was demanding its interest; and the only way he could come up with the cash was finally to instruct the bank to sell the property at Ihluku. Land that had had a considerable value when tobacco or cotton could be cultivated had virtually none when it reverted to grazing. This is how Newton later summed up the end of his South African farming adventure: 'I was just able to meet my commitments, though there was nothing at all left over. So after twenty years' good work in the country I was worse off than when I landed.'

He badgered officials in Pretoria, and in March he was offered an interview with Hertzog himself. It lasted no more

55

than ten minutes, with the Prime Minister insisting that as the government had not in any way acted illegally, it was not obliged to offer Newton any compensation. Then, to make matters worse, Newton received a letter from Pretoria on 2nd April stating that while the government was under no legal obligation to pay him anything, Hertzog had in fact been open to the possibility of making a gesture on the grounds of equity, but that Newton had blown his chances by the way he had behaved at the meeting. This is what the official told him: 'Had you yourself, when you interviewed General Hertzog, not *demanded* your full pound of flesh, you would not have lost the golden opportunity of securing a settlement on an equitable basis. It seems rather unjust to blame the government considering the unreasonable attitude you took up.' In May – immediately after winning the Comrades Marathon for a fourth consecutive year – Newton upped the stakes by arranging for the letter from Hertzog's office to be published in the Natal press. The response was just what he wanted. Within a week the *Natal Advertiser*, under the headline 'Justice for Newton', had called for a province-wide 'Committee of Sportsmen' to be formed to raise money for his cause, and had also published the text of a petition that they hoped would be presented to the Union parliament. The paper now referred to Newton as 'the World's Greatest Runner'.

Arthur Newton wanted to become famous, and perhaps one definition of fame is having one's personal case taken sufficiently seriously for it to be debated in the national parliament. Newton had his moment on 18th June 1925, when his MP, J.S. Marwick, managed to table the Natal petition in support of his case during a debate on farming in Zululand. But Newton, one imagines, can only have regretted the occasion because none other than

Prime Minister Hertzog took the floor to denounce him as certainly a simpleton and possibly a liar. In immediate response to Marwick, Hertzog said, 'I do hope this question will not be taken up by the House or the country. I gave the Hon. Member the assurance that I was most sympathetic when I first heard of Mr Newton's case. He came to see me, and really if I were to put all the facts before this House I think everybody would laugh heartily. I have it from Mr Newton himself that he had bought a farm in the midst of land held by natives.' Marwick interrupted to question this last remark, saying that Newton had bought Crown Lands. 'Yes, Crown Lands situated among natives,' replied the Prime Minister, who was evidently enjoying this opportunity to rubbish and ridicule an English settler who had set out to make sport into a pulpit, from which he could rain down moral condemnation on the government.

Hertzog must have seemed convincing to the majority of MPs who did not come from Natal, as he had surprising command of the detail of Newton's situation. He spelt out how, in his view, Newton had tried to exploit the Africans who lived near his farm by making them work on his land in return for dipping their cattle; and that the Native Affairs Department had deemed it both fairer and 'more economical' for them to have their own dip. The root of Newton's grievance and his claim for £4,000 in compensation was, Hertzog said, his belief that 'the government had interfered with his lucrative dip'. The Prime Minister then described his meeting with Newton. 'Let me say that Mr Newton really put his case before me so simply and without any attempt at hiding anything that I openly told him that I had got him to come in the hope that I might do something for him, but I gave him the assurance that if I were to comply with his request and pay him any of the money he asked for, I would be simply laughed out of Parliament if I had to account for it later.'

Marwick did his best to correct what he had the courage to describe as 'an entirely jocular and by no means accurate description of the case of Mr Newton', but the House, unsurprisingly, sided with Hertzog and decided that it would take no further interest in 'the case of Mr Newton'. This is how the athlete himself was later to sum up his situation in June 1925: 'six years of a real sporting fight had changed me from an active and prosperous farmer to an energetic and all but penniless tramp'.

II

On 30th July the residents of Maritzburg woke up to find a banner headline across the front page of the *Natal Witness*: 'THE MYSTERY OF ARTHUR NEWTON, THE FAMOUS MARATHON MAN'; then, below; 'Where is Newton? Famous Runner Vanished'. The next day the *Johannesburg Star* joined in with 'A. Newton Disappears'; and it says much for the impact Newton had made on the Brighton road in the autumn of 1924 that the London press soon picked up the scent of a possibly extraordinary story. 'The disappearance of the famous athlete has caused a sensation in Natal,' stated the *Daily Express*; while the *News of the World* went with the headline 'Athletic Mystery'. But 'mystery' was perhaps an exaggeration. Newton had let it be known privately that he was soon going to leave South Africa: he had intimated that this would be for 'a British country', which, in terms of accessibility, could only mean Rhodesia; and he had told one Natal journalist, 'I cannot go on running much longer; I must go to work, and one cannot do both.' To make the most of his departure (and of the supposed ending of his running career), Newton had persuaded the local athletic authorities to arrange a one-off run from Durban to Maritzburg – the sole purpose of which was to set some new world records. They would be a pointed 'leaving present' to the Union. He duly set new records for thirty, forty and fifty miles – as well as beating his own best time for the Comrades distance. That was on a Saturday. He 'disappeared' on the Sunday night, hardly more than twenty-four hours later.

While it was common knowledge that he had said he would soon be off, almost certainly to Rhodesia, the local press could not hide its anxiety over Newton. The assumption had been that he would leave openly, probably by train. A sudden flight in the early hours of the morning seemed entirely out of character. He had no known creditors, and he had paid his hotel bill. In fact it was the proprietor of Maritzburg's Warrington House Hotel who first alerted the press, telling the *Natal Witness* that '[Newton's] practice was to get up at 3 o'clock each morning and go for a run: on Monday morning he went out at the usual hour, but did not return.' He had told the hotel that he had virtually no money left, and he had left all his personal effects behind. Durban radio station immediately put out a request for people to look out for Newton, and some of the papers speculated that the athlete might have been contemplating suicide. 'Until his whereabouts are established there is room for anxiety, because there can be no doubt that he was suffering from a deep sense of injustice in regard to his alleged grievances,' suggested the *Johannesburg Star*. The next day, 31st July, with still no news from or sightings of Arthur Newton, the *Natal Advertiser* tried to calm the speculation: 'To those who know him well, the thought that Newton has done injury to himself is not to be countenanced, as he is of well-balanced mind and strong character.' But the paper thought it wise to print a detailed physical portrait of an idiosyncratic man whom its readers might see walking the high road: 'In appearance he is of medium height, square-shouldered, bronzed, and he has a small toothbrush moustache. He walks with a peculiarly hurried stride, taking short springy steps, and usually wears a khaki-coloured topee, which appears to be a size too big for him.'

What the paper could not say, because it did not know, was that Newton was carrying a suitcase strapped uncomfortably round one shoulder or the other. He had left Maritzburg under cover of darkness, and his aim was to walk to Rhodesia. As he put it later, he set off 'knowing I had got to make an entirely new start in life, and the sooner I was in a position to begin, the better'. He had no money for either trains or hotels, and he seemed to believe – naïvely – that he could manage the journey without being recognised. Before leaving he had asked a friend to wire him some funds to a town called Estcourt, addressed to a Mr Hamilton – his middle name. He decided to walk at night and sleep during the day: his route went over the mountains and it was far too cold for him to sleep rough at night, and he would also avoid the possibility of someone who recognised him passing in a car. But the strategy proved far more difficult than he had imagined, and after forty-eight hours he was completely exhausted. (It is worth remembering that only two days before he set off he had established a world record for running more than fifty miles.)

When he came to the small town of Mooi River, forty miles from Maritzburg, he could not resist the sight of a small tea-shop. 'I had blundered badly this time: I was recognised as soon as I entered the place and, of course, obliged to admit my identity. Just try to imagine how frightfully embarrassing it was.' Once her famous client was on the road again, the owner of the tea-shop, a Miss MacAllister, sent an immediate telegram to the *Natal Witness*. 'Newton Found' ran the head-line the next day, 1st August. The runner himself seemed to think that he could avoid this happening again, which would have been possible had he been able to do without any human contact at all. As it was, he accepted a lift one afternoon; 'we hadn't gone four miles and he suddenly asked if my name was not Newton'. He stopped at 'a little country post-office to send some letters'; 'making for the box I was spotted right away by the official. Was I not Mr Newton? Well, yes, that was my name, but what about it?' The postmaster invited him in for a cup of tea and a look at the last week's papers. 'Heavens! A glance was sufficient to show me what had occurred: I was supposed to have disappeared, which, of course, was what I had meant to do: but the last thing I had intended was that the disappearance should be noticed: the publicity was deplor-able.' Did he really think so? His 'disappearance' was the best publicity that his campaign against the government ever had.

Cold, insomnia, hunger, poverty and sore feet – those seem to have been the dominant characteristics of Newton's long walk to Rhodesia. He reflected later, no doubt accurately, that if he had not been what he called 'a particularly well-trained athlete', he would have given up within days. As long as he was within reach of Maritzburg he continued to walk only at night; but at times he found the conditions 'perishingly cold and confoundingly dark'. Finding it impossible to sleep for any length of time during the day, he established a nocturnal rhythm of two hours' walking followed by twenty minutes' rest. During the day he would find a place to settle down near the road, and if possible close to water. He passed the time reading his small edition of Shakespeare. He had banked on picking up modest amounts of money that he had arranged to be sent to certain post offices along the way; but he rarely got the timing right, and he came to depend every now and then on the hospitality of old friends or white farmers who noticed and recognised him.

He lived on biscuits: they were light, full of the sugar he needed, and they were cheap. But by the time he reached the boundary between Natal and the Transvaal he was down to his last half a crown. He decided to follow the railway tracks, hoping to find small rural stations where there might be a waiting-room fire that was kept going through the night. It had not taken him long to realise that a suitcase was a hopeless impediment, so he had left it at a station with instructions for it to be sent on to 'Mr Hamilton' later on. But no case meant few clothes – an embarrassment for such a punctilious man. His scruffy and dirty appearance became another reason for his walking at night. He was confident that no one in the Transvaal would recognise him, but he had 'no wish to appear in public as a tramp'. A crucial turning point in the journey came after Newton had been on the road for eight days, during which he had covered 250 miles. Early one morning he came across a family who were having problems fixing a burst tyre on their car. In return for his help they insisted that he accept a lift, which took him a good hundred miles to a small town not far from Johannesburg. His feet were in such a state that his hosts kept him for a week while they recovered. His way of proving to them that he was fit to continue his journey was by going out for a twenty-mile 'jog'. They also agreed to keep his presence at their home a secret, because the Johannesburg press was speculating that Newton was in the area. As a parting gift they presented him with a bicycle, complete with a pannier full of provisions. One can only hope that their kindness and hospitality went some way to tempering Newton's attitude towards the Boers!

He sped through Pretoria, which he had last visited for his uncomfortable meeting with Prime Minister Hertzog, and soon entered countryside that was new to him. It was dangerous for anyone on foot who was obliged to camp out at night, because it was 'lion country'. But Newton found it exhilarating after the endless flat lands of the Transvaal veldt: 'Great piled-up rocks, huge silent buttresses, vistas of precipices high above your head, an awesome gorge with the road blasted out of the cliffs and built up with concrete – the whole more or less covered with an intricate and tangled mass of tropical forest: nature in a fit of careless and stupendous extravagance.' He devoted more time than previously to collecting firewood, knowing that he had to keep the lions away from his camp. Even so, he found sleep impossible. He marvelled at the first baobab trees he had ever encountered, finding them like 'some uncouth prehistoric growth'. The strangeness and novelty of nature matched and reinforced Newton's sense of embarking on a new adventure in his life, of having left behind the known and the comfortable.

The closer he got to the mining town of Messina, the last settlement in South Africa before the Limpopo River and the crossing to Rhodesia, the more desperate he realised he was to leave the Union. Apart from anything else, he simply had to find work. But he arrived in Messina before his suitcase, and this time he had no option but to wait for it.

His lack of money meant that he still had to camp, and a fortuitous meeting in the bush not far from town led to his spending time in the company of an entertaining and hospitable prospector, hunting each day for their food. This was not a major crossing point from South Africa into Rhodesia, and the only way for Newton to leave the Union was to be taken across the Limpopo in a small boat rowed by local villagers, with his precious suitcase precariously balanced on the stern. His life and his belongings were in the hands of 'kafirs', and one cannot think of a more appropriate way for Arthur Newton to take his leave of South Africa. But within hours the athlete was being rowed back again. He was refused entry to Rhodesia. Newton obviously had not bothered to enquire whether there might be any preconditions or requirements for being allowed into the colony; one imagines he assumed that, as a British citizen wanting to go to Rhodesia precisely because it *was* British, he would be welcomed with open arms. He was told by the border police that he had to have either £50 in cash or written evidence of a firm offer of a job in Rhodesia. Having done his best during the long journey from Maritzburg to hide his identity, he now tried to cash in on it. He produced an old newspaper article about one of his record runs that carried his photo and showed it to the policeman. It had no effect at all. The officer had never heard of the 'Newton Case'.

This must have been one of the most sobering moments in Arthur Newton's life. He was forty-two years old; he had neither money nor the immediate prospect of earning any; he had completed an exhausting and hazardous journey only to find his long-anticipated destination barred to him; he had devoted himself to becoming 'famous' and now found himself in a corner of Africa where no one knew who he was. He was rowed back over the river and went once again to camp out with the lone prospector. The only work in Messina was in the copper mines, and Newton had no option but to offer himself as physical labour. He was eventually taken on in a supervisory position, and within weeks had negotiated a transfer to one of the company's mines in the most northern part of Rhodesia, hard by the border with what was then the Belgian Congo. Once again he was rowed over the Limpopo, this time armed with hard evidence of a job offer. The border police waved him through.

III

From the moment Arthur Newton embarked on his career as a professional athlete he always wore the same logo on his running vest: diagonal blue stripes framing two words, 'Natal' and 'Rhodesia'. The former remained his romantic homeland throughout his life – the English place a perfidious 'Dutch' government had obliged him to abandon. He lived in Natal longer than anywhere else; it was where he spent his young manhood, and where he had almost married. It held complex memories of both failure and success. Rhodesia meant different things to him. He had initially thought of trying to re-create his South African farming life there, of becoming a white Rhodesian settler; but in the end he only spent two and half years in the colony – years in which he was able for the first time to devote his life almost entirely to the business of running. In 1921 he had taken up athletics because its status as an amateur sport gave it a particular meaning and importance in colonial life. In the late autumn of 1927 he left Rhodesia, and Africa, to become a professional runner. The two words on his vest encapsulated his unexpected life – and were also a constant reminder to others of why he had become a runner in the first place.

Newton's Rhodesian sojourn began in a most ironic way. Messina, where he had crossed the river, was a hundred miles from the nearest railway station at West Nicholson, from which a twice-weekly train could take him on to Bulawayo. The distance was no problem for Newton, but there was no proper road and he needed to employ two local 'boys' as bearers and guides to get safely through the bush. Though he met one or two white settlers on the way, he was dependent on his boys' local knowledge, and he camped in native kraals because of the danger from lions. Towards the end of their walk one of the young men injured a leg and had to pull out, and Newton was then alone with a 'kafir' whom he evidently found too talkative and insufficiently deferential. He kept an aloof distance because, as he later wrote, 'the white man has to be becomingly reserved among the natives'. It is not a sentence that does him much credit, given that his safety was in the young 'kafir's' hands.

Arthur Newton might not have been known in Messina, but he certainly was in Bulawayo, where his train arrived on 27th October, almost exactly three months after he had set out from Maritzburg. The local *Chronicle* immediately sent a reporter to talk to him. 'Famous Runner in Rhodesia', the next day's headline read. Newton insisted that he was in the colony to stay; that he had no intention of ever returning to the Union of South Africa; and that his plan was to get back as soon as possible to farming cotton and tobacco. He was quoted as saying, 'I do not intend to keep up running. My future is to do farming, and I am very grateful for the offer of employment in Bwana M'Kubwa.' If he was serious in saying all of this, then his life in Rhodesia did not turn out as he hoped.

Newton would have found Bulawayo a welcoming and comforting place after the hardships of the road. He would also have found it reassuringly British, with its white population of more than 7,000. This was an increasingly prosperous community. Bulawayo benefited from its rail links to South Africa, and from the rich yields of cotton and tobacco that the farmlands of Southern Rhodesia produced each year. The white population occupied the central part of the town, while on the periphery were the townships where the African servant classes – and a growing number of immigrants from India – lived. Newton makes no mention of Rhodesian politics in his letters or writings, yet he must have been aware of a growing racial tension in Bulawayo that was to explode in communal riots the year after he left the country. Bulawayo was also, by the standards of colonial Africa, a cultured town, and Newton could have spent evenings at the theatre or the opera.

But the pleasures of Bulawayo would have to wait, because the near-penniless athlete had to get to work – and this meant a long journey, across the Zambesi River, into the different, and much more hostile, landscape and culture of Northern Rhodesia. His destination, to take up the job that had been arranged for him at Messina, was Bwana M'Kubwa – and even for a man as stoical and resilient as Newton, Bwana M'Kubwa would have come as a shock. It was not really a town, hardly yet a properly organised human settlement. It was just the beginnings of a giant copper mine, deep in a forest that a British geologist who worked there at the time, J.A. Bancroft, described as a 'snake park': 'Puff adders were very numerous, including some specimens of the gaboon adder type. Spitting cobras were common and occasionally green mambas made their appearance.' He also suggested that it was quite difficult to settle down to sleep with much confidence. 'Rarely a night passed without hearing the roaring of lions in the distance, and subdued coughing of prowling leopards in closer proximity.' In his 1940 memoir Newton provides a brief and matter-of-fact description of his time at the mine, which was situated near the present-day border between Zambia and the Congo:

> Up at the top of Northern Rhodesia my job was that of supervising gangs of natives on a copper mine. It kept me busy for eight hours each day, sometimes more when overtime was required, though I still managed to fit in a considerable amount of training. Work being the more important item, the training had to take second place, and my running was switched from the early morning to the late afternoon . . . I was always careful to get back before it was quite dark as there was too much wild life about for safety.

Newton found himself – and he cannot have known how long he would need to stay there – in an extreme outpost of European imperialist adventurism. The Rhodesias, both North and South, were political and administrative anomalies. They had not been created as formal 'colonies', but as geographical expressions of the ambition and greed of Cecil Rhodes. During the 1880s Rhodes, like many others, became convinced there must be large deposits of gold to the north of the Afrikaner territories of the Transvaal and the Orange Free State. The Colonial Office in London was, of course, keen for any such mineral wealth to end up in British rather than German,

Portuguese or Belgian hands; but it simply did not have the financial resources to take any formal responsibility for the vast tracts of African-occupied land that were involved. So the government did a deal with Rhodes. Under the terms of a Royal Charter awarded in 1888, his British South Africa Company was given exclusive rights to exploit whatever minerals it found north of the Limpopo, but in return would have to take responsibility for policing and administering the territories. The hoped-for gold was not found; but copper ore was, in potentially extraordinary quantities, just at the time when the electrical and automobile industries of Europe and America were becoming desperate for as much of the mineral as they could lay their hands on. Arthur Newton's arrival in Bwana M'Kubwu was part of a mad 'copper rush'.

The firm he was employed by was the Rhodesia-Congo Border Concessions Company, which in 1924 had been granted the prospecting rights over 52,000 square miles of territory. This deal was part of a decision by Cecil Rhodes's old company, the British South African, to get out of Rhodesia as quickly as it could. Despite its failure to discover any gold, the company was still obliged to pay for administering and policing the 'colony'; and its British shareholders were up in arms at the meagre returns on their investment. The company wanted Southern Rhodesia to become part of the Union of South Africa, but, understandably enough, this was rejected by the overwhelming majority of its British settlers. After consultations with the Colonial Office in London, a small Legislative Assembly was elected (with its seat in Bulawayo), and in 1923 Southern Rhodesia formally became a self-governing colony of the British Empire. The British South Africa Company was paid handsomely for renouncing its rights. In Northern Rhodesia the outcome was slightly different: the Company relinquished control over the territory in 1924, and it took on the uncertain status of a British protectorate. But the BSACo retained its mineral rights, which in turn it passed on to other concerns – one of which gave Arthur Newton a much-needed job in 1925.

This was not what he had come to Rhodesia for. There were as yet no proper roads to Bwana M'Kubwa, though there was a branch railway line to serve the mine. There was no white settler community, no shops or newspapers; almost certainly no one to talk to about Shakespeare or Beethoven. There would have been instead the daily brutality that was African labour in the mine, which Newton had to 'supervise'. No wonder he hoped he could leave as soon as possible. As he wrote later, 'I neither wanted nor expected to remain very long at this mining work, knowing that sooner or later I should be sure to find something else for which I was better suited.' Newton need not have worried. He had been in the far north for less that three months when a letter arrived from the Caledonian Club in Bulawayo asking if he would be interested in moving there and devoting himself to 'reviving' athletics in the city. If he was, the letter suggested, 'work' could be found for him within the club's administration. He did not hesitate. This was a crucial turning point in his life. From now on, it would be from running – its practice, its promotion, its coaching, its literature and philosophy – that Arthur Newton would make his living. Perhaps he knew that by accepting the invitation to Bulawayo he was finally renouncing his dream of farming the land.

But one thing he was not yet renouncing was his campaign against the South African government, and he kept in touch with his former MP in Natal, J.S. Marwick. The politician, though, was scrupulously honest in his refusal to give Newton any false hopes over his case. In March 1926 he wrote to the runner – who had recently arrived in Bulawayo – saying that he doubted very much 'whether there is any likelihood of redress from the Union Government, even if our own party were returned to power again'. Perhaps Arthur Newton was hanging on to some hope that Hertzog's Nationalists would be voted out, but Marwick's warning that even this might not shift things in his favour made no difference. January 1927 found Newton receiving a letter from the South African Prime Minister's private secretary in response to yet another appeal from the athlete over his lost farm. 'I need only reiterate,' the official wrote, 'what was said on the former occasion to you by this Department, namely that your case was thoroughly investigated but that neither the Department nor General Hertzog saw their way clear to act in harmony with the suggestions made by you.' It was rather an elegant way of saying 'Please go away and don't contact us again.' There must have been amazement in Pretoria at Newton's obsessive behaviour; after all, it was by now five years since he had started his campaign.

If his sinecure in Bulawayo gave Newton time to reopen hostilities with the South African government, it also gave him time to reflect and write about the one thing in his life that had not been a failure – long-distance running; and in January 1926 the *Bulawayo Chronicle* published a series of long articles that represented Newton's first attempt at articulating his theories about training. The articles, the paper insisted, 'do not only apply to what might be termed the intensive athlete, but will be read with interest by every man and woman who has the future health of the colony at heart'. There were six of them, each one arguing a 'common-sense' position that Newton felt – and would continue to feel – was perversely ignored. They dealt with how to build up stamina; how to preserve energy for racing; what to eat; what to drink; how to get a 'second wind'; and, finally, smoking. 'To Smoke or Not to Smoke, That is the Question' was its title, and Newton clearly relished its controversial conclusion: 'If I raised a flutter in the dovecotes of the professional trainers with my outrageous ideas on drinks and diet, it was a mere flea-bite to what I am after here. Thank goodness the police are ever with us. I must trust them to keep a fatherly eye on me. Should athletes smoke? By all means if they enjoy it.'

In the context of Arthur Newton's career as a whole the most important event of his time in Rhodesia was his first 100-mile run in the winter of 1927. It was its success that convinced him that what he called 'extra long runs' were what he should concentrate on, where his real singularity would reveal itself. He had never, competitively, run more than the fifty-four miles of the Comrades course, and he felt he could not suddenly attempt almost twice the distance. So he first planned a sixty-mile run, and among his papers is a typewritten sheet recording how he trained for it. It shows how meticulously he was planning his assault on a whole cluster of long-distance records. The sixty miles began and ended at the King's Grounds Gates, and Newton had set up 'posts' at ten, thirty, forty and fifty miles. There are three columns on the paper: one for the mileage, one for his time, and a third listing the existing amateur records. He started at five in the morning, reaching the ten-mile post just after six, and that for thirty miles at twenty-five past eight. The first record he lists is that for forty miles: 4.46.54, set at Birmingham in 1884 by J.E.F. Dixon. Newton, at this distance, was only marginally quicker, reaching the marker in 4.46.30, less than half a minute to the good. But, as he knew, the further the distance, the greater his superiority. At fifty miles he was two minutes ahead of Lloyd's 1913 record of 6.13.58, and by the time he got back to the King's Grounds he had broken W.C. Davies's 1880 record for sixty miles by just under *fifty* minutes. Ever the Empire loyalist, the route Newton chose for his run was from Bulawayo to the grave of Cecil Rhodes and back. He says that he was back at his desk for an afternoon's work.

The sixty miles were a solo effort, but Newton knew that he needed both company and competition to be able to deal with 100. Given the fact that, as he put it, 'there wasn't a spate of 100-mile men in the country', he organised for a relay team of four runners from the Bulawayo Harriers to provide the opposition. 'As they were all men whose normal distances were between one and ten miles they were, in their own way, taking on just about as big a job as I was, and they knew it.' As has been mentioned already, Newton had a profound aversion to running around tracks – they bored him to death – so a route was chosen over the relatively flat road to Bulawayo from the small town of Gwelo. The 100 miles were measured meticulously, with Newton insisting that a further quarter-mile be added just to make sure. After a large breakfast he set off at ten past six in the morning, with the relay team, at Newton's request, starting several minutes later. 'It was dark at first of course, but an official car about fifty yards behind me floodlighted the road which had quite a decent dirt surface, and I ambled along at a serenely easy seven miles per hour, knowing I had to save every atom of energy lest I should fail from exhaustion.' His own philosophy of running dictated that he could not, while on the road, worry about the outcome of the race, because the anxiety would sap his energy. So he would have worked out beforehand the pace he had to maintain, hour after hour. At about the halfway mark he stopped at a hotel for a pre-ordered lunch. 'My fodder was soup, chicken and vegetables, and fruit pie (pastry!): I worked it back as quickly as I dared for no time must be wasted. Twelve minutes later I was on the road again, climbing a gentle gradient on my way to Bulawayo.' By the time darkness fell he still had not reached the city, so once again the headlights of a following car showed him the way. 'Unlimited hot tea from inexhaustible thermos flasks' kept him going over the last miles of desperate exhaustion that ended at the King's Grounds, where – to his usual embarrassment – a considerable crowd had gathered to greet him. He had not only beaten a relay team of four well-trained men, but had taken more than an hour and a half off the existing world amateur record. Hardly surprisingly, he found it difficult 'even to talk and answer the many questions fired at me'.

This was to be Newton's last competitive run in Africa. If his autobiographical writings are to be taken at face value, a decision was made very soon afterwards that he should go to England as soon as possible to run another 100-mile race. What was at stake here was colonial pride, and it was a repeat of the situation Newton had faced in relation to his earlier South African records. His run from Gwelo would not be formally recognised by the British Amateur Athletic Association (AAA), nor therefore by the international athletic community, because of doubts over the expertise of Rhodesian officials. So unless Newton went to England and repeated his feat, Rhodesia would be denied its only world record. This is how the runner himself later described the decision and the thinking behind it:

Bulawayo, and Rhodesia, generally, rose to the occasion. From all quarters subscriptions came in to the Rhodesian A.A. asking that arrangements should be made to despatch their 'guide and mentor' overseas to make good the time, or perhaps even beat it, on some well-known course such as the Bath Road. As I was more than willing to do anything I could to show my appreciation of all the kindness I had met with in this splendid country, it wasn't long before I found myself sailing for England.

That description comes from *Running in Three Continents*, and it was a scenario he repeated in his later book, *Races and Training*: 'The improvement on the [existing record] was so unbelievable to many of these good people that they there and then decided to take steps to send me to England to attempt a better time under more favourable conditions. Feeling that I now knew something of what was needed for this type of race I willingly agreed.'

But these accounts fall short of telling the whole story; and by the time Newton sailed for England at the end of November 1927 his reasons for wanting to set another 100-mile record on British soil were to do with more than putting Rhodesia on the sporting map. We know that he had contacted Joe Binks at the *News of the World* to ask him to organise a record attempt over the classic Bath Road course at the earliest possible date. But why should Newton have been contemplating such a run in the depths of an English winter? He was used to running in African conditions, and English winters were predictably far colder in the 1920s than they are in the early twenty-first century. Why not wait at least until the spring? The answer to these questions lies in a disingenuously simple sentence from Newton's 1940 memoir. 'Just before I left Rhodesia,' he writes, 'I had seen in the papers that a promoter in the United States was organising a race from the Pacific to the Atlantic, for which considerable prizes were offered.'

The promoter in question was a brashly confident American by the name of C.C. Pyle, who had dreamed up the extraordinary project of a non-stop running race across the American continent from Los Angeles to New York; and Pyle had been desperate to contact Newton after reading of his record-breaking sixty-mile run. An article appeared in the *Bulawayo Chronicle* in September 1927 under the headline 'Mr Newton's Records. Invitation From America'. It said that Newton had just received a letter addressed to 'Mr Arthur Newton / Champion Long-Distance Runner / Bulawayo / South Africa'. 'Enclosed in the envelope were a cutting from an American paper reporting Mr Newton's success in his 60-mile record-breaking run, and an invitation to him to participate in the International Transcontinental Foot Race which is being organised by a Mr Charles C. Pyle.' After giving details of the dates for the race and the prizes on offer, the report finished by saying: 'Participation in such a race would, of course, imply Mr Newton's abandonment of his amateur status, which he will not consider. It might be possible to secure permission to run as an amateur, but it is very doubtful.'

Pyle's race was due to start in March the following year, and the promoter needed to sign up some famous distance runners to give his event athletic credibility. There was potentially no one more famous over 'long journeys' than Arthur Newton, but he would be far more of a 'catch' for Pyle if an unofficial record established in a small British colony in southern Africa had been transformed into an official one established in Britain itself. So did Pyle offer Newton any financial inducement to try and set another 100-mile record in England? Did he offer him money if he entered the Transcontinental? Did he say, 'If you set a new record in England then I will pay you to take part in my race?' We do not know. What we do know is that immediately after Newton's success on the Bath Road in January 1928 he received a telegram from Pyle's agent and right-hand man, Hugo Quist, that read simply, 'Congratulations Wonderful Record'. More telling still was one that arrived four days later from Pyle himself. It read, 'Congratulations. May we announce your entry our race?' So there can be no doubt that Newton and Pyle had been in touch with each other before Newton took on the Bath Road; and this means that he set about establishing a new amateur record knowing that he was on the verge of turning professional; and, more damningly, that he had accepted financial help from friends and supporters in Rhodesia under possibly false pretences. One thing is certain: in all his published writings Arthur Newton was very economical with the truth when it came to his financial dealings with C.C. Pyle.

Just before Newton left Rhodesia in late November the Bulawayo Harriers put on a special social evening in his honour. Advertisements for it in the local press explained that it was 'to show the club's indebtedness for what he has done for it and to give members and friends an opportunity to say au revoir to Mr Newton on the occasion of his departure for England'. They may have been saying 'au revoir'; Arthur Newton probably knew he was saying farewell.

IV

In his memoir *Running in Three Continents*, Newton devotes one short paragraph to what he did on 7th January 1928: but the *News of the World*'s Joe Binks, who was there, described what he witnessed as 'the greatest running feat the world has ever seen'. Newton's arrival in England the previous month had coincided with the onset of the coldest winter anyone could remember. He went to stay with his sister Ursula, who lived in the Chilterns between London and Oxford, and Newton hoped this would be a base from which he could explore the Bath Road and get used to its particular challenges. But the weather was too bad. 'I remember one day when I gave it up entirely,' he wrote:

> I had managed to flounder part of the way through a four-to-five-foot drift that blanketed the path from the house for fifty yards or more, but as it appeared running would be quite impossible I worked my way back again. Next day, however, I was able to reach the road by getting over a fence, which was invisible in the snow, and crossing a flat field. Once on the highway I found that traffic had hardened the surface sufficiently to allow me to get along. I went over towards Stokenchurch and from there down to West Wycombe, and was surprised to see cars alongside the kerb on the London–Oxford highway deserted and half-lost in the drifts.

This was hardly ideal preparation for a man who had just left the heat of a southern African summer; and he was worried about a niggling tendon injury. But pulling out was never an option. Joe Binks had organised a four-man relay team to run against Newton, each doing twenty-five miles, and had made sure that there was huge excitement about the record attempt, both from the press and the public. (There was also, quite probably, C.C. Pyle to satisfy.) To please the photographers, who wanted Newton to arrive at Hyde Park in daylight, he had to set off from the village of Box, near Bath, at 2 a.m. and run the first few hours in the dark. He said after it was over that he had felt ill most of the way, and there were certainly moments when he seemed in real difficulties. *The Times* reported that after about seventy miles Newton 'was sick and his progress over the last thirty miles was unusually slow. He kept plugging away doggedly, though obviously distressed.' To make matters worse, the snow had turned to rain in the days immediately before the run, and some parts of the route – Maidenhead in particular – were deep in flood water. Newton had hoped to break fourteen hours, but failed by just over twenty-two minutes; and this perhaps explains his own flat and perfunctory summing-up of the run: 'I was pleased enough to get through it in twenty minutes less time than the hundred in Rhodesia, but that was all that could be said for it.' His lack of enthusiasm was not shared by tens of thousands of Londoners who flocked to see him as he dragged himself over the last few miles through west London to Hyde Park. The police were stretched to the limit as Newton came close to being mobbed along Hammersmith Broadway, and there was pandemonium when he reached the finishing line near St George's Hospital. 'Amazing scenes were witnessed at Hyde Park Corner when, in semi-darkness, Newton completed his great run', wrote Joe Binks; 'thousands of people were there to greet him, and the greatest excitement prevailed.' The runner briefly thanked the crowd, and slipped away.

3

Sport and Endurance, Fans and Voyeurs

C.C. Pyle and the Origins of the Transcontinental

I

The 1920s were golden days for the American sporting press, and writers across the country went to town with both alliteration and condescension in trying to portray the bizarre and unprecedented array of athletes who set out from Los Angeles on that March day in 1928 to run across America. They came up with the 'blister brigade', the 'callous caravan', the 'asphalt arabs', the 'macadam mashers', the 'pain procession'; but when inspiration deserted them, their default description was usually 'Pyle's Plodders'. C.C. Pyle was the race's inventor, its organiser, its boss and its paymaster. It is no exaggeration to describe him as a revolutionary figure. He more or less single-handedly invented the job of sports promoter; and until Pyle came along the words 'sport' and 'professional' sat uncomfortably in the same sentence.

In 1928 C.C. Pyle was forty-eight years old, and for nearly three decades he had been criss-crossing the American continent, constantly reinventing himself in a vain search for the fame and wealth that he regarded as his due. His energy and imagination were admirable; his moral probity somewhat less so. He had been born in Delaware, the son of a Methodist preacher, and from the time he dropped out of college he seemed intent on leading the sort of life such a father could only regard with horror. He had been a salesman, a boxer, a vaudeville actor and a cinema manager; he had been twice married and twice divorced, and he had a habit of running away from his creditors. He was an imposing, good-looking and very vain man. This is how he came over to one of his clients: 'He liked to hear his name mentioned. He'd ride the 20th Century Limited between Chicago and New York and whenever one of the waiters would say "Mr Pyle, how are you", he'd give him a ten dollar tip. If he didn't know his name he wouldn't give him a nickel. He loved that acclaim.'

March 1928 was, for C.C. Pyle, a moment pregnant with possibility. He intended the Transcontinental Foot Race to become an annual event: he thought it would transform American ideas about sport, and he thought it would make him, finally, both deeply respected and extremely wealthy. Given how Pyle was eventually to treat many of the runners who slogged their way across the continent with *his* name on their running vests – both in 1928 and again the following year – it is hard not to regard him with a certain distaste. In the final resort, he was a con-man and a liar. But he did things that no one else in America dreamed of doing. His speciality was convincing the most famous amateur sporting personalities of the day that they should renounce all they had hitherto believed in and stood for, and should turn professional under the tutelage and guidance of C.C. Pyle. Arthur Newton found himself in illustrious company.

To understand the scale of Pyle's ambition one just has to look at the Transcontinental Foot Race's official starter, the man who set off a firecracker to send 200 men trudging through the Californian mud. His name was Harold 'Red' Grange, and in 1928 he was probably the most famous sportsman in America. His game was football (the American variety) and for a handful of years his name could be mentioned in the same breath as the likes of Babe Ruth or Jack Dempsey. He had made his name as a college player, as an amateur, and then C.C. Pyle had 'turned' him. His mother had died when he was five, and Harold 'Red' Grange – the nickname came from his ginger hair – had been brought up by his policeman father in the small town of Wheaton, west of Chicago. He had a younger brother, and family life was close, but spartan. From his days at high school what set Grange apart was simply his speed. As he told an interviewer in 1984, 'It was God-given; I couldn't take any credit. Other guys could make 90s and 100s in chemistry. I could run fast. It's the way God distributes things.' It was natural that he would go to the local college, the University of Illinois at Champaign; it was also natural that he would devote his time there to playing football. Illinois was one of the Big Ten Midwestern and eastern football colleges. The coach earned as much as any professor.

Grange owed his fame to what he did in the opening minutes of one particular game. Against the mighty University of Michigan in 1924 he scored four touchdowns inside the first twelve minutes. Each came after he had run at least half the length of the field. Within days the sporting press made perhaps its first instant hero, and Americans rushed to the cinemas to see newsreel footage of the stern-faced young genius. Grange's running was, by all accounts, mesmerising in its speed and subtlety; and it inspired Grantland Rice, America's most influential sports writer, to some of his most evocative prose. He saw Red Grange as a 'streak of fire, a breath of flame, a grey ghost thrown into the game'. Within weeks *The New York Times* was writing (albeit more prosaically) of Grange as a figure of national significance: 'It is seldom that a player's fame spreads so rapidly and so definitely throughout the country. Grange is known and his deeds are followed from coast to coast with almost the same interest as in his own section of the country.' But someone in his 'own section of the country' was soon to take a very particular kind of interest in the young footballer.

In September 1925, almost a year after his extraordinary game against Michigan, Red Grange – who was beginning his last year at college – went out to the cinema one Saturday evening. This is his own account of what happened.

I was about to take my seat when an usher approached me. Handing me a slip of paper with a few words scribbled on it he said, 'Mr Pyle who runs this theatre wants you to have this. It's a pass that'll get you in at the Virginia Theatre as often as you want for the rest of the year. And you can use it for the Park Theatre too, since Mr Pyle operates both places.' I was very pleased with the offering not only because I liked going to the movies but since this was the first time I had ever received anything free while I was in Illinois.

Several days later I went to the Virginia again. As I

entered the theatre I was greeted in the lobby by Mr Pyle and invited up to his office. I had heard his name mentioned a few times before, but never met him. After exchanging a few pleasantries, he got round to the real reason for wanting to see me.

'How would you like to make one hundred thousand dollars, or maybe even a million?' Pyle asked. I was momentarily stunned. Regaining my composure, I quickly answered in the affirmative. When I attempted to find out what Pyle had in mind he told me he had a plan, but wasn't at liberty to reveal the details at the time. He said he'd contact me in a few weeks and made me promise that after leaving his office I wouldn't mention our conversation to anyone.

This account comes from Grange's 1953 ghostwritten autobiography that was published to read like an all-American inspirational story. So perhaps it is hardly surprising that the athlete was being less than entirely truthful as to his dealings with Pyle. Later evidence has revealed that he certainly knew Pyle in the spring of 1925, and that the Champaign cinema-owner had been working for some time on ways to market the country's most famous footballer – getting him a movie contract seemed to be his first idea. Grange had always been acutely aware of his family's relative poverty; and he was also aware, as any athlete is, that his earning power might not last for long. So he was open to persuasion, and C.C. Pyle could be very persuasive. It is now commonplace for prominent sportsmen and women to negotiate with the world via an agent; but in 1925 such people did not really exist. The job had not been defined. Yet what Pyle was doing over several months that year was to persuade Red Grange that he should allow him, C.C. Pyle, to arrange his life for him – to become in effect both his manager and his agent.

When Pyle got back to Grange after their meeting at the cinema in the autumn of 1925 he offered him something that both of them knew would cause a furore. Instead of suggesting some way for Grange to cash in on his footballing fame after he graduated from college, Pyle suggested that Grange walk out of the university in November at the end of the college season and immediately start playing football for money. Pyle had negotiated a deal with the co-owners of the Chicago Bears professional football team that Grange would play for them for the rest of their season, and that after it was over Pyle would organise a special national tour on the back of Grange's presence. The star was not to be paid a wage; rather, he and Pyle were to be given half of all the gate receipts. 'Pyle had been around: I was just a country boy,' said George Halas, one of the Bear's co-owners, admitting that C.C. had driven a hard deal.

No wonder Pyle insisted that not a word about the deal should be leaked to the press. There were enough rumours flying around anyway as to Grange's possible interest in the pro game – ones he had to continuously deny. Why this was so delicate and potentially embarrassing was that in 1925 the worlds of college and professional American football occupied two different moral universes. Pyle was offering Red Grange an opportunity to become a rich man in a very short period of time; but for the mass of football fans in America their hero had made a pact with the Devil. 'Football isn't a game to play for money,' Grange's coach at Illinois told him. College football was the American equivalent of cricket, in the moral

85

weight that middle-class educationalists placed on it. It was character-forming, turning boys into the right sort of men. It taught courage, self-sacrifice and dignity in defeat; young men learned to put team before self, and the team itself was a symbol of institutional pride. All this was perverted, the argument went, if money was involved.

The trouble was that college football's very success in the 1920s raised questions about how 'clean' it really was. Across the country huge stadia were built, often designated as memorials to alumni who had died in the Great War. (Red Grange's inspired performance against Michigan in 1924 was during the first game played at the Memorial Stadium in Champaign.) The game benefited from the huge cultural changes of the 1920s – the automobile enabled people from far and wide to come to games; the radio served those who could not make it. It was to become a cliché, but in the 1920s it was new and startling for people to describe college football as a secular religion. There was no suggestion that colleges were actually paying their footballers game by game, but, with so much at stake, there were persistent suggestions that talented players were being offered under-the-table financial inducements to go to one particular university rather than another. These eventually led the prestigious Carnegie Foundation for the Advancement of Teaching to investigate what was really going on in elite university sport; and after several years of research their report was finally published in 1929. It did not pull any punches. 'The subsidised college athlete of today connives at disreputable and shameful practices for the sake of material returns and for honours falsely achieved. Arguments in support of such practices are specious, calculated to mislead, and fundamentally insincere. Viewed in the light of common

(*Left*) Peter Gavuzzi, soon after he decided to become a professional runner.

(*Right*) Arthur Newton when he first became a sporting hero in Britain.

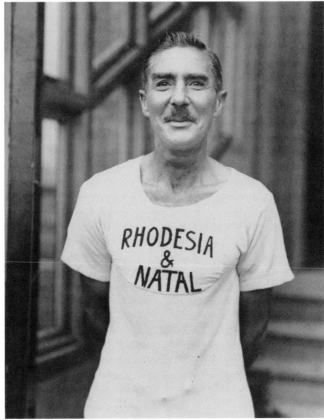

(*Left*) Newton took up running in South Africa – to make a political point.

(*Below left*) Newton breaking the first of his many world records.

(*Below*) Newton raced against a horse in 1925 as a publicity stunt. He'd do so again, years later, for the money.

(*Above*) Huge crowds would turn out to watch Newton in South Africa. His fame highlighted his campaign against the government.

(*Below*) Newton in Rhodesia, after his notorious 'escape' from South Africa.

(*Above*) It was still the middle of the night near Bath when Newton began his attempt on the world 100 mile record in January 1928.

(*Left*) Newton stops for the tea that he always insisted was piping hot.

Nearing the end of his 100 mile run in 1928 Newton had to deal with a major Thames flood.

Right) Gavuzzi first began running on board the transatlantic liner where he worked as a steward. He became a star in races between the crews of different boats.

(*Above*) The two Transcontinentals were the hardest and most extraordinary foot races ever held. Here, in 1929, the competitors gather around race creator C.C. Pyle's luxurious motor-cruiser.

(*Right*) Neither Newton nor
Gavuzzi had a wife or partner
to help them on the long treck
from New York to Los Angeles
in 1929. But Gavuzzi's great
rival Johnny Salo did.

Sincerely
Mrs & John Salo

Superior
Arizona
1929

(*Left*) Not just
a steward any more
Gavuzzi returns to
England on the SS
Majestic in 1929.

Le Chef. Mons Darcourse, Signor Biscasoe e Pietro Gavuzzi
A Bordo del "Majestic" 10 Settembre 1929

decency, this fabric of organised deceit constitutes the darkest single blot upon American college sport.' Football, the Foundation concluded, was the 'darkest' sport of all.

So no wonder professional football was so looked down upon – not just by the amateur elite, but by the paying public and the press. The leading sports writer, John Underwood, called it 'a dirty little business run by rogues and bargain-basement entrepreneurs', while Grantland Rice's condemnation of Grange's 'defection' was withering: 'It might seem that if a college education was worth anything at all it was worth something more than a pro football career.' Where upwards of 60,000 spectators turned up for a big college game, matches in the National Football League struggled to attract one-tenth of that number. When Red Grange signed for the Chicago Bears there were eighteen teams in the League, but, as he later admitted, 'there wasn't enough activity at the turnstiles to support half that number'. Yet if anyone could change the public's perception of the professional game it was Grange. The largest ever crowd for an NFL game, 36,000, turned out for his Bears debut; and, crucially, the elite of the sporting press – men like Damon Runyon – started covering Grange's every match.

The terms of his contract were hard-headed and brutal. They stipulated that Grange had to play at least thirty minutes of each game, even when injury demanded that he be rested. It was 'Red', after all, whom the public would pay to see. And pay they did. Over the winter and early spring of 1925–6 C.C. Pyle's gamble paid off with startling ease. A frantic December schedule had the Bears playing in St Louis, in Pittsburgh, in Philadelphia, in Washington DC, and in New York: ten games in seventeen days. After the New York game, which was watched by professional football's biggest ever crowd, Pyle and Grange spent the evening at their hotel arranging commercial endorsements. As the footballer later wrote: 'we collected about $25,000 in certified checks for endorsements of a sweater, shoe, cap, doll and soft drink. We turned down a tie-up with a cigarette company because I didn't smoke.'

Then, with hardly a rest, the team headed south to the Florida sun and the start of Pyle's hastily arranged tour of exhibition matches. They played in Miami, then went west to New Orleans. Travelling by train in their own Pullman car, they crossed the desert to Los Angeles before ending the trip late in January in Seattle. Twice during a two-month period Pyle had presented Red Grange with a cheque for $50,000. As George Halas put it, 'Red came to the Bears famous. Ten weeks later he was rich.' There were plenty of people who worked with and for Pyle – Peter Gavuzzi and Arthur Newton among them – who would condemn him as someone who did not pay up, and who felt cheated by him. But with Grange, Pyle kept his word; and throughout his long life America's first superstar footballer would never hear a word against the man who manufactured his career. 'Down through the years many unkind remarks have been made about Charlie Pyle', Grange wrote in 1953, 'he was pictured as a notorious money-hungry promoter who ruthlessly exploited and used me to further his own ambitions. Nothing could be further from the truth. Pyle was always more than fair to me and one of the finest men I have ever known. It was a genuine pleasure to be associated with him. I wouldn't have missed the experience for the world.'

For a shy Midwestern young man from a humble back-ground it was quite an experience. Only the best hotels would do for Pyle, only the top restaurants. In Los Angeles he introduced Grange to the likes of Mary Pickford and Harold Lloyd. While there he negotiated Grange a $300,000 film contract, and the footballer spent a good part of the summer of 1926 in Hollywood. The film was a romantic comedy called *One Minute to Play*, and Grange played the male lead; a college football star, needless to say. The football scenes were by no means incidental to the film, and this created a problem. Crowd shots were needed, but how could you hire thousands of extras in the heat of a Southern Californian summer and expect them to look like spectators at a game taking place on an autumn afternoon in the Midwest? It was C.C. Pyle, of course, who came up with the solution. He put an advertisement in local papers announcing that a team led by Red Grange would play a real match against one led by local football hero George Wilson, and that admission would be free to anyone turning up 'in full apparel'. 'The results of Pyle's brainstorm were unbelievable,' Grange remembered; 'fifteen thousand die-hard football fans turned out in felt hats, scarves, coats and jackets, and when seen on the screen couldn't be distinguished from a crowd on a chilly fall day in Ohio or Illinois.'

A sideline as a budding film star was not the only new thing to come out of the summer of 1926 for Red Grange. The other, and far more significant, development in his professional relationship with C.C. Pyle was their formation of a separate professional football league, one to rival the NFL. The co-owners of the Chicago Bears had been keen to continue the existing arrangement for another season, but Pyle – negotiating, he thought, from a position of strength – insisted on Grange and himself acquiring an ownership stake in the club. When this was refused, he decided to walk away and set up his own franchise, but his plan for a New York team was blocked. What happened next was typical Pyle: if the existing structure could not provide what he wanted, his response was to create a new one. But by the time the alternative American Football League, and his own and Grange's New York Yankees team, were up and running, much of Pyle's attention was elsewhere. He had become the agent for someone whose fame, on both sides of the Atlantic, put that of Red Grange in the shade.

II

She was greeted everywhere by masses of awed and adoring fans. She travelled exclusively by chauffeured limousine or private rail car. She draped herself in the white ermine of royalty and crowned herself with a unique jewelled bandeau. Her wardrobe was created by France's leading designer, and what she wore set the style for women throughout the Western world. What she said, did, ate, how she felt and where she lived were all reported in painstaking and adoring detail in the newspapers. She was the best known and most admired woman in Europe – perhaps in the world.

So her biographer, Larry Engelmann, described the impact in the 1920s of the French tennis player Suzanne Lenglen. Lawn tennis in the years after the First World War was without a doubt an important international sport, if as yet in only a handful of countries. Its great championships at Wimbledon, Paris and New York were fiercely contested and widely reported; the best players took part in the Davis Cup. But the sport was staid, middle class, socially conservative, properly dressed and suburban. It was also dominated by male administrators for whom amateurism was next to godliness. Then came Lenglen. She fitted the sport's class profile, coming from a comfortable bourgeois family in Nice. But that was as far as her conformity went.

Groomed for success by her obsessive father, she played tennis in a startlingly 'unfeminine' way, being physically both flamboyant and aggressive. She shocked spectators with the audacity of her tennis clothes as much as with that of her strokeplay. She arrived on court wrapped in an ermine stole, and she drank brandy between games. She put as much energy into her nightlife as into her tennis, and became a focus of the fascination with sport that characterised French artistic life for much of the 1920s. She was by no means 'pretty', and all of this would have made her, in tennis circles, an object of suspicion, if not ridicule, but for one thing – Suzanne Lenglen was so good as to be almost unbeatable for much of the decade. She was Wimbledon champion every year between 1919 and 1925, and she became – whether she liked it or not – a potent symbol of the revival of France after the trauma of the First World War.

'The fact that people hated her was enough for me. People will pay to see someone they hate.' That, reportedly, was how C.C. Pyle responded to Damon Runyon when the writer suggested to the promoter that Lenglen could make big money playing professionally in the States. 'Hatred' might be too strong a term, but there is no doubt that American fascination with her was laced with a certain measure of vitriol. This went back to 1921 when the French star had made a disastrous trip to the States. At the French Championships in June that year

Lenglen had beaten the much-vaunted American player Molla Mallory. The score of 6–2, 6–3 suggested that the victory was almost embarrassingly easy, but Lenglen rubbed it in by claiming that she had only lost the five games because new shoes had given her blisters. This confirmed a common view among America's top players that she was simply too big for her plimsolls, and Mallory was convinced that she could gain her revenge were Lenglen to play her on the other side of the Atlantic. The 'Goddess', she believed, would lose much of her power when deprived of her retinue and her daily dose of adulation. Lenglen, for her part, made known her disdain for all things American and her desire not to visit the country. Yet she had a powerful reason for doing so. The US Lawn Tennis Association refused to accept that the winner of Wimbledon had the right to call himself or herself 'world champion' unless they also won their own championships at Forest Hills; and Suzanne Lenglen wanted to be able to call herself just that without anyone being able to question it. So she agreed that after Wimbledon – which she won for the third consecutive year, with Molla Mallory losing in an early round – she would contest Forest Hills for the first time. The cost of the trip would be covered by playing a few exhibition matches on either side of the championships. But what could have been a great sporting occasion turned out to be an embarrassment.

Suzanne Lenglen could be both neurotic and hypochondriac, so it is hard to judge how genuine was the 'illness' that delayed her departure from France and that caused her first exhibition matches to be cancelled. Perhaps it was real; perhaps it was caused by nerves; or perhaps she was getting in some mitigating circumstances in advance of a possible defeat. Whatever the reason, when Lenglen arrived at Forest Hills it was unnecessary for her to tell people that she was not feeling at her best; those who saw her practising reported that she seemed tired and listless.

The tournament was still, surprisingly, unseeded; and – much to the disappointment of both fans and officials – Lenglen and Mallory were drawn to meet each other in the second round. Then the former's first-round opponent withdrew at the last minute. So it was without any recent match practice, as well as without the usual courtside presence of her father, that Suzanne Lenglen stepped out to face Mallory on Tuesday 16th August 1921 in front of a capacity crowd of 8,000. The American showed neither sympathy nor respect for the legend on the other side of the net, rushing to take the first set 6–2. Lenglen, by all accounts, looked physically and mentally beaten from the beginning, with a hacking cough that got stronger and stronger as the points mounted against her. She started the second set with a double fault; she went up to the umpire's chair and whispered something; then she left the court. The most-anticipated match of the championships was over; and, in little more than half an hour, Suzanne Lenglen had gained a reputation as a quitter. There was nothing more disreputable in the eyes of the American sporting public. Yet, just short of five years later, C.C. Pyle decided that he could make money by marketing a professional Suzanne Lenglen tour across the United States.

For years her detractors had been accusing Lenglen of already being, to all intents and purposes, a professional tennis player. She had no occupation other than the game, and she hardly pursued a modest lifestyle. But those detractors were very largely Anglo-Saxons – players and administrators who were ideologically committed to strict amateurism. Competitive sport in France, while gaining in social significance and prominence after the First World War, had never carried the same philosophical baggage. After all, schools along the lines of Rugby, Eton or Marlborough simply did not exist. Suzanne Lenglen was certainly not paid directly for winning tennis matches, but there can be no doubt that she was quietly and handsomely 'sponsored' by the elite clubs of the French Riviera, especially the Nice Tennis Club. On both sides of the Atlantic the early and mid-1920s were a period of frantic, relieved exuberance, as younger people, having experienced the death of so many of their contemporaries in the war, celebrated the simple fact of being alive. Sport was part of this; so were travel and tourism; and the two came together on the Riviera. For the best players in the world the most attractive tournaments in spring and early summer were those in Nice, Cannes, Menton and Monte Carlo. For the wealthy of London, New York or Paris those were the most attractive destinations for escaping the tail end of long, grey winters. For years Suzanne Lenglen was the main attraction at Riviera tournaments. She sold tickets, and she also sold expensive hotel rooms. So, as a matter of course, the great and good of Nice made sure that she and her family remained loyal to their home town and were able to devote themselves entirely to tennis.

But 1926 was a year of crisis for the French champion – a crisis that C.C. Pyle was sharp enough to recognise and then to exploit. In purely tennis terms, Suzanne Lenglen's year was dominated by an intense, emotionally exhausting rivalry with the brilliant young American, Helen Wills.* In Europe, and

* The following paragraphs are indebted to Larry Engelmann's *The Goddess and the American Girl; the Story of Suzanne Lenglen and Helen Wills*, Oxford, 1988.

especially at Wimbledon, Lenglen had remained unchallenged during the years since her traumatic visit to the States in 1921. But the American sporting press had continued to question her status and her character, and the Forest Hills tournament in 1923 finally gave them a home-grown player they were convinced would put the egotistical, unsporting, alcohol-loving and dubiously amateur Frenchwoman in her place. The Californian Wills was seventeen that year; blond, classically attractive, athletic, serious-minded and modest (if rather humourless), she was everything that Lenglen was not. She said she just played tennis for fun and was more interested in pursuing a career in fine art; and she was just the sort of sporting heroine the country had been waiting for. In the final at Forest Hills that year the young woman whom Paul Gallico had already christened 'Our Helen' crushed the defending champion Molla Mallory 6–1, 6–2. Grantland Rice was enthralled by her 'peacefulness and perfection', insisting that 'no woman player today would have even the slightest chance against her, for no woman player could come close to matching her power and control'. He was not just talking about American players. He was saying that Helen Wills would have no difficulty in beating Suzanne Lenglen. A gauntlet had been thrown across the Atlantic. It landed on the French Riviera.

It was not until two and a half years later that Wills and Lenglen finally met across the net, by which time it was perhaps the most-anticipated sporting contest that had ever taken place. The event was the final of the Carlton Club tournament at Cannes on 16th February 1926. The world's press were there, and special stands were erected overnight; huge sums had been spent on acquiring the filming rights; dedicated trains arrived from Paris; tickets changed hands at ten times the asking price. 'A game that made continents stand still' was how the American journalist Ferdinand Tuohy described it. Other writers found it hard to avoid 'clash of civilisations' rhetoric. This is how Paul Gallico looked back on the way he and fellow Americans covered the match: 'we were whooping it up in those days, and it was ballyhooed into the battle of the ages, with the cool peaches-and-cream-skinned, clear-eyed beautiful Helen fighting for the forces of youth and light, democracy and right, against the unattractive Suzanne. A foreigner representing the menace that is always met and defeated by our fine American manhood and womanhood.'

The match exceeded all expectations. The tennis was dramatic and daring, with the lead repeatedly changing hands. Lenglen won the first set 6–3, but had been required to play with such consistent intensity that she only got through the second with the help of regular shots of iced cognac from her mother's courtside hamper. She prevailed 7–5, but only after she had celebrated a premature victory when she mistakenly thought a Wills drive had been called out. Lenglen had won, but she knew as well as anyone what the real meaning of the match was – that Helen Wills, six years younger than she was, would soon be able to beat her as a matter of course. The American was calm and graceful in defeat; the French champion went home to Nice and sank into an exhausted depression.

In retrospect one can see the 'match of the century' in Cannes as the beginning of a long crisis that would result in Lenglen's stunning decision later that year to take Pyle's money and turn her back on amateur tennis. The next act in the drama was played out on the most famous tennis courts in the world, those at Wimbledon, where Suzanne Lenglen had not lost a singles match in seven years. What happened was this. It was Wimbledon's jubilee year, but Lenglen arrived in south-west London feeling unwell. After her first-round match she sent a message to the tournament referee, F.R. Burrow, asking if her next one could be put back. Assuming that the champion's request would be granted, she did not turn up for the match at the initially advertised time. The problem was that Queen Mary, a devoted Lenglen fan, did: and she waited for more than a hour before pointedly leaving. Burrow, insisting that he never received Lenglen's message, made it be known that he had given her a severe dressing-down for insulting the Queen. A shaken Lenglen appeared the next day for a doubles match, to find that the crowd that turned against her. They booed and hissed as her game disintegrated. The following day she informed Burrow that she was withdrawing from the tournament. This time the message did get through; and Suzanne Lenglen had played her last game of competitive amateur tennis.

III

Three weeks later C.C. Pyle arrived in France. He brought his lawyer with him, and an already drafted contract. They settled into a luxury hotel near Dieppe, and waited for Suzanne Lenglen to be ready to negotiate. She already knew who he was, as earlier in the year Pyle had employed a prominent Californian promoter, William Pickles, to go to Nice and explore possibilities with the Lenglen family. Pickles had initially had their villa's front door slammed in his face, until he assured them that what he wanted to talk about did not involve professional tennis. He mooted various tantalising but vague scenarios of Lenglen touring the States as a celebrity, and of her being given a movie contract. None of this was serious, but he was sowing the seed in the Lenglens' minds that Pyle might represent their future in some way, and he was finding out what he could concerning both the family's financial situation and Suzanne's own frame of mind. He was able to report back to Pyle that they were extremely worried – about the implications of Suzanne's dominance of the women's game being threatened, about her father's rapidly declining health, and about the fact that Suzanne had no obvious way of earning a living other than as a tennis player. It was all she had ever done. This was what Pyle knew *before* the extraordinary events at Wimbledon. Afterwards he thought he could also play on Lenglen's desire to have some sort of revenge on the ruling elite of amateur tennis.

C.C. Pyle was impressed by what he saw. 'Why, if she were merely to rise from this chair and walk over to the door,' he was reported as saying after his first meeting with the tennis player, 'it would be, well, it would be like a seagull leaving a wave.' Suzanne Lenglen, for her part, was impressed by what she heard. There were suggestions in the press that Pyle was offering her something in the region of $200,000; and he was still, disingenuously, encouraging her to think about the possibility of a Hollywood career. Pyle, as Red Grange could have told her, was a persuasive man. Before the end of the month Lenglen issued a brief statement to the press: 'To whom it may concern: I have just signed a contract with Charles C. Pyle of America for a four months' tour of exhibition tennis. My engagement will start in America on October 1, 1926.'

So Suzanne Lenglen became a professional. It was an extraordinary moment for tennis; and it was an extraordinary coup for a relatively small-time sports promoter from America to sign up the world's most famous sportswoman, who was European to boot. *The New Yorker* characterised Pyle as 'a cannibal king who devours amateurs as the Minotaur gulped Athenian youths'. When the French liner the *Paris* docked in New York on 30th September C.C. Pyle hosted a dinner on board in honour of Lenglen, with Red Grange acting as the master of ceremonies. Ten days later what was marketed as 'The Suzanne Lenglen North-American Tour' got under way at Madison Square Garden, and over the next four months Lenglen was to play forty professional exhibition matches across the continent. But whether the match was in Pittsburgh, or Chicago, or Toronto, or Los Angeles, or Havana, her opponent was always the same – Mary K. Browne, who when she signed with Pyle was America's fifth-ranking female player. On the first night of the tour Browne was beaten 6–1, 6–1, and though on occasions she was to make more of an impact, she never once beat the Frenchwoman. It was even suggested that it had been in her contract that she was not to. The 'Tour' also featured a men's match between the American Davis Cup player Vincent Richards and a young Frenchman, Paul Feret.

Who knows whether C.C. Pyle thought there would be a stampede of financially frustrated amateur players queuing up to join his squad. If he did, he was rapidly disillusioned. Professional tennis was as roundly condemned in the press as professional football had been. The US Lawn Tennis Association refused to allow any of its members to act as officials for the Pyle matches, and Lenglen and her colleagues were told in no uncertain terms that they would no longer be welcome at tournaments where they had once starred. The five-times Wimbledon champion had her membership of the All England Lawn Tennis Club revoked. By the time the tour ended in

February 1927 it was obvious to all involved that there was no point in trying to do it again. It was clear that professional tennis had no immediate future. Suzanne Lenglen, who by all accounts had become desperately bored, returned to France with about $100,000 to put in to her Nice bank account. C.C. Pyle made about the same amount. When asked by a reporter whether he was downhearted at how it had ended, Pyle said no. 'I was in the Suzanne Lenglen business,' he was quoted as saying, 'not the tennis business.' And in the early spring of 1927 he was already thinking of his next scheme, and his next famous amateur to 'gobble' – Arthur Newton.

IV

C.C. Pyle's remark about being interested in Suzanne Lenglen rather than in tennis is a telling one. It provides a clue as to what he was setting out to achieve with the Transcontinental Foot Race, and as to why he thought such an extraordinary and unlikely event could make him money – because that, in the final analysis, was why he created it. Perhaps he never quite got the theatre out of his blood, because he was not interested in sport that was not spectacle at the same time. He probably could not appreciate whether or not Lenglen was playing good tennis when he was managing her, and he would not have worried if he were assured she was not. He was in search of a new audience – people who would turn out on a cold winter's night to watch Lenglen because she was a phenomenon, not because she was a good tennis player. In fact he bragged about attracting people who knew nothing about the game. He wanted to remove the distinction between sport and entertainment, between sport and spectacle. To achieve this he needed athletes who were celebrities (for whatever reason) as much as they were great performers, and he needed audiences who were voyeurs as well as fans.

In his Transcontinental race Pyle was trying to bring together two things: mainstream sport, and what can loosely be termed 'competitive physical events'. The two existed side by side in 1920s America; ordinary people were increasingly passionate about them both, but they appealed to different sections of the community. On the one hand, there were the accepted 'sports', defined to some extent as such because they were what 'sports journalists' wrote about – football, baseball, boxing, golf, basketball, ice hockey, and to a lesser extent tennis and 'track and field'. These had all taken root in American society, or at least in certain areas of the country; they were all capable of creating 'heroes'; and they were all in the complex throes of transition from amateurism to professionalism. On the other hand, there were a cluster of novel physical competitions – long-distance swimming events, dance marathons, pole-sitting contests – that had no history and no traditions, that sports writers ignored, but that somehow touched and expressed the spirit of the times. The American sports historian Mark Dyreson has spoken of a public fascination in the 1920s with feats of endurance and with 'long distance of all sorts'. He sees the passionate response to Charles Lindberg's transatlantic flight and an obsession with marathon dances as two sides of the same cultural coin. He also suggests – with particular reference to Pyle's transcontinental runs – that the extraordinarily rapid creation in the 1920s (thanks to Henry Ford) of a motoring society produced a fascination with what the limits of human endurance might be, with what 'human bodies could still conquer'.

The historian of the 1920s dance marathons, Carol Martin,

argues that initially they were simply part of a larger craze for setting world records. She sets them in a context of competitive marathons for kissing, hand-holding, gum-chewing or egg-eating. 'If the records of the world-class athletes were beyond the dreams of ordinary persons,' she says, 'the promise of fame and perhaps wealth was still possible through endurance contests.' But before long promoters like New York's Milton Crandall (a close associate of Pyle) began to see the commercial possibilities of dance marathons, if the human drama of extreme endurance could be taken to its limits. Over a long period of time, he thought, spectators would come to identify with a particular person or couple and would keep coming back to watch how they were getting on. It did not take long for 'innocent' marathons to become horrific exercises in exploitation, contested by the desperate and fuelled by a prurient press on the lookout for tales of despair and disappointment. Crandall's big moment as a dance-marathon promoter came in June 1928, only weeks after Pyle's first transcontinental run had ended, when he mounted what was billed as the 'Dance Contest of the Century' at Madison Square Garden. This is how *Time* magazine reported on it:

> For the first week, practically no notice was taken of the proceedings. It was regarded as uninteresting, futile, vulgar. On the tenth day the New York *Evening Graphic* published 'doctored' photographs of contestants, showing faces that were thinned and blackened with exhaustion, suggesting that the dance marathon was not only silly but cruel. At this, a vast throng of persons rushed to Madison Square Garden and bought their way in. The marathon, which had hitherto been a financial failure,

bloomed into success. The dancers, whose ranks were by this time greatly reduced, became famous and excited; they whirled and shuffled happily, receiving donations from the audience.

C.C. Pyle wanted to attract the people who made up the marathon audience; but he also wanted to attract those who followed college athletics or the Olympic Games. He wanted to create a unique sporting fusion.

Perhaps the best way to understand what Pyle was after is to look at the two sporting events that he used as models. On the one hand, there was the Tour de France – epic, symbolic, highly competitive, creative of national icons, a celebration of the landscape; on the other hand, there was the six-day bicycle race at a venue like Madison Square Garden – dangerous, claustrophobic, urban, on the edge of the illicit. What was common to both was pushing the human body and spirit to the edge of complete exhaustion. Looking back from the vantage-point of the late 1940s, Fred Hawthorne of the *New York Herald Tribune* produced a wonderful description of the world of the six-day bicycle race.

The hardiest athletes in any sport and of any era were the six-day riders. This has been attested time and again by the track physicians who do the 'repair' work on injured riders. Falls that would either kill an ordinary man or put him in hospital for several weeks are merely incidental in the life of a six-day racer ... In [the 1920s], in addition to the advertised prize money, the six-day riders used to reap a harvest every night of the race by winning 'primes'. These were special sprints requested by spectators with more dollars than sense. Many a night the announcement would go over a loudspeaker in this fashion: 'Mr McGoofie offers $500 to the winner of a one mile sprint', or 'The Gents clothing firm of Ginsburg, Levy, O'Houlihan and Ginsburg offers a two-pants suit and a hand-tailored overcoat to the winner of a one-lap sprint', and the race for an extra pair of pants would be on. Refrigerators, washing machines, lamps, long flannel underwear, dog biscuit, hair restorer, a year's subscription to a fashion magazine, or a set of aluminium kitchen ware – all of these were grist to the riders.*

This was sport with the frisson of possible death. Pyle wanted runners who had the same hardness as the six-day cyclists, the same lack of shame or embarrassment at showing themselves in public as marathon dancers did when they were reduced by exhaustion to dirty, sweaty, hobbling wrecks. Pyle, it is worth saying again, wanted spectators who were also voyeurs.

The components of the Transcontinental were simple. There were the athletes; there was the unimaginable distance; and then there was the route, the actual roads on which the plodders would plod. But C.C. Pyle was faced with a fundamental problem. He had no stadium, or track, to which he could charge an entrance fee; and he could not block off sections of the public highway and charge people to stand by it as his

---

* It's worth mentioning that Pyle initially intended his Transcontinental race to feature just such sprints; and Peter Gavuzzi suggested that it was their inclusion in the programme that encouraged him to enter. His ironic description of himself in 1928, after all, was as 'a budding miler, ready to slaughter all and sundry at 3,000 miles'.

runners went by. There were no television rights to be sought in 1928, and though radio was newly important and ubiquitous in American life, the Pyle race – in which several minutes, if not hours, might separate one competitor from another – would hardly make for gripping listening.

The solution to Pyle's dilemma (and it seems fair to say that without this the event would never have been imagined, let alone organised) was that while he had a race to sell, there were others who had a road to sell. It had recently been designated US Route 66. 'If you ever plan to motor west, travel my way, take the highway that is best. Get your kicks on Route 66.' It was in 1946 that Booby Troup came up with the lyrics for what soon became one of America's iconic songs – a hymn both to the motor car, and to the landscape of Midwestern and south-western America. But it had been precisely two decades previously, in 1926, that the US Federal Government had recognised the need for a rational, universally accepted system of numbering for the new roads that were linking state to state, and that were just beginning to provide an alternative to the railways for those seeking to discover their own country. Numbers were up for grabs, and Cyrus Vance, an Oklahoman who was President of the American Association of State Highway Officials, wanted a catchy and memorable one for the road that was to link his rural backwater of a state to Chicago in the east and Los Angeles in the west. He chose 66, and he also took the lead in forming a US 66 Highway Association, which brought together delegates from the eight different states that the road crossed on its 2,000-mile journey from Lake Michigan to the Pacific. They came up with the matchless slogan 'The Main Street of America', and set about advertising the road's attractions – especially that it gave those who lived in the somewhat humdrum Midwest access to the romantic 'Wild West'. The Association put on 'Indian Shows', rodeos and regional craft fairs. Expectant motels sprung up by the side of the road in provincial towns like Springfield in Missouri, Amarillo in Texas or Albuquerque in New Mexico. But what the advertising did not emphasise was the quality of the road itself. It was not to be fully paved until 1938, and in 1928 less than 20 per cent had been surfaced with either asphalt or cement. The further west one went, the more primitive its condition became, and from the Texas Panhandle to the outskirts of Los Angeles it was little more than a much-hyped dirt track.

Accounts differ as to whether it was Pyle who first contacted the Route 66 Association in 1927 or the other way round. No matter, both saw advantages in linking the Transcontinental road race, for the first two-thirds of its distance, with the Route itself. Promoting one would be promoting the other; and Pyle thought he had found the key to his making money out of the race in the desire of businessmen and city elders along the way to be associated with his heroic venture. This is what he told *Time* magazine a few weeks before the 'long grind' got under way:

> We'll run through hundreds of towns, cities and villages. Spectators by the thousands will be attracted to these places to see the race pass through. That will mean money for local merchants and advertising for the towns. It will help the sale of everything from mouse traps to grand pianos. Each town will be assessed so much by me for advertising, or we won't run through, but through a rival town. Then we'll sell a million programmes, easy. You

can't tell the runners without a programme. I'll get a hundred thousand for the advertising in that. I'll have a travelling amusement show with the race. Admission will not be free. I'll make money on that too. In fact it's about the easiest thing I've ever seen.

The master of ceremonies for the amusement show, who was to accompany the race all the way across the continent, was none other than Red Grange. It was a potent way of saying that the Transcontinental road race would be sport of the very highest quality.

4

Los Angeles to New York, 1928

The First Transcontinental

I

Peter Gavuzzi, aptly enough, arrived in Los Angeles by boat via the Panama Canal; and in his suitcase was a running vest with one word emblazoned on its front: Southampton. Gavuzzi, with an Italian father and a French mother, never quite knew which country was 'home', and for much of his life he expressed no great loyalty to Britain, preferring to live either in France or in French Canada. But to the city of Southampton he did feel loyal because it was there, when he was nineteen, that he got his first job – as a steward on the White Star liner *Majestic* crossing the Atlantic to and from New York. He wanted to travel, he said later, to help him overcome the disappointment of having become too tall and heavy for a career as a jockey. He had left school as soon as he could and had been apprenticed at two horse-racing yards, the first in Wiltshire, the second in Newmarket; and it was at the latter Suffolk horse-racing town that Peter Gavuzzi first realised he had a special gift as a runner. Each year the racing community held an athletics meeting there, and in 1923 he won what he called his first 'big race', a twelve-mile 'Marathon'. He had no clear idea of an alternative career, but family connections helped him make the transition from Suffolk to Southampton, from racing to sailing. An old friend of his father's, Magno Boscasso, had recently been appointed manager of the *Majestic*'s first-class dining room.

The *Majestic*, at nearly, 57,000 tons, was the biggest vessel in the world; and she was the second fastest, after Cunard's *Mauretania*, across the Atlantic. She could carry more than 2,100 passengers, and her operators were particularly proud of the first-class dining room, which could serve 654 at a sitting and which featured, the publicity brochure boasted, a 'frescoed dome springing from slim Ionic pillars'. But the ship had a curious past. Her maiden voyage from Southampton to New York took place in 1922, yet she had been launched eight years previously – in Hamburg. She had begun life as one of three planned superliners, which were to show the world that German shipbuilding was equal – if not superior – to Britain's; and she was to be named the *Bismarck*. But her launch by the Kaiser's granddaughter in the summer of 1914 was soon overtaken by war, and her hull was left rusting in the waters of Hamburg docks. Under the terms of the Treaty of Versailles her two sister ships were handed over to the Americans, while the *Bismarck* herself became British. The order was that she was to be completed, and a team of engineers from the Belfast yard of Harland and Wolff was sent to Hamburg to oversee the work – which, despite various attempts at sabotage by the German labour force, was completed early in 1922.

The *Majestic* had one design idiosyncracy that was to suit Peter Gavuzzi down to the ground: the whole of the promenade deck was open along the entire length of the superstructure. This made it ideal for running laps around the boat – which was something Gavuzzi's bosses were, it seems, keen for him to do. In 1961 he gave the British Road Runners Club a brief description for their newsletter of his youth and his first experiments with athletics, and this is what he said about White Star life: 'Competitions were held amongst the crews of all the liners and believe me the competition was stiff. Each company likes to win the Blue Riband in athletics. The races were held in the Van Courtland Track in New York. I tackled two events, the 200 yards and the mile. The mile was of course the Blue Riband and I proudly have the cup I won outright for three consecutive years. It was given by Lord Dewar the whisky magnate.' These inter-company sports days were fiercely contested – a vehicle for the rivalry between Cunard and White Star in particular. But athletic competition was also shipping-line policy for individual boats, a way no doubt of keeping crews fit and occupied while they waited in port. Southampton's local paper, the *Southern Echo*, makes frequent mention of them during the later 1920s. On 1st November 1928, for instance, the paper reported on the Cunard ship *Aquitania*'s sports day in New York. It was held at the famous Pier 54 on the Hudson, 'where the course was laid out on the upper pier, which, being asphalt, was somewhat hard and fast on the legs'. Individual events were sprints, the mile, a 'ladies 80 yards', special races for officers and chefs, and a tug-of-war in which 'great rivalry existed between the Catering and Deck departments'.

It was in the White Star's own paper, the *Ocean News*, that Peter Gavuzzi noticed an advertisement that offered a very large sum of money to the winner of a road race from one side of the USA to the other. He was intrigued, and when he mentioned the event to his boss on the *Majestic,* Magno Boscasso immediately offered to sponsor him. When asked years later why he had entered the race Gavuzzi just said, 'I thought it would be a good way of seeing the country.'

Arthur Newton, by contrast, crossed America by train; and the fact that he was accompanied all the way by Hugo Quist – the man who had masterminded the great Paavo Nurmi's tour of America in 1925 and who was now working for C.C. Pyle – says much about his status as a special competitor. So does the fact that he was given dispensation to arrive well after the stated deadline of 12th February.

II

This deadline was a full three weeks before the race was due to start, and Pyle insisted on it for reasons of safety. He had required every entrant to agree in writing that during this period they would 'be willing at all times to submit to a physical examination by official physicians'. The American medical profession was both terrified and enthralled by what 'Pyle's Plodders' were about to do to their bodies and their minds. To them the race amounted to an unexpected, fascinating and possibly revelatory clinical trial that no research team could have dreamed of putting together: 199 men, of widely differing age, physical type and athletic experience, were setting out to run an average of forty miles a day for eighty-four consecutive days. They were going to be crossing the highest mountains of the continent and its harshest deserts; they were going to be running in extremes of heat and cold, and of wind and rain; and they were setting out to do this without any sophisticated backup from trainers, physiotherapists or dieticians.

In July 1929 the prestigious *Journal of the Medical American Sciences* published two studies that resulted from observing and testing the transcontinental runners. The first, which involved ninety athletes, was entitled 'Observations on the Apparent Adaptability of the Body to Infections, Unusual Hardships, Changing Environment and Prolonged Strenuous Exertion'. The second, which studied a smaller group of twenty-three participants, wanted to assess the 'Effects of Exercise on the Size of the Heart'. The researchers were based at the Jefferson Hospital in Philadelphia, and one of them, John C. Baker, signed up with Pyle as the race's official doctor. He accompanied the run from coast to coast. The preamble to the first of these studies reveals a general medical unease at the prevalent cultural obsession with competitive endurance events: 'The possibility that certain untoward effects may occur following prolonged exercise has been considered seriously in recent years. The interest is due largely to the increasing number of endurance contests (swimming and running) and the fact that a number of prominent athletes have succumbed to heart disease and pulmonary tuberculosis.' The development of these conditions by these particular athletes could, the authors acknowledged, have been accidental and nothing whatever to do with the effects of endurance events. What was needed was a long-term study that could establish whether, over time, extreme exercise was good or bad for people; and that was what Pyle's race offered. Follow-up studies in later years would track the lasting effects of the Transcontinental's unprecedented physical demands.

The first thing for Dr Baker to do was to make a pre-race assessment of his ninety runners (whether they volunteered or were selected is not known). He asked them for detailed information on their medical history, and took basic blood and urine samples. But Baker's job as race doctor meant that he also had to make a basic assessment of *all* 199 entrants, and Pyle gave him the authority to bar those he felt should not run. The last thing the promoter needed – given the way the race was going to be financed – was for a contestant to collapse and die during its early stages. But one can only say that Dr Baker was extremely relaxed in how he interpreted his brief. Given what they were about to embark on, his assessment of the entrants' physical condition seems chilling. He found 50 per cent of them to be 'undeveloped physically'; and could only find forty or so who 'appeared capable of withstanding strenuous athletic competition'. He identified serious gastrointestinal problems, and a range of respiratory weaknesses that included bronchitis and even emphysema. Arthur Newton, too, was far from impressed by the physical calibre and athletic experience of the men he would be running against. 'A little investigation,' he wrote later, 'revealed the fact that the great majority of [them] were quite unaware of the magnitude of the task ahead of them and were not sufficiently trained: those who, on one occasion only, had done as much as fifty miles in a single day, could almost be counted on the fingers of a single hand.'

It was not just his fitness that made Arthur Newton stand out from the majority of his fellow competitors in Los Angeles in February 1928. So did his class and education. Though he was eventually to come to like and greatly admire several of them, such a gathering of hard-bitten and very largely working-class men can only have underlined to him the unsettling course that his life was taking. Everything he had done up until this moment had been premised on being an 'amateur', yet here he was on the cusp of becoming a professional runner. His whole relationship with the world was being turned upside down. 'I hate and loath this turning professional,' he had written to a friend from his liner in mid-Atlantic on the way to New York, 'but the South African government has left me no choice.' His embarrassment at having to start running for money soon passed, though, and when he came to write *Running in Three Continents* he was able to rationalise his decision to take part in Pyle's race:

> Naturally enough, I did not wish to relinquish my amateur status, but common sense always struck me as being worth more than anything else. As a man of over forty, with no outlook and no pension, it was obvious that, being one of the best-trained men in the world for long distances, I should do well to consider it . . . I had my living to think of before anything else, and this race offered a better chance of safeguarding it than any other opening available to me.

Newton knew, however, that he was carrying a weak Achilles tendon and would be lucky to reach New York. This strongly suggests that he had been offered some sort of retainer by Pyle, because it is inconceivable that he would have travelled all the way to California knowing that he was unlikely to pick up a prize-winner's cheque. He later suggested that he was sanguine about not winning anything, given that 'the event was expected to be an annual affair and I should be able to learn sufficient about the conditions to ensure making a good job of it on the next occasion'. But Arthur Newton was not in a financial position to wait more than a year for the prospect of any money;

and that he was in a special position was shown clearly by his being asked by Pyle to address the field a few days before the race started. Exactly what he said, we don't know; but he remembered stressing to them that they were embarking on a 'desperately serious affair', and that those who best applied their *brains* to the task ahead would be the eventual winners. On the other hand, Newton mucked in on an equal basis with everyone else. Among his papers was his race Identification Card, which stated that he agreed 'to abide by all rules in training and race', and showed that he was allocated bed no. 16 in Tent 8. His race number was 135. On the back of the card was a written receipt for the $5 he had paid to cover his accommodation before the race got under way. Food, though, was on the house, and all competitors were given coupons that they could cash in at the central canteen.

The Ascot Speedway was an appropriate place for Pyle's runners to congregate for their pre-race assessment and preparation. Horse-racing had been banned in Los Angeles in 1910, so auto-racing of one sort or another became a popular obsession. (Los Angeles first grew into a city in the 1920s, and it was laid out with the car in mind: by 1927, remarkably enough, one out of every 3.2 inhabitants of the city owned an automobile.) Ascot had been opened in 1924, and by the time Pyle's runners arrived there four years later it had already established a gruesome reputation as a 'killer' track. It had a five-eighths of a mile steeply banked circuit, whose gravel surface was mixed with motor oil to provide better grip; on the straights specially adapted Model Ts reached speeds of well over 100 miles an hour. This was a dangerous place. 'The principal hazard,' writes Mark Christiansen in his history of auto-racing in Southern California, 'was "the marbles", the pebbly surface along the fence that would cause drivers to skid out of control high on the turn, tumble end over end over the fence, and plunge down a steep embankment.' It was yet another venue for the spectator as voyeur, especially as drivers shunned protection. One of the best-known of them, Ed Winfield, became a laughing stock in 1926 for starting to wear a football helmet at the wheel. 'It became the joke of the day,' he said later, 'any protection the driver used was considered chicken.' Ascot Speedway was closed down in 1936, by which time twenty-four drivers had been killed there during races.

The local press, as one would expect, took a certain amount of interest in what was being prepared at Ascot Speedway. C.C. Pyle, after all, was not unknown to West Coast sports writers, who had covered his adventures with both Grange and Lenglen. But Pyle was putting on what he regarded as a *national* event, which he hoped would become part of America's regular sporting calendar; so it must have been galling for him to see the race virtually ignored by the important East Coast papers. Take *The New York Times*, for example. The austere paper certainly did not ignore sport, but the majority of its coverage was of university and post-university amateur events. For instance, on 4th March, the day Pyle's marathon set off, the paper's sports pages carried reports on curling, bowling, indoor polo and fencing; there were photos of indoor college athletics and of the Swarthmore College Girls' basketball team. It also mentioned that a six-day international cycle race was starting that evening at Madison Square Garden. The following day it acknowledged the Pyle run, but did so in a short paragraph that was both inaccurate and condescending. Claiming that there were 275 starters, it went on, 'No sporting event ever drew a stranger entry list. Old men jogged alongside youngsters; a sixteen-year-old boy matched steps with a grey-haired man of 63. Nearly every race and colour was represented.'

Indeed. C.C. Pyle might be open to all sorts of criticism and condemnation, but he deserves real credit for putting on an event that *did* bring together 'every race and colour'; and that was a remarkable and brave thing to do in the America of 1928. Two of the pre-race favourites were Ed Gardner, whom the press always referred to as 'the Seattle negro', and the Oxford-educated West Indian/Canadian Philip Granville, who was to become a close friend of both Arthur Newton and Peter Gavuzzi. There was also a strong Jewish contingent.

III

The race finally got under way just after 3 p.m. on Sunday 4th March. Despite torrential rain, Pyle stage-managed a portentous send-off for the 199 starters. They had a police escort, and were followed by dozens of cars carrying the press and local dignitaries. The first stage, ending in the small town of Puente, was a mere taster of seventeen miles, and it was to be the shortest of the whole epic. For much of the way the runners were dodging traffic and crowds of curious spectators, and the run then developed into a tense battle between the Finn Willi Kolehmainen, one of the favourites, and the Swede Gunnar Nilsson. By all accounts they had developed a far-from-friendly rivalry while training at Ascot Speedway, and this led to their setting a pace that wiser heads like Arthur Newton knew to be too fast. He finished in twenty-fourth place, with Peter Gavuzzi further back in forty-fourth.

In Puente, with the rain still falling relentlessly, the runners settled down for their first night in the travelling tents. These leaked, but that was not the main reason Newton found sleep impossible. He was used to solitude and the privacy it brings, and he now found himself in the sort of dormitory that he would not have experienced since boarding school in Norfolk. He was also used to the deep silence of African nights, and not far from the runners' tents the vaudeville show, with Red Grange as master of ceremonies, was doing good business. The show was a mixture of music-hall and circus and was due to accompany the runners all the way to New York. Its success was a key element in C.C. Pyle's financial planning. The noise it made was unbearable for Newton: 'what with the drumming, banging, whistling, and screaming which it kept up until midnight, none of us had a chance to get to sleep however much we might have wished to'. If a runner did get to sleep by midnight, he would only have got five hours' rest. Then they were all woken; breakfast was at six, and the day's running began at seven. This was to be their relentless routine. The second stage was exactly twice as long as the first. It was a kindness that the runners had not yet been told that the eighth, at fifty-seven miles, would be almost twice as long as the second.

Willi Kolehmainen dominated the field again on Day 2. So much so that by the time he reached the town of Bloomington he had covered the first fifty miles of the race in forty minutes less than anyone else; and despite the fact that there were well over 3,000 miles still to go, some of the accompanying press began to confidently predict the Finn's ultimate victory. But the very next stage proved them to be as impatient as Kolehmainen himself. It saw the first serious climb of the race, as Route 66 hairpinned its way out of the San Fernando Valley. The leader suddenly lost his pace, with runner after runner overtaking him; and when he finally limped home in thirty-ninth place it was obvious that he had pulled a muscle in his groin. He tried again the following morning, but it was no good. His race was over. Its future belonged to those who were approaching the challenge with greater caution and greater humility.

'With my usual unconcern, I started off very gently with seventy or eighty ahead of me in the first mile or two, and counted on picking them up one after another as the day wore on. Twenty-five miles generally found me getting near the front.' That was how Arthur Newton remembered his strategy during the early stages of the 1928 Transcontinental. 'I always ran at my usual training speed, knowing that it gave my damaged leg its only possible chance to hold out.' Newton's training speed was just under seven miles an hour, and if he rarely went any faster, he equally rarely went any slower. It was, as he had worked out in Africa, a way of running that assured him complete mental relaxation; and it paid off, as Pyle's men suddenly found themselves confronted by the start-ling and unexpected heat of the Mojave Desert. On Day 4 Newton came in second; on Day 5 he won a stage for the first time and found himself in the overall lead by four minutes. By winning the sixth stage he increased his lead to three hours. But by the end of the seventh stage, when the caravan had penetrated deep into the desert, almost a *quarter* of the runners had already withdrawn, knowing that they had made a mistake in thinking they could manage the event. It seemed that those who had predicted the Transcontinental would be an embar-rassing failure had been right all along. A reporter for the *Los Angeles Evening Herald* summed up an increasingly common opinion among the press corps: 'They'll never make it. It's impossible. They're burning themselves out right now, and

Pyle has made the laps so long and so tough that he'll wind up without a runner in his race before they get to the Rockies.'

Pyle did make one concession to his runners' needs – not that it cost him any money. The Maxwell House Company (whose slogan 'Good to the Last Drop' had been trademark-registered in 1926) was keen to establish its coffee as a national brand, and it saw the Transcontinental as a way to do so. Anticipating more press coverage than in fact materialised, the company came up with a classically American advertising ploy: a vehicle shaped as a giant coffee cup that followed the race, providing the runners with free coffee and sandwiches every day at the halfway mark of the stage. Arthur Newton appreciated it: 'That famous Coffee Pot was one of the outstanding comforts of the race, and every competitor who came through has good cause to be grateful to the kindly men who managed it, and who always seemed to be on the spot when most required. I've never enjoyed better coffee.' Peter Gavuzzi was less impressed by what it had to offer: 'Not very good sandwiches. It was peanut butter, and if there's anything in the desert you don't want it's peanut butter, it's so dry.'

By winning the ninth stage Newton increased his lead to five and a half hours. When he won the eleventh stage – fifty-one miles from Kingman to Peach Springs – his lead over the Oklahoman runner Andy Payne in second place was not far short of eight hours. This was why C.C. Pyle had been so keen for Arthur Newton to take part in his race. It was distance running of a quality that gave the Transcontinental itself a certain stamp and a certain glamour; above all, it gave the event sporting credibility. The group behind Newton in these relatively early stages of the race contained several athletes who had also been expected to do well: Ed Gardner; Arne

Souminen, the Finnish doctor from Detroit; Philip Glanville; and the Americans Andy Payne and Len Dilks. But by the end of the first week there was another, and entirely unexpected, name among the leaders – that of Peter Gavuzzi.

No one, least of all himself, could have predicted his ability to run long distances; but it soon became clear that he was no one- or two-stage wonder. On Day 5 he came fourth; on Day 7 second; on Day 9 fifth. By then he was sixth in accumulated time, and he was not to be classed any lower than that throughout the rest of his race. Perhaps, as with Newton, the key lay in his ability to be relaxed even in conditions of extreme hardship and exertion. The older man had learned over time how to do this, while for Peter Gavuzzi it was a function of the fact that initially there was no pressure of expectation on him. No one knew who he was, or what he could do, and – as he himself said – he was there to see the country. 'I wasn't worried,' he said later of his first few days in the race, 'I just ambled along at the back with a few other chaps; we'd laugh and play the banjo, and come in hours after the leaders.' This was an exaggeration, but it is an accurate reflection of an easy sociability that was one side of his character. He also, thanks to his parents, had the advantage of being fluent in three languages; so he could talk to the handful of Italians in the race and to the French Canadians. The press, especially small-town reporters, found it difficult to make him out. He was variously English, Italian or 'the Italian from England', and during the course of the race he was identified as Peter (or Pietro) Gavuazzi, Gazuzzi, Guzazzi, Cavuzzi and Gauvuzzi. He was admired for his invention – he donned an outsize Mexican sombrero to run across the Mojave Desert and saved himself the agonising sunburn that affected so many others. He was admired for an unaffected friendliness. But above all he was admired for the ease and grace of his running style. This is how Arthur Newton summed it up: 'His action was delightful and caused comment wherever he appeared: he seemed to just glide over the ground like a swallow glides through the air without a suspicion of effort or concern.'

IV

The Transcontinental Foot Race of 1928 was to be a transforming event in the lives of both Arthur Newton and Peter Gavuzzi. The former – who always had an easy fluency with words – was to describe it at length; but it was also with the first Pyle race that Gavuzzi, who was never a writer, found his voice. In the years before his death a handful of people realised belatedly that he was someone who had done unique and extraordinary things in his life. They asked him to talk about them; and, from what he said, it was obvious that nothing he had done subsequently meant as much to him as the Transcontinental runs of 1928 and 1929. It was as though he had been carrying a newsreel of them in his head for decades.

'We had to cross the Colorado River. Now the trucks and all couldn't do this. They had to go round a different route, some forty miles, and we were rowed over the Colorado River by some Indians in punts. A funny thing about that too. We all got stuck in the middle, we had to get out and push these punts to get to the other side. But anyway we got over. And this is the run we called the Jungle Run because when we got to the other side the officials gave us each two oranges. And these two oranges were all we were going to get till we met our trucks. Lord knows when we were going to see them because they'd gone round a completely different route.' This was Peter Gavuzzi talking to John Jewell of the Road Runners Club in 1976, five years before his death, and just short of fifty years after the first Transcontinental race. The tape of their conversation provides a priceless insight into Gavuzzi's personality and his sense of himself.

The crossing of the Colorado River took place on Day 9; and it seems that the 'Jungle Run' that followed was an important moment, in personal terms, for both Gavuzzi and Newton. They both mention their meeting in that Arizona wilderness. Here is Gavuzzi's spoken recollection: 'During this run all the roads were always marked with red arrows so that we would know where we were going, but here in the jungle nothing was marked. But there was a sort of goat trail. And, well, I decided to wait and see what the others were doing, and I followed behind. But we were all over the place, and who should come up to me but Arthur Newton. Up to this moment Arthur Newton, who was known as the Rhodesian Rambler, was way in front in the lead. He was some six hours in front of the second man and he was really running away with the race. Anyway, I met him on the road and he said to me "Peter", he said, "where are we?" I said "I don't know". So there was a bit of a tree there and I climbed up the tree to look around and all it was just trees and jungle. So anyway Newton and I ran together but Newton seemed to go better than I did that day, and he left me.'

Newton himself described the track they had to use as 'villainous'. This was how he recalled his collaboration that day with the young runner from Southampton: 'I remember twice waiting at different spots until Gavuzzi, who I knew was not far behind me, came along; and together we discussed the probability of a certain track being the right one before setting off along it. He afterwards told me he was exceedingly glad to find me each time, as he fancied he had also lost the official route.'

With uncertainty as to how long it would take to cross the Colorado River, the run that day was 'only' twenty miles; but it was a crucial stage, as it marked the transition from desert to mountains. Over the next week the runners climbed and crossed the high Rockies, stopping in small mining towns like Oatman, Peach Springs and Seligman. It was high enough for there still to be patches of snow by the roadside, and the nights in the tents were freezing. 'The cold weather bit into our sunburnt limbs and gave many of us a bad time,' Newton remembered. He, at least, was an experienced mountain runner, and the hills of Natal had given him a taste of what it was like to cover long distances at high altitude. But for the over-whelming majority of the field, Peter Gavuzzi included, crossing the Rockies was something terrifyingly new. This is how he recalled it half a century later: 'At the beginning of the race we had been warned that sooner or later we would be climbing the Rockies, and that the altitude would vary from six to seven thousand feet. Of course we were all afraid a little bit about it because we didn't know what to expect. Anyway we began to see we were climbing all the time, and also a lot of the runners were beginning to bleed either from the ears or the nose. Now I was never affected by it, but a lot of other runners were; and we had to do quite a shift in the way of running. Instead of running our usual way we had to adopt what you would call a lower gear and just crawl up a bit at a time.'

The Transcontinental's official doctor, John C. Baker, must have been deeply worried. This was uncharted territory, and ultimately his job was to ensure than no one in the race died because of it. But at the same time it was against his research interests to step in too quickly and insist that a runner withdraw. At least he must have felt compelled to dispense some medical advice, because from what he wrote afterwards, few of the runners had any idea of how to protect themselves against the unavoidable ravages of the event:

> The first three weeks of the race were characterised by almost every violation of the accepted principles of diet and hygiene and disregard for physical injury, infection and human endurance . . . The general appearance of most runners after completion of the daily mileage was that of exhaustion with cold perspiration, drawn facial expression, hunger, thirst and a desire to sleep. Tonsillitis, diarrhea, shin splints, injuries to the feet, pains in the abdomen, red and white blood cells in the urine and increased heart rate were among some of the manifestations noted.

The pain of the mountains brought out tensions between some of the runners and C.C. Pyle. Many found the facilities that he provided them with both inadequate and insulting: the tents were cold and damp, the food basic. Men doing what he was demanding of them needed nourishment and rest; but they were getting too little of either. Even their laundry was rarely seen to. Pyle, by contrast, was accompanying the race in the luxury of a specially constructed motor-home that he had ostentatiously christened the *America*. It had plush upholstery with wooden panelling, two double bedrooms, a bathroom and shower with hot running water, a fully equipped kitchen and – most extravagantly of all for the times – air conditioning. It had cost $25,000, and was perhaps justly described by one journalist as 'the most pretentious land yacht ever built'. To exhausted, dirty and hungry runners the *America* must have seemed a provocation. After a hard thirty-six-mile stage from Flagstaff to Two Gun Camp, word got around that Paul Rodeta, a trainer who was working with some of the Finnish runners, was going to lead a delegation to C.C. Pyle to protest at the conditions they had to put up with. But Pyle apparently threatened to disqualify all Rodeta's runners, and the trainer backed down. As professionals desperately seeking dollars, Pyle's runners were, in the final resort, dependent on him. But the incident at Two Gun Camp was not the last 'mutiny' on the long road to New York.

It was, though, the last place that Arthur Newton would pass through as a competitor in the 1928 Transcontinental race. He had reached Two Gun Camp in terrible and worsening shape. 'Both ankles were so swollen that the ends of my legs were mere shapeless chunks,' he wrote later, and he was beginning to find it almost impossible to persuade his body into motion in the mornings. He was nine and a quarter hours in the lead, but he was forty-five years old and had covered more than 550 miles in little over a fortnight. The sixteenth stage was a relatively short one, twenty-four miles from Two Gun Camp to Winslow, and Newton was intent on trying it. But it was no good: after only three miles he was forced to stop by agonising pain in his right ankle. His Achilles tendon had torn. He sat by the roadside as dozens of runners passed him by, until he was picked up by C.C. Pyle, who was aboard the *America* checking up on the field. The promoter insisted that Newton stay with him in the motor-home for a few days to give his legs a complete rest and his tendon a chance to heal.

Pyle had lost the one genuine star athlete from his race; but he obviously still wanted Newton's involvement in some way, and having him as a convalescing house-guest gave Pyle an opportunity to make the runner an offer. Money must have been part of it – and perhaps this was the sort of situation that both parties had envisaged before the Transcontinental even started – but Newton made no mention of it, just saying that he accepted the position of 'Technical Adviser to the Management' for the rest of the race.

It was probably up to the runner himself to interpret what this job description might mean, and Newton was to devote himself over the coming weeks to helping those men at the back of the field who were in real difficulty, encouraging or cajoling them and offering them practical advice. It also seems, though, that Arthur Newton had been persuaded by C.C. Pyle to use his name in the service of PR for a race that was still subject to occasional ridicule or abuse in the press. As we have seen, while still in Los Angeles, Newton had been critical of what Pyle was demanding, and dismissive of many of his fellow runners. But not long after taking on his new 'management' position he explained to a journalist why he was so happy still to be part of the Transcontinental. 'I live in the middle of the cheeriest bunch of men it has ever been my good fortune to meet. [These men] are the cream of the world's finest distance runners, and that alone is enough to make any man realise that Mr Pyle and Mr Grange were doing their country a very good turn when they engineered the event.' One can only hope Pyle paid well for the expression of such sentiments.

At the end of the race the surviving fifty-five runners clubbed together and bought a silver cup, which they presented to Arthur Newton as a token of their gratitude for what he had done to help them. He was always averse to prizes; but he kept this one. Once his tendon had healed sufficiently, Newton developed a routine of running for ten or twelve miles each morning among the stragglers, 'discussing their troubles and offering what advice and help I could'. Each evening he went out again in search of any men who were struggling to finish the stage by the deadline of midnight. (A runner who failed to complete a particular day's distance was not disqualified; but he had to start the next day from the point he had reached.) As the race descended from the Rockies and crossed the high plains of New Mexico on the way to Texas, Newton must at times have had his work cut out to convince exhausted men that there was anything to be gained by continuing – because the further the race went, the more Pyle's plans for it unravelled. His ambition had created something that he was proving incapable of managing, for the simple reason that he was not able to raise any money. The whole venture was premised, as we have seen, on towns along the route being prepared to pay for the privilege of having Pyle's men run through them and, ideally, stay in them. A handful of towns had paid in advance, while others had 'promised' to come up with the cash when the runners actually materialised – which, of course, meant they were hedging their bets against the event turning out to be a damp squib. Pyle's developing crisis was summed up by what happened in Albuquerque on Wednesday, 28th March.

With a population of more than 25,000, the capital of New Mexico was the first 'large' town one met heading east on Route 66 from Los Angeles, and C.C. Pyle had high hopes of it providing him with a much-needed injection of funds. He sent Red Grange's vaudeville on ahead, to drum up excitement for the arrival of the runners, and to remind the town's business leaders of their responsibility to use the Transcontinental as a way of promoting Route 66 itself. They did not get the reception they, or Pyle, were expecting. Albuquerque's ambitious mayor, Clyde Tingley, had decided there was political mileage in standing out against all that his predominantly conservative electorate might object to about Pyle's operation, or at least about what they had heard about it. Rumours were repeated – for instance, about the vaudeville's female dance routines being a front for organised prostitution; and lies were told – for instance, that Pyle's whole caravan had been run out of town by the citizens of Gallup, New Mexico. The mayor also claimed that he had been told of a spate of house burglaries in the Arizona town of Holbrook on the night Pyle's men were there. Tingley ordered the vaudeville tent to leave town, and told the town's police force to arrest anyone trying to sell programmes for the race. Albuquerque had shut its door in Pyle's face, and he had nowhere else to take the ninety-six men who were still running and who needed food and shelter on a bitterly cold night. While a furious promoter drove on in the *America*, the runners were taken on a detour around Albuquerque and were then told they had a further fourteen miles to cover, most of them steeply uphill. They finally arrived at a small settlement called Seven Springs, where they experienced what Arthur Newton succinctly described as 'the worst night of the whole trip', with many eating and sleeping outdoors. When the runners set off again the next morning, most, he wrote, were 'numbed with cold'.

V

But if on the one hand the 1928 Transcontinental Foot Race was threatening to descend into farce, on the other it was beginning to take on the dimensions of a real and absorbing *race*. Arthur Newton was no longer in contention, and it became clear in the week or so after he was forced to withdraw that a small handful of runners were showing themselves to be of a different quality from the rest of the field. The race, to use the terminology of the Tour de France, was breaking up into 'leaders' and 'peloton'. The leading handful was made up of four very different, but equally determined men. There was the slight, somewhat bookish doctor from Detroit's Finnish community, Arne Souminen; he was forty, and no one in the field had trained as long or as 'scientifically' for the Transcontinental as he had. There was another Finn, the stocky and muscular Johnny Salo, who had fought in the US navy during the First World War and worked as a longshoreman in New Jersey; he was thirty-five years old and had been part of the winning team at the 1926 Boston marathon; in the early stages of the race he had been 'adopted' by the American Legion, which provided him from time to time with the privilege of good food and comfortable lodgings. There was the powerful twenty-year-old farmer's son from Oklahoma, Andy Payne, who had Native American blood in him and had spent his boyhood running eight miles to school each day and eight miles back. Finally there was the effortlessly graceful Peter Gavuzzi, who had developed the superstition of not shaving, so becoming for the press 'the whiskered Englishman'. On occasions another runner might win a stage: but from Day 17 until the end of the race on Day 84 the leader on accumulated time was always one of these four.

Behind them were talented runners like Eddie Gardner and the diminutive Finn Ollie Wantinnen, who continued to run with prize money within realistic sight; and further back was a group of fifty or more with no hope of winning a single dollar, but who had ceased to think about giving up. It was as though the race was becoming a way of life for them, a painful but enriching experience of friendship and mutual help. They were no longer running to beat one another; they were running to be with one another. This was something that neither Pyle nor the press understood about them. Perhaps they had fantasised at the beginning about winning thousands of dollars and transforming hard lives; but after weeks on the road what kept them starting out again each morning was that they were, at least for a time, escaping those lives – the unemployment, perhaps, or the demeaning job or the unhappy marriage. Some too, no doubt, kept going because they knew Pyle wanted them to drop out, and they had come to despise him. So when a writer for a New Mexico paper got on his moral high horse and said, 'I would like to see the race called off as unfair and inhuman and Pyle forced to pay the men for the misery he has caused them', he was missing the point.

It took the field six days to cross the Texas Panhandle. All the men had to put up with mud, freezing rain and unexpected snow; but the black runners like Gardner and Granville also had to put up with insistent racist harassment. On more than one occasion they were threatened by farmers with firearms; and C.C. Pyle had no option but to obey Texan law and make them sleep in a 'blacks only' tent. The fact that Gardner's trainer followed him in a large and expensive car was an almost unbearable provocation to poor whites, who shouted abuse as the 'Sheik' from Seattle ran by. Arne Souminen held his overall lead all the way until, on Easter Sunday, 8th April, one of his tendons gave way and, like Newton before him, he had no option but to pull out. The finishing point for the stage that day was the small Oklahoman town of Texola, and Andy

Payne's performance – he took over the overall lead from Souminen – excited more popular interest in the race than at any time since Los Angeles. One thousand dollars had been raised as a prize for the first runner to cross the Oklahoma state line, with few doubting that the runner would be Andy Payne. It was, but only after Eddie Gardner had decided it was wise to relinquish his lead that day; he and his trainer had received too many threats as to what might happen to them if a black man was first into Oklahoma.

The airport in Oklahoma City is named after a man who, in 1928, was without doubt the state's most famous citizen – Will Rogers. Through his syndicated newspaper columns and his radio shows he had become America's best-loved comedian, dispensing a unique form of down-home rural humour. He was the antithesis of urban chic, and in Oklahoma above all he was lionised. Rogers, who had once been close friends with Andy Payne's father, was also besotted with sport, and C.C. Pyle had made a point of seeking him out. The comedian was the official starter of the second Transcontinental Foot Race in 1929, and in the *American Magazine* early that year he published a defiant justification of Pyle's races, furious at the majority of sports journalists who regarded them with scorn:

> A sporting writer will rave his head off over some football player making an 80-yard run. What would he do if he had to run 80 miles, and do it again the next day, sick, sore feet, bad colds, bum feet, cramps, blisters, no time to lay up and cure 'em, always had to get out in the morning, rain, snow, sleet, desert heat, always be there, ready to go? A marathon that they train for years for is a little over 26 miles. Then they come in and faint, and

crowds carry them off. You couldn't faint in this race, nobody to carry you off. If you did, you just layed there, maybe some car run you over, but that was about all you could expect.

Rogers wrote as he spoke: and he made sure he was in Oklahoma City on 13th April, waiting for Andy Payne.

Payne was shy and introverted, and he found the attention of the Oklahoma press invasive and embarrassing. He gave curt, monosyllabic answers when cornered by reporters – some of whom tried running a few miles with him to see if he might open up when on the road. He disappointed them, just as Oklahoma City disappointed C.C. Pyle. The promoter had been expecting a huge pay day: the Depression was yet to bite, the state capital was a rapidly expanding oil town of more than 35,000 people, and there was a local man in the lead. Payne was a farmer's son, and thousands made the journey from deep in the countryside to welcome him. The *Daily Oklahoman* reported that 'Horny-handed farmers were gathered with their wives and their almost unbelievable flocks of children along the edges of the great highway No. 66. Most brought their lunches, and children ran about the landscape with peanut butter and bread crusts and decaying bananas.' Pyle thought he could take advantage of this crowd by moving the finish of the stage from the centre of town to the State Fair Grounds, where he could charge admission – 50 cents for adults, 25 cents for children. Flyers were quickly printed, and distributed around the town. 'Today, see the finish of a Lap of the International Foot Race,' they screamed: 'There was never a race like this in the history of the world! Be in the grandstand at the Fair Grounds before 8 o'clock. Something doing every minute. Music, Vaudeville, Presentation of auto-graphed footballs and photographs by "Red" Grange. Be there.' An estimated 5,000 responded to the command, but Pyle had failed to realise that there was no way to fence off the Fair Grounds completely at short notice, so the large majority of the spectators got in free. The finish of the race itself can only have disappointed them, as Andy Payne seemed determined to avoid any heroic moment. He came home in fifteenth place, tied for the second day running with Peter Gavuzzi. 'The show was a flop,' was the opinion of the following day's *Oklahoma City Times*. 'There is nothing interesting in seeing a mob of sun-blackened runners straggle in miles apart.'

For C.C. Pyle, Oklahoma City was a premonition of things to come. He arrived to find that a suit had been filed against him in the District Court by a disaffected former employee from the New York Yankee football team, who was claiming he was owed nearly $4,500 in unpaid wages. On top of this, the city's Chamber of Commerce decided that Pyle's event did not, after all, warrant a cent of the $5,000 they had said they would pay him. So a deal was done behind closed doors at the courthouse. The suit was dropped; and so was any expectation that Pyle would receive his money from the city. The promoter also had to renounce any claim on the meagre takings at the Fair Grounds.

If local interest focused on Andy Payne, less partisan followers of the race were becoming increasingly impressed by Peter Gavuzzi. As Route 66 went north and east from Oklahoma, into Kansas and then Missouri, 'the bearded wonder from Southampton' made sure that Payne's slender overall lead did not increase. Often they would run much of a stage together, content to protect their thirty-hour advantage over Johnny Salo in third place, and they came to like and respect each other. They came from different worlds, but they were both young, resilient working-class men. Doubtless Payne told Gavuzzi about Vivian, the young woman in Oklahoma whom he hoped would be so impressed by his running across America that she would agree to marry him. Whether Peter Gavuzzi told Payne about Nellie, whom he would marry in Southampton later that summer, is less certain. Gavuzzi did not know he was about to get married, because he did not know that Nellie was pregnant.

Both men insisted to anyone who asked that they would be first to New York, but as Route 66 entered Illinois, with only 300 miles to go until Chicago, Peter Gavuzzi, in his own words, 'started to run'. The late April weather was benign, the terrain mercifully flat and the road properly surfaced. Gavuzzi, who, like most of the remaining field, was getting fitter and fitter as the race went on, lengthened his elegant stride and for a succession of days startled both his rival and the press by maintaining a pace of seven or seven and a half minutes per mile.

Gavuzzi first took the overall lead on 25th April, with an advantage over Andy Payne of thirty-three minutes. He held the lead until 10th May, by which time he was more than six hours in front of his rival from Oklahoma. He seemed unstoppable: an improbable and unforeseen victory for the young 'whiskered Englishman' began to seem inevitable. But then, in Fremont, Ohio, Gavuzzi suddenly withdrew from the race, unable any longer to mask his growing distress. His crisis had nothing to do with his strength or his stamina or his general fitness. It was tragically prosaic. This is how he remembered it in 1976.

'Before the race I had several teeth that were in a bad way, and I had been to the dentist, but he wanted to extract the lot. I said to him if I have them out, what am I going to eat on the road? I said I can't do that. I said as this race is only less than three months surely I can get through? So he said to me, well, take a chance. Well, eventually it didn't work out because, as you know, runners take a lot of sugar in. They're drinking orangeade, tea, coffee. A tremendous amount of sugar is used up, which gives us our energy. So this worked on my teeth. I started to get abscesses in the mouth; I couldn't eat any solid food at all. I had to just drink soup, drink tea, that sort of thing, and I was getting weaker and weaker. And there was a condition in the contract. The doctor, at any time if he saw a man that was unable to continue, he'd be pulled out and the promoter couldn't do a thing about it. And the doctor examined me and he told me "Peter, you'll have to give up. You're doing too much mileage and you're not getting any stronger, you're getting weaker all the time." And so at Fremont, Ohio, I was in a really bad way. Not only that, I was in the lead by six hours and I had done over three thousand miles. There were only four hundred and twenty-two miles to go, and it was no use. The doctor pulled me out. That was the end of me.'

VI

There were still two weeks to go before the remaining runners could reach the safe haven of New York, but Gavuzzi's exit had drained the contest of any sporting excitement. Unless something unforeseen happened to him, Andy Payne would win. He had a twenty-hour lead over Johnny Salo – who at least had the consolation of a full civic welcome when the penultimate stage ended in his home town of Passaic, New

Jersey. C.C. Pyle was delighted at the prospect of victory for Payne, rather than Gavuzzi or Salo: he saw him as someone it would be easy to market as a small-town all-American hero. But Pyle was also deeply worried about the state of his finances and his ability to pay the promised prizes. This led him to a callous calculation that Peter Gavuzzi remembered with disgust. 'The last week was the hardest, three hundred and ninety-eight, nearly four hundred, miles. And what was the reason for that? The promoter wanted to get rid of a lot of men but he just couldn't get rid of all of them. So that was why the mileage was so big . . . to have made such a great mileage for the last few days it was complete murder. These men were reduced to walking and struggling along.' Gavuzzi was right. C.C. Pyle had become desperate for as many as possible of the 'peloton' of runners with no hope of winning anything to drop out. As long as they were there, finishing each day within time, he had to provide them with food and lodging. That had always been the deal, and he could not renege on it, however much he wanted to. Perhaps unsurprisingly, he had underestimated the power of camaraderie.

In the final week there were successive stages of fifty, fifty-two, fifty-nine, seventy-three and fifty-seven miles. The consequence, Arthur Newton later wrote, was that 'it was a mob of listless and exhausted men who reached the goal'. Sections of the press were merciless in their ridicule of the event as it came to its close – none more so than John Kiernan, leading sports columnist of *The New York Times*. This is how he welcomed the remaining runners on 26th May:

Just when many good people were beginning to believe that the C.C. Pyle Transcontinental foot race was merely perpetual motion under another name, word comes that the end of it is in sight. If all goes well the quaint caravan that started in far-off California many years ago – or so it seems – will trek into Madison Square Garden this evening, and having scampered all the way across the country, will gallop ten extra miles around the Garden for no good reason at all, which is quite in keeping with the spirit of the whole affair. What Bill Pickens, chief assistant to the Hon. C.C. Pyle, called 'this titanic struggle' either shoved off or was pushed off from Los Angeles some time ago, the exact date being a matter of bitter dispute among historians . . . Since Polybius makes no mention of it in his history of early Roman days, it is probable that the race started some time after the Third Punic War and before the signing of the Magna Carta.

Kiernan could also not resist a dig at a recent sporting hero's involvement with the event: 'The side-show had "Red" Grange as master of ceremonies at all performances, and Red is now letter perfect in his orations on the marvellous, inimitable, exhilarating and astounding merits of the dancing snakes, the sword-swallower, the five-legged pig and the Wild Man who eats nothing but broken bottles with just a dash of pepper and salt.'

The next day, on a news rather than a sports page, the paper reported the arrival in Manhattan of the fifty-five surviving runners, who came across the Hudson River by ferryboat from New Jersey. The mocking tone of the previous day's column was still there: 'For their New York appearance most of the Transcontinental hoofers had undergone considerable barbering and grooming: many of them had left their beards in Passaic. Some ran on their toes to save their heels and others on their heels to save their toes. A few still wore bandages and tape where dogs and other fauna had bitten them.' New York provided C.C. Pyle with a rare opportunity – that of charging the public to come and see his 'plodders'. It seems almost inhuman, given what his runners had been through, but Pyle – instead of organising a valedictory run up Fifth Avenue or a circuit of Central Park – insisted that they complete a final twenty-six-hour relay at Madison Square Garden. But why should people pay good money when the outcome of the race was not in question, when New Yorkers had no local runners in contention, and when the event had failed to make any of its participants into figures of national interest? The Garden had a capacity of 20,000, and at best only one-fifth of that number turned out for Pyle's exhausted men. They deserved better; and they certainly did not deserve a seemingly desperate promoter standing at the side of the track from where he was reported as exhorting them to 'streak it, boys, streak it'. Pyle did honour his commitment to pay the promised prize money. Andy Payne went back to Oklahoma with $25,000, which he used to pay off the mortgage on his father's farm; and Johnny Salo took the ferry back to Passaic with a cheque for $10,000 in his pocket. But C.C. Pyle had had to borrow the cash.

One well-known doctor had predicted that 'the marathon will shorten the life of each competitor by five to ten years'. He had argued that 'the musculature of the blood vessel and the muscle of the heart will be terribly aged by the ordeal. The capacity of the lung of each man has been taxed to the limit.' But this was just a prediction, based on no examination of the competitors; and when such an examination *did* take place, it came to very different conclusions. Before they all dispersed, race doctor John C. Baker and his team took twenty-five runners who had completed the whole coast-to-coast run down to the Jefferson Hospital in Philadelphia and subjected them to a rigorous series of tests – 'electrocardiographic, ophthalmoscopic, orthopaedic, laryngeal, and roentgenographic'. There they were able to compare data with the results of tests done on the runners before they set off from Los Angeles; and whereas a disapproving press had seen a group of shuffling skeletons, the medics were pleasantly surprised at what they found. For example, 'the lungs in general were found to be normal . . . the bones were essentially normal except in the older runners . . . only one heart is increased in size'. Overall their data told them that 'the comparatively normal human body, provided with adequate food and rest, may acquire during prolonged exercise unusual capacity for work apparently without serious untoward effect'. In other words, running an average of forty miles on eighty-four consecutive days had made most of the runners fitter and stronger than they had been at the beginning of the race.

The medical team also asked their sample to respond to a series of questions over the weeks and months that followed, to find out what the longer-term effect of the Transcontinental had been. 'After returning to my home I climbed a 12,000 feet high mountain and experienced no difficulty' was one answer; 'I am running every morning at least 40 miles and the Sunday before Christmas I ran 72 miles and finished in excellent shape' was another; while a third simply said, 'I am in good health, in fact I never felt better in my life.' Regular distance running as a boon to health and well-being – it was something Arthur Newton had been propounding for years.

5

New York to Los Angeles, 1929

The Second Transcontinental

I

It is hardly surprising that it has been the first of the two Transcontinental races that has attracted most attention. It was both novel and contentious, as unlikely as it was heroic, and for most Americans it was their first encounter with the phenomenon of C.C. Pyle. But as sporting contest, as athletic achievement and as tragic human drama 1928 pales into insignificance in comparison with the second race a year later.

The 1929 run was to cement the friendship and professional partnership between Arthur Newton and Peter Gavuzzi, and it very nearly made them both extremely rich. Gavuzzi himself had no doubt as to the difference between 1928 and 1929. 'All of us in the second race were well-trained men, and believe me we were well trained,' he told John Jewell in 1976, 'not like in the first race where we were all really a whole bunch of amateurs.' (He did though, both tactfully and accurately, exclude Arthur Newton from this, describing him as 'the only really trained man' in 1928.) C.C. Pyle emerged from the near-fiasco of his first Transcontinental Foot Race adventure asserting confidently that he had inaugurated what was to become a regular landmark in the American sporting calendar; and, convinced that Pyle would deliver on his promises, a handful of those who had survived the run from Los Angeles decided to devote themselves to professional distance running and to preparing themselves for the 1929 Transcontinental. Newton and Gavuzzi were among them, though initially they went about their preparation on different sides of the Atlantic.

In his autobiography Arthur Newton stated simply that 'after the first Transcontinental race I returned to England, determined to carry on training so as to be in real good fettle for the next year's event'. True enough, but he omitted to mention that his return was not until six months after the race, and that he was initially very ambivalent about the idea of running across America again. He decided to stay on in the States to see if he could make a living as a professional runner – a trade that had been anathema to him only months earlier. He had of course crossed his ethical Rubicon by agreeing to take part in the 1928 race, and he had to take any opportunity he could find to make money from running, before middle age finally caught up with him. He was in close contact with both C.C. Pyle and Hugo Quist in the days and weeks after the end of the run, as they all tried to work out whether a professional distance running circuit could be created that would be sufficiently profitable for athletes, managers and promoters alike. Newton was to spend six anxious months, uncertain as to where he should be and where he could best earn his living.

C.C. Pyle must have been worried that, were Arthur Newton to decide to go back to southern Africa – as he often threatened to do – it would be all but impossible to persuade him back for the 1929 Transcontinental. Pyle needed Newton on board; but in more immediate terms, Newton, to be able to stay in the States, needed the promoter. Pyle himself, though, had to accept that at least in New York he would always play second fiddle to the man who controlled Madison Square Garden – the veteran boxing promoter Tex Rickard. Rickard, who had made his name and his fortune during the 1920s, was at the height of his fame. He had promoted all of Jack Dempsey's major fights, and in 1925 had won a special place in the hearts of thousands of New Yorkers by persuading the city's mayor to overturn a long-standing ban on live boxing. In response Rickard redeveloped Madison Square Garden as a tailor-made venue for the biggest fights. He had helped Pyle put on the desperate marathon that had brought the Transcontinental to such a cruel end, and in the autumn of 1928 Rickard decided to move seriously into running on his own account. On 24th October the Garden hosted a marathon that was billed as a head-to-head between the reigning Olympic champion, the French Algerian Boughera El Ouafi, and America's popular hero at the distance, Joie Ray. That both were prepared to turn their backs on amateurism at the height of their powers and fame would show the sporting public, Pyle undoubtedly hoped, that the best athletics was now to be found on the professional circuit.

El Ouafi's victory in the Olympic marathon at Amsterdam earlier that summer had been no fluke; he had come seventh in Paris in 1924, and his employment in the French army allowed him a privileged amount of preparation for the 1928 Games. To the American press and public he could only be regarded as an exotic curiosity, and he was referred to as 'the brown-skinned desert runner' or 'the camel driver from the deserts of Algeria'.*

His headline opponent, Joie Ray, had turned professional almost immediately after coming third in that year's Boston marathon, the Blue Riband event in the American distance running calendar. Ray, who was nicknamed the 'Kankakee Kid' after his home town in Illinois, had become an American sporting institution during the 1920s. He had represented his country in each of the decade's three Olympic Games, competing at every distance from the 1,500 metres to the marathon, and had come fifth behind El Ouafi in Amsterdam. He had also held world records at both the mile and two miles. Professional though he now was, Ray insisted on running at Madison Square Garden in the official US Track and Field Olympic strip.†

The race was billed at 'Tex Rickard's First International Marathon Championship'. The fifty-eight-year-old promoter was to die suddenly the next year – from complications after appendicitis – so we will never know how deep his commitment to professional distance running would have turned out to be. But it says much about the sport's possible appeal

---

* With the money he made in America in 1928, El Ouafi returned to Paris, bought a café and disappeared from public view. In 1956, when another French Algerian, Alain Mimoun, won the Olympic marathon, the press tried to track down his once-famous predecessor. They found El Ouafi virtually destitute. Three years later, during the final terrors of the Algerian War, the veteran runner was gunned down in a Paris street by an FLN hit-squad. He had apparently refused to support publicly the cause of an independent Algeria.

† Joie Ray is included in the US Track and Field Hall of Fame, where his biography makes *no mention* of his having run as a professional.

that Rickard was prepared to put his name to it. El Ouafi, who signed a six-month contract, was obviously central to the plans, and the French North African earned his first pay cheque of $4,000 by beating Joie Ray into second place at Madison Square Garden on the evening of 24th October. Though neither of the star attractions had taken part in the Transcontinental, C.C. Pyle was able to offer Rickard a stable of 'Bunioneers' to make up a decent field, and prominent among them was Arthur Newton. He came in third, quite possibly under orders not to come any higher than that, in front of a crowd that he estimated as being 13,000.*

After the race Newton admitted in a letter to Len Dilks – a railwayman from Pennsylvania with whom he had become good friends during the 1928 race – that El Ouafi had been 'of course too good for any of us', and revealed how Pyle had intervened on his behalf to make sure that he received a decent fee:

We all signed on beforehand – win or lose – to compete for sums varying from 100 to 200 dollars. I was allowed 200. They offered me 100 and I told them I couldn't consider it . . . They then offered me 150, and I said if they make it 200 I would accept. They politely told me to go to blazes, so I went off to book my passage to England and on the way called to say goodbye to Mr Pyle. When he heard the position he said 'What! You leave 'em to me.' So I came back without calling again and sure enough a paper arrived offering me $200 to run.

* Pyle runners came to be known as Bunioneers after a dismissive description of the Transcontinental as the 'Bunion Derby' caught on in the American press.

But Newton's mood was dour. Marathons were never his distance; they were far too short; and he hated running on banked indoor tracks. Peter Gavuzzi claimed later that his older friend and partner 'had been offered a contract to do several twenty-six mile races indoors', but this does not seem to have been the case. Rather, Newton had to negotiate his involvement in Rickard's new venture race by race. He felt belittled and undervalued. Giving his address as 'Pyle's New York hotel', he spelt out his despair in a long letter to Len Dilks a week after the Madison Square Garden race:

> I cannot continue to stay in America if there is no living to be made, and unless I can hear of something in the very near future I shall be obliged to ship for England and Africa. I just hate this continued threat of having to pack up and get out, but things seem to be anything but favourable for long distance runners in this country just at the present. They told me outright in New York that El Ouafi and Ray were 'the goods' and that nobody else counted for anything worth mentioning.

But it seems that even 'the goods' were not proving to be a worthwhile investment for Tex Rickard. In the middle of November Pyle wrote to Newton to try and reassure him: 'They are not doing very well with El Ouafi and are evidently holding down the expenses. I know that if anything turns up Quist will immediately get in touch with you and he is hoping that they will use you in some other towns.'

After a race in Boston, where he came third, Newton was seemingly so disillusioned with what he found himself doing that he talked openly of retiring. Questioned by the *Boston*

Herald's sports columnist, Arthur Duffey, he said that he wanted to have one more go in England at reducing his 100-mile record, and after that 'I then expect to hang up the running pumps for keeps'. It was walking pumps that he needed on board the SS *American Banker*, as it crossed the Atlantic. 'I did eleven miles of walking round and round the deck this morning,' he wrote to Len Dilks on 2nd December, 'and shall have to do about as much again this afternoon. I do not at all fancy this sort of work aboard ship, but of course it has to be done' – for his sanity, one suspects, as much as for his anticipated record attempt. He also confided in Dilks that he *was* intending to go back to the States for the next Pyle race, though not as a runner: 'I have told Mr Pyle I will try to arrange to wait in England until next March and then shall probably come over again to act as Referee in the Transcontinental.' But Arthur Newton's running career was far from over. In fact perhaps its most singular part still lay in the future, and it was to centre on the unique partnership that he built with Peter Gavuzzi. In the midwinter of 1928–9 Gavuzzi was in Southampton, hoping for Newton's return.

II

While Newton had been coming to terms with life as a professional, Peter Gavuzzi had been having to come to terms with something entirely different: life as a married man and as a father. It is a great frustration for anyone writing about Gavuzzi that those who interviewed him while he was alive were only interested in his running, and not in his wider life – though one must doubt that he would have had much truck with any questions about emotional or sexual matters. Those who met him invariably mentioned his joviality and his open friendliness, yet he spent most of his adult life in a state of deep loneliness. The minimal diaries he kept when working in France during the later 1940s reveal his susceptibility to depression. (Things that were somehow too personal, or that embarrassed him in some way, he wrote down in French, as though this might hide them. His depression was always '*le cafard*', the blues.) His diaries, as we shall see, also reveal his appetite for affection and for sex, but they are almost silent when it comes to his wife and son. There were deep connections, it would seem, between Peter Gavuzzi's apparent addiction to the 'aloneness' of long-distance running, his preference for an expatriate existence and his arms-length approach to emotional attachments.

His son, also named Peter, was born in Southampton on 30th September 1928, so he would have been conceived, perhaps, during his father's celebrations for New Year in the city with a young local girl by the name of Nellie Woodward. We do not know when Gavuzzi became aware of Nellie's pregnancy. We also do not know what sort of family pressure he came under to marry her as soon as he could. It would seem likely that he did, because otherwise he would surely have stayed in New York with Newton and joined the Tex Rickard professional troupe. All he tells us is that as soon as the Transcontinental was over he worked his way back to Southampton on his old ship, the *Majestic*, and that once home he immediately set about training for the 1929 Pyle event. On marriage and parenthood he is silent.

Gavuzzi was not present when his son was born. In fact he was not even in town. He was, significantly enough, about as far from the south coast as it is possible to be within the

British Isles, setting out to run from John O'Groats to Land's End. The timing could not have been accidental: he was not going to let having a baby get in the way of his running. The fact that he had been so convincingly in the lead of the first Transcontinental when his dental crisis forced him to pull out had obviously convinced the young Gavuzzi to devote himself to preparing for the 1929 run. He was making a decision that would have been unimaginable a year previously – to become a professional distance runner. He was giving up his job as a ship's steward, and he recognised that the Transcontinental needed a specific sort of preparation. This is how he expressed it to John Jewell of the Road Runners Club in 1976: 'I decided that I was really going to have a go at this second race and I wasn't going to make a mistake. So I thought, well, I must do some real hard training. Now this business of training from home and going out ten or fifteen miles and coming back home and that sort of thing didn't appeal to me at all because it wasn't anything like the actual race. So what I did I went to the *Southern Daily Echo* in Southampton and asked them if they would help me out a little bit. I wanted to do John o'Groats to Land's End. This was not for a record of any kind but just for the amount of work that would be done. Over a thousand miles of running and all kinds of weathers and ups and downs. This was the sort of thing that would prepare me for the run.'

Gavuzzi's local paper *was* prepared to help, though it gave his long run surprisingly little coverage. The *Echo*'s front page on Tuesday, 11th September carried a photo of Gavuzzi setting off by car for Scotland. He was smartly dressed in jacket and tie, with a neat moustache and his trademark pipe in his mouth. At the wheel was his manager-cum-press officer, who was provided by the paper, and who over the next few weeks phoned in periodically with news of Gavuzzi's progress. But, as there was no race involved – even against the clock – reports that the athlete was 'making excellent progress' or 'travelling splendidly' hardly made for gripping reading. When Gavuzzi arrived in Southampton on 20th October he was formally greeted by the deputy mayor; and one wonders if the runner went that evening for a first meeting with his three-week-old son.

A more significant indicator of Gavuzzi's emerging status as an athlete was that he also got sponsorship for his run from the Ovaltine company. These were pre-steroid, pre-blood-doping days, and Ovaltine – a recent Swiss invention – marketed itself as the ideal supplement for adventurers and sportsmen. Its advertisements, which appeared in the *British Medical Journal* as well as in the mainstream press, boasted that the malt drink contained 'all the nutritive properties required to build up body, brain and nerves and to create abundant energy'. In the mid-1930s the company was to become best known for its 'League of Ovaltineys', which attracted the participation of thousands of British children, but in 1928 it seemed to be focused on identifying itself with exploits of endurance. Peter Gavuzzi's was one, while others were the first journeys by both car and aeroplane from London to Australia. British Ryder Cup golfers were quoted as putting their success down to their consumption of Ovaltine; and a few years later the company itself was to publish a short book entitled *Lessons in Athletics*, in which photos of prominent 'stars' of track and field were interspersed with testimonials as to the efficacy of the wonder-drink. From 1932 until the 1960s Ovaltine was a significant

Olympic sponsor, and it was in 1928 that the company started advertising in the United States.*

In January 1929 Peter Gavuzzi and Arthur Newton moved into a set of rooms above a pub in the village of Shirley, just outside Southampton, and started their preparations for C.C. Pyle's second Transcontinental Race. As Newton put it, 'the two of us settled down and got busy'. The arrangement between them went much further than mutual support with training. This is when their 'partnership' really began. It was based on the simple principle that they would share all expenses in their preparation for the race, and during it, and they would also share any winnings either of them might get. There was, it seems, complete trust between them. But before they got back to the States there turned out to be competitive running for them to do in Britain.

There was even less of a culture of professional distance running in Britain at this time than there was in the United States. But it was only a year since an amateur Arthur Newton had been lionised by both press and public for his exploits on the Bath Road, and Joe Binks at the *News of the World* was keen to see how far he could go in marketing the South African phenomenon. Binks knew that if there was one place

---

* In 1955 Gavuzzi's run was used in a newspaper advertising campaign by Rowntree's Fruit Gums. 'Down at Land's End an excited crowd is cheering long-distance runner Peter Gavuzzi as he completes the last few yards of an amazing run – from one end of Britain to the other . . . Running six days a week, covering between 30 and 60 miles a day, Gavuzzi took a total of 167 hours, 37 minutes, 34 seconds for the 1,089-mile journey; a record that has lasted since September 1928 – unbeaten for twenty-seven years! And Rowntree's hold the long-lasting Fruit Gums record with Five delicious flavours – the longest-lasting 3d. worth you can buy!

in Britain where people would turn out to see professional athletes competing in the depths of winter it was at the Powderhall Stadium in Edinburgh's northern working-class quarter. Powderhall, named after a nearby gunpowder factory, had been opened in 1870 during the heyday of pedestrianism and was home to the internationally famous 'New Year Sprint', a 130-yard handicapped dash that attracted the world's best professionals. Binks was not suggesting to Newton that he sprinted. He wanted him to run to Powderhall from Glasgow – a distance of forty-three miles – and then make up a fifty-mile event by doing seven miles round the track. His opponent, who was as yet unknown to Joe Binks, would be Peter Gavuzzi; because, as Newton later wrote, 'there were no others in the country capable of putting up decent time over such a long course'. They agreed that they would split the £100 on offer 60/40. Not that this mattered; it was all money for their American campaign.

The two runners travelled first-class to Edinburgh, and both there and for the night before the race in Glasgow they were put up in the best hotels. More than 1,000 spectators saw them off. But the British winter of 1928–29 was famously cold, and even on the main Glasgow-to-Edinburgh road conditions were almost impossible. 'Every atom of the road was a criss-crossed maze of ruts in hardened snow and ice,' Newton wrote. They must have been tempted to call it off, as they undoubtedly risked serious injury just three months before the start of the Pyle race. But that would have been discourteous and unprofessional. As Newton said, 'the officials kept to their timetable and of course we could do no less'. They agreed between themselves to run the first quarter of the race at a steady nine miles an hour, exchanging the lead every now and then, but found it was simply too cold to keep up that sort of pace. Over the second part of the race Gavuzzi gradually got away from his older colleague, but as Newton approached the outskirts of Edinburgh he suddenly came across the young man from Southampton slumped by the roadside, beaten by 'bad roads and numbing cold'. Arthur Newton went on and remarkably, given the conditions, set a Glasgow-to-Edinburgh professional record. Gavuzzi's faithful local paper had sent a reporter north across the border for the event, and his despatch suggests clearly that there was, at least in Scotland, a real public appetite for this sort of contest. 'Newton passed his fallen rival, and entered the city accompanied by a great crowd of cyclists and motorists. He received a great ovation when he took to the track to complete his run and record a fine victory.' The race took its physical toll. The end of the month found Newton in Brighton, from where he wrote to Len Dilks in Pennsylvania: 'Gavuzzi and I ran on roads sheeted with ice, the result being that we both damaged legs. Gavuzzi tells me that a week put his right, but it is a month now since we ran and mine is still anything but well. However I am now doing no more than some 15 miles a day and hope that another week will have it right once more.'

Evidently it did, because within a fortnight Newton and Gavuzzi were presented with another challenge. Again they could not afford to turn it down, although this time they would only be receiving a proportion of the gate money. The challenge came from a Welsh runner, R.E. Cole, who wanted to sort out whether or not he could claim to be the British professional marathon champion. He held the record on the track, but Arthur Newton had beaten his time on the road during the course of a longer race. He wanted a head-to-head, but by now if you got Newton, you got Gavuzzi as well. They agreed to race Cole – whom Newton described to a friend as a 'fast ten-mile man' – on his home patch in Hereford, setting out by coach from Southampton on a morning of withering cold. Frightened that they might stiffen up too much on the journey, they decided to do it in stages, so that they could get out and exercise a bit before taking another coach. Their first stop was Bath, where they ran a quick ten miles and then went on to Bristol for the night. Before dawn the next morning they were out running again, but the cold drove them back.

When they woke up in Hereford on the day of the race they found there to be twenty-two degrees of frost with leaden skies. It soon started snowing. This is how Arthur Newton described what had been prepared for the race: 'We found it was a slightly tilted field, round which a 440-yard track had been measured. The snow had been so prolonged and heavy that whoever had been attending to the preliminaries had been unable to keep the fairway clear, and to start at all we should have to trample down about three inches of it.' He and Gavuzzi both ran in 'two sweaters as well as gloves'. As in Scotland, it was the younger man who found the conditions more difficult, and Gavuzzi retired at about the halfway mark. Newton ran on, but was eventually well beaten. He later suggested that they had set off too quickly just to get warm, but this was not a defeat – or indeed a record – that he was much concerned about. As he put it, 'the 26-mile marathon was not my distance – my style of running was suited only for fifty miles and upwards'. He was about to take part in a race that admirably suited his style.

III

Newton and Gavuzzi knew that the next Pyle race would be tougher and more professional in athletic terms, and competitors also needed to be more professional in the way they planned for it. Pyle was to persist with the accompanying vaudeville troupe, but 1928 had taught him that he could not afford to provide the runners with either accommodation or food. They would have to make their own arrangements. This meant that competitors – if they were really serious about the race – needed to employ a manager-cum-trainer-cum-driver to look after them on the road, and Newton and Gavuzzi thought they had found exactly the right man in a former athlete by the name of George Barratt. Their relationship with him was eventually to break down, but in early 1929 they were confident in their choice of a man whom Gavuzzi described as a 'top-class mechanic' and a 'fairly good cook'.

Pyle wanted a smaller, more dedicated field; so he increased the entry fee from 25 to 300 dollars. This was no mean sum, and for Newton and Gavuzzi the prospect of having, on top of this, to pay hotel and restaurant bills for three people for three months was both daunting and depressing. They were not rich men. So as soon as they got to New York (with less than a fortnight to go before the start of the race) they started hunting for what they had decided could save them a great deal of money: a DIY camping van. This is how Arthur Newton remembered their quest:

We went round to various garages until we found a suitable van for our purposes. This was a one-ton Chevrolet, and we immediately had it fitted with two Simmons beds, ice-chest, portable stove, shelving and so on; a collapsible bed for Barratt also forming part of the equipment. We wanted to be as comfortable as possible, for a great deal depends on freedom from worries of all sorts during a long-drawn-out race of this kind. Everything had to be thoroughly sound and good, as there would be no time for tinkering along the road. Fortunately, in spite of the shortage of time, we managed to make a really decent job of it, thanks mostly to the efficient work of our Manager. Among other things, a gramophone and a couple of dozen records of classical music were taken aboard, a foresight which gave us a great deal of pleasure later on.

It was not quite C.C. Pyle's ostentatious land yacht, but their strange vehicle was to serve Newton and Gavuzzi well over the next three months.

'Multitudinous wisecracks of a heartless nation scorch the vertebrae of some one hundred stooping athletes who set off at three o'clock from Columbus Circle this afternoon. The best observation of a sorry lot seems to this writer, at least, to be the notion that the race has missed its appropriate opening by twenty-four hours. Tomorrow, you might be reminded, is April Fool's Day.' This cruel cynicism from a sports columnist in the New York *Sunday Post* on 30th March 1929 suggested that the US press was picking up from where it had left off nearly a year previously – condemning Pyle's Transcontinental as a somewhat sad farce. But some reporters at least could not quite convince themselves that that was all there was to say about it. The anonymous author of the article just quoted went on to acknowledge the enormity of what those 'stooping athletes' were setting out to do, and that he admired them for it:

It is all very well for columnists and funny sports writers and the like to hold the lads up to ridicule; but the fact remains that theirs is certainly a gruelling feat, not duplicated by footballers, boxers, or six-day bike riders. Many an Indiana farmwife will see dark silhouettes of these boys patiently plodding over the country road after sunset, rushing to make the next encampment and food. Oklahoma ranchers will find the bandaged, jerseyed stragglers, burned the deep chocolate of the tropics, swinging over their prairies.

It was, he sneered, 'a professional enterprise, pure and simple', and so could not quite qualify as sport, but he knew that these pros were doing something no amateur athlete would dream of attempting. 'We think a marathon of 26 miles is something. These men laugh at the first lap of 24 miles. Most of their days call for runs of 70 miles. A man who can run 70-milers daily for a week is an athlete worthy of more consideration and respect from the sports world than his mere establishment as a joke butt.' Another indication of this shift towards recognition of the event was discussion in the press as to who might win it; and both Arthur Newton and Peter Gavuzzi were routinely listed among the favourites. One journalist summed them up patronisingly as 'semi-famous names'.

C.C. Pyle did his utmost to ensure a high-profile send-off for his runners. For a start, he had negotiated with the New York Police Department for the race to begin at Columbus Circle, in the very heart of Manhattan at the south-west corner of Central Park. It was Easter Sunday, and Pyle guaranteed himself a large crowd by asking Will Rogers to be the official starter. Rogers, as we have seen, had already gone public in his admiration for the event. *The New York Times* reported that 'a milling, pushing, gathering of 50,000 thronged Columbus Circle. A detail of forty policemen was practically powerless in the face of the disorganised but enthusiastic crowd. Rather than get his highway hoofers tangled up in the throng C.C. Pyle gave orders to get the race going without any ceremony. The runners weaved in and out of the traffic tangle, fighting their way through the crowd and the dense jam of cars.' Newton remembered that no one could hear Rogers's starting pistol.

Pat Robinson of the more populist *New York Daily News* was at his alliterative best, describing how '61 corn cultivators' were embarking on 'the Mad Marathon'. He had Pyle sporting a 'grin like the cat that dined on the canary' and complaining that he had not been able to enclose the Circle and charge an entry fee. The promoter – who was out of pocket after a disastrous season with his New York football team – was, as always, bullish about the financial prospects for the race. 'I look to make quite a bit of money this year,' he was to tell a Maryland paper a few days after it started: 'I have about $60,000 coming from Chambers of Commerce along the way, and I'll get $10,000 from the Los Angeles Chamber of Commerce for finishing the race there. I have a better bunch of runners than last year: the $300 entrance fee and the require-ment that runners must care for themselves along the way has kept out the "dogs".' He added that he hoped 'to make the race a national institution'.

He was certainly skilled at persuading individuals who could be described as 'national institutions' to associate themselves with the event. He had Will Rogers as his chief cheerleader in the press, and in 1928 there had been 'Red' Grange as his leading travelling celebrity. By the spring of 1929 Grange had moved on from his association with Pyle and was in Hollywood trying to map out a new career. But Pyle had another, perhaps even more iconic, sporting ace up his sleeve: Jim Thorpe. Thorpe, whose ancestry was an exotic mix of French, Irish and Native American, came from a poor background in Oklahoma. When he was sixteen he was recruited by the Carlisle Industrial School, a philanthropic 'Indian' institution in Pennsylvania that was extremely serious about its football. Thorpe became the team's star, and also revealed an extraordinary natural all-round ability as a track-and-field athlete. He could sprint, hurdle, long- and high-jump, pole-vault, while also throwing javelins and discuses for serious distances. In 1912, when he was twenty-four years old, he became the unexpected hero of the Stockholm Olympics – perhaps the first modern Games that provided competition of the highest quality. It saw the introduction of the modern pentathlon, which Jim Thorpe won easily. Only five days later he was back on the track for the even more demanding decathlon. Again Thorpe demolished the opposition, which led to a famous exchange on the podium when he was presented with his second gold medal by the Swedish king, Gustav V. 'Sir, you are the greatest athlete in the world,' the monarch said. 'Thanks, King' came the reply. When the US team returned home after the Games, Thorpe was certainly treated as the 'greatest athlete in the world', with ticker-tape parades being put on in his honour in New York, Boston and Philadelphia.

But the Olympic movement before the First World War was struggling to establish itself and to forge an identity in the context of increasing international sporting competition.

Central to this was an almost paranoid anxiety about amateurism, emanating from IOC headquarters in Switzerland; and Jim Thorpe became its first high-profile victim. It became known that in 1909–10, while taking a break from his studies at Carlisle, he had been paid to play minor-league baseball in North Carolina. The sums of money had been tiny, but they were enough for Thorpe to be summarily stripped of his two Olympic medals in 1913. The athletes who had come second refused to accept the gold medals.*

Thorpe's only possible response was to embrace the emerging world of professional sport, and he immediately signed for the New York Giants baseball team. Over the next fifteen years he was to mix this with American football, and before he finally retired in 1928 he was named the 'Greatest Football Player of the Half-Century'. The esteem that the American sporting public held him in became obvious in the Olympic year of 1932. Word got out that he was living in Los Angeles, but did not have the money to buy himself tickets for the Games that summer. The necessary sum was raised by public subscription, and when he first took his seat he received a standing ovation from 105,000 people. Signing up with C.C. Pyle in 1929 was the beginning of Jim Thorpe's non-playing career, and his job was essentially PR. He did not have all that much to do; Pyle just wanted his fame to rub off on the Transcontinental.

Among the papers Peter Gavuzzi left at his death was a small, coverless blue notebook. It was his diary of the 1929 race from New York to Los Angeles. It was sadly incomplete

---

* In 1983, thirty years after his death, the IOC restored his position in Olympic history and returned his medals to his family.

– there were no entries after Day 62 – and strangely moving. Gavuzzi would have got back to the 'caravan' after a day's run of anything up to seventy miles, and during the evening he would put down, in pencil and in a rounded childlike hand, the bare bones of the day. He noted the weather, the mileage and the state of the roads, with occasionally a comment about his competitors. He was by no means a natural writer, but he had made an agreement with his local Southampton paper to send them an occasional progress report and he needed to keep notes. He was also, of course, sharing his domestic space with someone who certainly *was* a natural writer and who could see the future potential of a detailed account of the extraordinary race in which they were involved. Day 1 found Gavuzzi noting down the chaos of the start in Columbus Circle and the easy distance of little more than twenty miles to Elizabeth, New Jersey. He also mentioned that 'those with no experience dashed off and just went mad, all to my delight'. That first evening he, Newton and George Barratt established what would be a pattern for the rest of the race. After completing the formalities of recording their times for the day and ideally, but by no means always, being provided with a bath, Barratt would drive the caravan a few miles out into the countryside away from whichever town they had reached, and there the three of them would eat and sleep. Both Newton and Gavuzzi were deadly serious about this race. They approached it as a job, one that could well set them up financially for the rest of their lives. They were not to allow themselves to be tempted by what the towns had to offer, and they wanted to be well out of earshot of the vaudeville tent.

They might not then have been aware until the next day of the deeply embarrassing events of the race's first evening. This was how the local paper described it: 'The bunion derby ran afoul of the New Jersey blue laws last night. The promoter, arriving at about noon, in advance of his hundred or more runners, began setting up tents for the sideshow which was to be given after the runners arrived, but Police Chief Michael Mulcahy made him take the tents down and said no show would be permitted. Chief Mulcahy likewise placed a ban on the sale of programmes containing the name and number of every contestant.' The Pyle organisation had made an elementary mistake. They had failed to find out that New Jersey state law prohibited public entertainments on Easter Sunday.

But this was just the beginning of an opening week that showed C.C. Pyle's organisation to be as amateur and chaotic as some of his runners were professional and focused. The second stage was a long one, more than forty-six miles, and it was due to finish in the industrial Pennsylvania town of Trenton. In the event the runners were diverted at the last minute to nearby Morrisville, because Trenton civic leaders had come to believe that Pyle's was a dubious outfit from which it would be best to distance themselves. Before the race began Pyle had hired 1,000 folding chairs for the audiences he anticipated would flock to see his Follies – a larger version of the vaudeville show that accompanied the first Transcontinental. The cost was $800, but the promoter's cheque bounced. When he arrived in Trenton he was met by officials who told him to settle the debt or his two vehicles would be seized. He somehow argued his way out of this, but was told, according to the local paper, that there was 'no parking space in Trenton for either his runners, himself or his show'.

Worse was to come. Pyle had hired an experienced circus

family, the Kunkelys, to be responsible for the big tent. Theirs was difficult, back-breaking work, assembling the tent each evening, taking it down the next morning and transporting it to the next town, before erecting it once again; and the job was made harder still by the wind and rain that accompanied the caravan during the first week of the race. After only five days the Kunkelys had had enough. The wages for their team of thirty 'razorbacks', who had practised to perfect their skilled operation for a week before the runners set off, were to be paid out of gate receipts. But virtually no one was paying to see the show, and the men had had no money for the best part of a fortnight. But as the Kunkelys headed back home to New York with a tent that had been nearly shredded by the wild weather, Pyle insisted that the show would go on. 'I don't care what they say as long as they don't misspell my name,' he told the *Baltimore Evening Sun*. 'As for that crack in the papers today about the show breaking up – that's some more baloney. We had a tent that was too big. It required too many men to handle it and it couldn't be gotten up in time to show at night. The only thing to do was to send it back and get another tent. In the meantime we'll show in any theatre available on the route.' For good measure he added that he regarded his Transcontinental as 'already one of the world's running classics. It will be even more so in years to come.'

Meanwhile Arthur Newton and Peter Gavuzzi were settling into the race. 'The scorchers are now all pooped and quite a few have already dropped out,' Gavuzzi wrote in his diary at the end of the second day, and on Day 4 – a run of thirty-seven miles – he decided for the first time to take the lead to see how the other main contenders would respond. But then, he jotted down that evening, 'owing to bad management on the part of the officials I took the wrong road, as did three others'. Newton also remembered the incident as a simple, if regrettable mistake: 'the official who was responsible for placing the arrows indicating the course was frequently very lax in the way in which he did his work; later on he was relieved and another man put on the job'. But a few years later, when Gavuzzi's trust in C.C. Pyle had completely broken down, he looked back on this 'mistake' and saw something more sinister. He was to tell a Canadian interviewer that he thought he had been intentionally sent down the wrong road, suggesting as well that on some occasions his drink might have been doctored. But at the time Gavuzzi felt no such paranoia; his problems were ones that he could share with his fellow runners – the distances they were being asked to cover on some days, and the fickle spring weather. His minimal diary entries give a sense of what they had to contend with during the first fortnight or so of the race:

Day 6: We started the run in torrential rain which lasted for four hours. I ran in my mackintosh and so'wester for thirty miles.

Day 8: The sun I must say was killing . . . The only way of keeping cool was to have a lot of cold water thrown over you every mile or so, in this way you could manage to jog along very slowly. Sunburn was another thing; we were actually baking, the skin was red raw, my word what pains we had to suffer afterwards.

Day 10: 63 miles. We started at 6.00 for this grind, and thank goodness we had rain to accompany us all the way.

You may imagine that was hard to run in, but it's much better than a burning sun broiling you up. Today we climbed an altitude of 4,620 feet; a lot of the men were sick.

Day 17: This was a very tiring run, the weather was very cold and a strong head wind. We also had 15 miles of loose gravel to run on, and this was very tiring and painful to the feet.

Among the men described by Peter Gavuzzi as being sick during the savagely long stage on Day 10 was Arthur Newton, one of several runners to be hit by a debilitating stomach bug. There was no possibility of a day off, of course, though Pyle did – just for that day – relax the rule that he had introduced the 1929 race which disqualified anyone not finishing a stage by midnight. But, seeing that they had started at six in the morning, an athlete still struggling on at midnight would have been on the road for eighteen hours. Newton found it humiliating that he was reduced to walking at times, and he was reported as needing medical attention before he could complete the stage. But the day had an impact on him that went beyond the physical. He considered a mountainous stage of more than sixty miles – even if all the runners were in good health – to be sadistic madness. 'The distance was overgreat,' he wrote twelve years later, convinced that it said much about Pyle's mistaken strategy for the event:

You would have thought that [the 1928] race would have taught the Management common sense with regard to this point, but . . . it seems to have been completely ignored. There's no doubt that the absurdly great distances we were called upon to cover were the cause of many of the best runners dropping out, just as they prolonged the suffering of others who could have recovered much more quickly from temporary injuries if they had no more than some thirty or thirty-five miles average per day to negotiate.

This was not just hindsight on Newton's part. He wrote to Len Dilks during the race complaining about the daily distances, saying that 'unless Pyle attends to this point very carefully there will not be another race as the men will be too cautious to enter again'.

Yet only two days after that sixty-three-mile stage Pyle was once again talking up his event to a small-town journalist, this time a reporter from the *Wheeling Register*: 'This race is the most remarkable marathon in present day history. I don't see how the boys keep up such a terrific pace. Just think, through New Jersey and Maryland the leaders averaged eight miles an hour. It was this pace that caused many internationally known stars to drop out. Although there are only 34 runners left, they are the cream of the distance marathoners from all over the world.' He went on to mention his concern about one in particular, the man whom he still felt gave his Transcontinental true athletic pedigree. 'I was afraid I was going to lose Arthur Newton today. He is suffering with a bad foot, and is having a tough time keeping pace with the others. Well, after tomorrow the pace will not be so hard as we hit some level country for a change.'

But it was not just level country that Arthur Newton was to hit as the Bunioneers progressed across the flatlands of southern Indiana. On Day 20 Peter Gavuzzi, who had been leading the race for a week, made a short and obviously heartfelt entry in his little blue diary: 'There is not much I can say about today's race concerning the actual running. I am much too upset, my friend Mr Newton was knocked down by a car and had to be taken to hospital. He naturally had to quit the race.' The accident happened in the small town of Brazil, on a Sunday, when America's roads were at their most crowded and dangerous. In those relatively early days of the motor car people drove for pleasure, not business; compulsory driving tests had yet to be introduced; and the rules of etiquette between motorists and pedestrians had still to be worked out. 'A car coming up from behind and on the wrong side of the road knocked me down and ran over me,' Newton said. George Barratt and the 'caravan' were nowhere near, and Newton was rushed by ambulance to the hospital in nearby Terre Haute. His right shoulder was found to be broken. The car was being driven by a local vicar, the Reverend A.F. Schmitz, whom Newton, at the time, refused to blame. He insisted that he would not be seeking any compensation. But six months later, in October 1929, when he was in a quandary yet again as to whether to stay in America or return to Africa, he wrote to Len Dilks saying, 'I am only waiting to hear from my American solicitor with regard to that accident I had in April . . .'

Newton's accident was not the only problem C.C. Pyle was confronted with on that Sunday in Brazil, Indiana. While the veteran athlete was being taken to hospital, the promoter spent much of the day locked away with his financial and legal team in a room at the town's best hotel. The 1929 Transcontinental Foot Race was facing a crisis on two separate fronts – both a consequence of the fact that Pyle was simply not making enough money. First, both his own luxury vehicle and the bus that was carrying the vaudeville's actors and dancers had been impounded a few days earlier in Columbus. Pyle had agreed to pay for them by weekly instalments, but now found himself unable to come up with the money. After several anxious days, during which the runners went on without him, Pyle found a couple of local businessmen willing to lend him enough for his own 'land yacht' to be released. But the cast of the Follies was still without transport. A St Louis paper described them the following week as 'riding catch as catch can, with no holds barred. They have lugged their own bags or left them to be expressed ahead: they have ridden in the automobiles of passing tourists, they have perched among the bedding and supplies in trainers' cars. They have travelled from town to town at times by street-car: some have hopped on the tailgates of trucks.' As we shall see, when Pyle's extraordinary travelling village finally reached Los Angeles he would face raw fury from several of his actors. Some would try to take legal action against him. But in late April, on the edge of the Midwest and only three weeks into the transcontinental adventure, they were still keeping faith with their employer. It was a loyalty, though, that could put them in deeply embarrassing positions – such as the one they found themselves in at Brazil, Indiana, when many of them could not pay their hotel bill and had their luggage impounded.

If C.C. Pyle could wriggle out of an awkward financial situation and reassure his potentially slighted actors, the second crisis he faced in Brazil that Sunday was more serious because it involved the runners themselves. In 1928 he had faced down near-mutinies from exhausted and hungry athletes whose basic needs he at times failed to provide for, and he had restructured his relationship with his runners in 1929 so that they themselves were responsible for the costs of daily living. But they were still *his* runners and some of them had not had the foresight, or the means, to make the sort of arrangement that enabled the likes of Newton and Gavuzzi to require nothing from Pyle and his team. So, for example, they still needed the management to find hotel rooms for them; and everyone in the field expected to be able to soak in a bath at the end of a day's running. A reporter for the local *Tribune* assessed their mood as they staggered into Brazil after covering a mere fifty-seven miles that day: 'When the runners arrived here they found no arrangements had been made to take care of them and no rooms or baths were available for lack of funds. Runners coming in with sweat pouring from their bodies were forced to stand around outside the theatre for more than an hour until Pyle's agents finally made arrangements for the opening of the theatre. The runners got chilled and stiff and they made public their opinion of Pyle and his crew.' None more so than the stylish and punctilious Philip Granville. He was travelling in even greater private comfort than Newton and Gavuzzi, and he expected a bath. Colleagues and bystanders alike were astonished at the violence of his language against Pyle.*

---

* A Pennsylvania paper had described Granville's living arrangements earlier in the race: 'He carries a chauffeur, a trainer, a coach, an automobile and $2,000 worth of equipment with him. In fact, it has been said that all he lacks is the *Encyclopaedia Britannica*. Here are some of the articles in his outfit: three camp beds, a cooker, gasoline lamp, mosquito netting, refrigerator, radio, phonograph, fishing rods, rifles, several pairs of handmade shoes, 24 changes of costume to suit climatic conditions, and a bicycle. When Granville left Canada he also had $400 in brandy, but he was relieved of this at the border.'

'Newton was out, and there was me with this race on my shoulders' was how Peter Gavuzzi later summed up the situation he found himself in after his partner's accident. But if he missed Newton, it was for his companionship and advice in their caravan, not for his company on the road. For the first ten days or so after the departure from New York the two had run together much of the time. On Day 3, for example, Newton had come in tenth, with Gavuzzi five minutes behind him in eleventh place. The next day Gavuzzi finished just ten minutes ahead. But then on Days 6 and 7 the younger man, undoubtedly with Newton's agreement, made his first move on the lead. They knew that their most serious rivals were Johnny Salo and Eddie Gardner, and even though there were weeks of racing to come, they could not let them establish too much of a lead on the cumulative time. After five days the Finn from New Jersey and the man still invariably described as the 'Seattle Negro' were locked together in terms of time, and they were already more than two hours ahead of Newton and Gavuzzi. So then, on the forty-four-mile stage from Havre de Grace to Baltimore, Gavuzzi made his move. By winning his first stage he put himself twenty minutes closer to Salo's overall time. Victory in his second the very next day cut the difference by a further fifteen minutes. Then it was Arthur Newton's turn to assert himself. On Day 8 he came in third, improving this to second (behind Gardner) the following day. After nine days they would have been happy enough with where they found themselves, in third and fourth places on cumulative time.

Then came Newton's stomach problems and the monster stage over the hills to Uniontown. Peter Gavuzzi finished second behind the Italian ultra-distance expert Guisto Umek, but he gained an hour on Salo (who was also affected by the bug), with the suffering Arthur Newton a further three hours adrift. The 'Rhodesian Rambler' never recovered from a stage whose severity, as we have seen, made him furious. When Peter Gavuzzi first took the 'Yellow Jersey' of overall race leader his partner was more than twenty hours behind him; and when the Reverend Schmitz ended Newton's race in Brazil, Indiana, there was a forty-hour gap between them. As a competitor, Newton was already out of the race when his shoulder was broken. He refused to stay in hospital for long and returned, 'trussed up like a fowl' as he put it to a reporter, to the caravan.

IV

Peter Gavuzzi was about to embark on the most important two months of his life; and it seems fair to say that between mid-April and mid-June 1929 he achieved something that places him among the very greatest of athletes. That he has been forgotten, that the history of British athletics can find no place for him, scandalises the historian and champion sprinter Peter Radford: 'We should have him on the highest possible pedestal. We should idolise him as a symbol of fortitude and success against the odds. He should be a national public hero. But we don't know about him. It is a tragedy. This man is monumentally strong, and not just a sporting hero but a hero in terms of human endeavour.'* The race that Peter Gavuzzi felt he had 'on his shoulders' after Newton's accident had become, by that stage, a battle between three or possibly four men: Gavuzzi himself, Johnny Salo, Eddie

* In conversation with the author.

Gardner and Guisto Umek. 'All of us wanted to win this race,' Gavuzzi told John Jewell in his 1976 interview, 'the prizes were very good. When you've staked practically a year's work in training the race becomes very important.' It was also important, Gavuzzi worked out, for him to tailor each day's run according to the differing strengths of his main opponents. 'From one mile to twenty-six miles there was one man no one could touch and that was Eddie Gardner. From twenty-six to forty miles there was no one to tackle me, and from forty-five to sixty miles no one could touch Salo.' Guisto Umek apparently came into his own when the stage was a minimum of seventy miles.

These were working-class men, running for a prize that would change their lives. They lived a daily life in which intense rivalry was tempered by a deep solidarity and mutual respect, which had first been forged in 1928 and was reinforced by every painful mile they covered on the way from New York to Los Angeles. The 1929 race was longer by about 300 miles, yet Pyle had given the runners seven fewer days to complete the distance. Simmering anger and resentment against the promoter underpinned the camaraderie of the athletes. 'There is a lot of discontent among the runners about the way the race is being conducted,' wrote Gavuzzi in a despatch to his local Southampton paper after a particularly long day on the road; 'they are giving us altogether excessive mileage. It was a good thing for Mr Pyle that he was not with us that night, as the runners would have spoken very heatedly on the subject.'

The fact that the leading runners were considerably fitter than they had been in 1928 also meant that the pace they could maintain was greater. 'Many was the time I had to battle with men at nine and ten miles an hour,' remembered Gavuzzi. But as the field crossed the Ozark Mountains into Missouri, in consistently appalling weather, Gavuzzi's battle became more focused as Eddie Gardner was forced to retire. A hamstring problem had been aggravated by days of running in the cold and wet, and on a Pyle Transcontinental there was never a chance to rest and recuperate. Gardner's withdrawal robbed the event of one of its most graceful runners, and – more importantly – reduced its appeal to the predominantly black communities through which the more southerly 1929 route took it. 'We were all sorry at Gardner's demise, for we all liked him,' recorded Arthur Newton. This left Peter Gavuzzi and Johnny Salo, and their battle against each other across the plains of Oklahoma and Texas, over the Rockies and through the deserts of Arizona and California – with first one and then the other in the lead – was one of the most extraordinary, moving, and ultimately, controversial contests in the history of sport. It lasted fifty-six days, during which they covered 2,633 miles. Gavuzzi initially held the lead for twenty-seven consecutive days, but could never achieve anything much more than a two-hour advantage over his rival. Salo clawed it back and then led Gavuzzi for eleven days. During the final fortnight – which included five back-to-back stages of more than fifty miles – the lead changed hands five times.* According to Andy Milroy, the leading British historian of ultra-distance running, such a duel must have been mentally as well as physically draining: 'Distance running at that kind of level is a kind of chess, human chess. What you're doing is you're pitting your

---

* These figures are based on Harry Berry's exemplary compilation of race statistics in his narrative *From LA to New York, from New York to LA*, Chorley, 1990.

resources against someone else's resources, but you've got to be careful how to position yourself. You've got to position yourself at each stage to get yourself ready for the end game.'* There is a telling photo of Gavuzzi and Salo running side by side through a desert landscape. It captures their radically different styles: the Englishman lithe and graceful, his stride long and comfortable, his eyes taking in the countryside around him, while at his shoulder the stocky Finn is all about power and effort, his face a grimace of concentration. But the image also captures their closeness in the vastness of the American West – two men on their own doing something remarkable. They were doing it as much with, as against, each other.

In his conversation with John Jewell in 1976 Peter Gavuzzi revealed that there were in fact days when he and Johnny Salo agreed *not* to race – both for their own sakes and as a gesture of kindness towards their trainers. 'Sometimes we did manage a day off. Salo would come and see me and if the race was only about forty miles which was an easy lap, no one could gain very much time on that, and Salo and I would shake hands. We did this sort of thing mainly because our trainers were very hard-worked people. When you consider they had to drive all day long, stop go stop go, give us drinks, go ahead and get supplies and come back again. We used to try and give them a day off as well. Salo and I would run together, so one of the trainers would be sent ahead to the next control station and could have a rest.'

As in 1928, the state that showed the most enthusiasm for the Transcontinental was Oklahoma, even though local hero Andy Payne was not running again. Perhaps it was Will

---

* In conversation with the author.

Rogers's influence, or perhaps the race brought a rare sense of excitement and national significance to simple and isolated communities. In Miami, Oklahoma, on 2nd May Salo and Gavuzzi were greeted by 'an unbroken line of spectators', with the Englishman receiving 'a more enthusiastic ovation than any others'. The next day's stage ended in the town of Chelsea. According to the local paper, 'great interest was displayed along the route by people in small towns and by farmers who lined the highway by the hundreds shouting encouragement to every runner, and laughing in derision at numerous small boys who attempted to keep up the steady pace of the marathoners in the hope of accompanying them into Chelsea'. When the leaders reached the town itself they found the buildings decked with flags and the main street cordoned off, 'so that the runners would not be delayed by the immense crowds that thronged the sidewalks for blocks'. C.C. Pyle must, for a moment at least, have felt vindicated. He told a reporter in Muskogee on 5th May that the Transcontinental was definitely set to become an annual affair, and that the prize money on offer would be increased until it reached $100,000.

But if Oklahoma was one thing, neighbouring Texas proved to be quite another. Both Newton and Gavuzzi found it an unsettling, alien landscape. 'This was the country of oil wells, and believe me it was a big stink,' recalled the latter, 'and the oil well smell was terrible. All you could see was these pumps going up and down and somebody told us that every time they went up and down it was a dollar in somebody's pocket. So there you are: we were poor and they were rich.' But owners of oil wells were not the sort of people Newton remarked on seeing as they passed a distressingly dirty workers' village. 'This was the sort of country,' he wrote, evidently rather shocked by what he saw, 'where many of the girls, both large and small, wore mechanics' overalls all day. Oh no, they were not mechanics: that was just their ordinary attire. Nearly all the boys and young men wore the same.'

Peter Gavuzzi's diary provides a minimal record of how hard those Texas days were for the runners:

Day 39: A terrible day. Raining cats and dogs, roads all slippery and muddy.

Day 41: Murder is not a good enough word for this treatment. After covering seventy-five miles we had to run around the town Dallas for five miles which made us all very mad.

Day 44: Everybody is very tired, mostly leg weary. Salo and myself are keeping close company.

Day 49: A terrible day again, more of that slushy muddy dirt road, and to top that we had to run several miles on the railway tracks.

After Texas came Arizona – 'the place we all feared', according to Peter Gavuzzi. The heat was such, he recalled, that 'when we used to get in from the laps we used to creep under the cars, that was the only shade there was in the place'. Arthur Newton expressed a fascination with the tiny remote communities they stayed in. There was Duncan, 'a few trees and perhaps a couple of hundred people marooned in a sandy stony desert'; and Bylas, 'but a small Indian settlement, with a tiny hotel, a large store and numbers of Apaches'.

Newton was now sufficiently recovered from his injury to be able to take part in the race again. Not as a runner, obviously, but in the same role of 'Technical Adviser' that he had filled in 1928. He was back, it is important to recognise in the light of how the Transcontinental of 1929 was to end, on C.C. Pyle's payroll. This was how he described his job: 'I would start out with them every morning and have a chat with each man as I caught him up, discussing difficulties and offering advice when required. After fifteen or twenty miles of this, by which time I had gone through most of the field, I took up a position by the side of the road and checked the runners as they passed. In the evening I generally got into an official car and drove ten or a dozen miles to meet and cheer up the last men along the road.' A reporter from Los Angeles was to spend such a day in the company of the man he described as 'perhaps the greatest runner of them all' once the Bunioneers reached California, and he summed Newton up as a 'one-man morale squad'. 'Gentlemen and sportsmen of this type,' he concluded, 'are all too rare.'

However, we should be wary of accepting too idealised a picture of Arthur Newton at this particular moment in his life. He undoubtedly cared about the health and welfare of the men taking part in this unimaginably hard feat of endurance, and he probably relished their respect for him as a world-record holder and an elder statesman of ultra-distance running. He was older and he was better educated. He was also, as they had seen, willing to complain when Pyle's demands were too great or his management inadequate. But we have also seen evidence that Newton and Pyle recognised a mutual interest in working together. If year-round professional distance running – which they both wanted – were to become established and to prove commercially viable, then they needed each other. So during the second half of the 1929 Transcontinental Newton was both Pyle's agent in relation to the exhausted and at times fractious competitors and *their* spokesman when it came to dealings with the management. But if this was not in itself a delicate enough position, he was at the same time the mentor and business partner of the man who was threatening to run away with the race. If Peter Gavuzzi were to go on to win, the terms of their agreement meant that Newton would receive 50 per cent of $25,000. Equally, if Gavuzzi were to win too easily, having been in the lead for too long, public interest in the event would dissipate and the chances of the race establishing itself as a regular part of the American sporting calendar would diminish.

In the interview he gave to the Road Runners Club in 1976 Peter Gavuzzi recalled a conversation he had with Arthur Newton during the latter period of the race – when his lead over Salo appeared unassailable. 'With two weeks to go I had something like an hour and forty minutes' lead. I was the younger man and some people would say, oh well, if you were the younger man you were the stronger, but not in this kind of race. It was really endurance that was needed. And so I discussed this thing with Mr Newton, and it was decided that I should not race Salo but do the best I could not to give him too much time each day. Sort of three-quarter speed while he was doing full speed. What I was trying to do was to get into Los Angeles, or at least the day before Los Angeles, with about fifteen to twenty minutes' advantage.'

The final day was to be a marathon of twenty-six miles round a track at the Wrigley Field baseball stadium in south-eastern LA, and Gavuzzi had complete confidence in his ability to beat Salo over such a 'short' distance. Which meant that a lead of fifteen minutes or so would be ample to assure victory.

In his autobiography Newton put it this way: Peter Gavuzzi did not want to risk exhausting himself over the last, long stages. But the argument is unconvincing. Gavuzzi had given no sign whatsoever of becoming exhausted, and would also surely have wanted the peace of mind of a more substantial lead over his rival. There was, after all, a lot of money at stake. So it is hard not to come to the conclusion that, if Newton advised Gavuzzi to slacken his pace a bit and so allow Salo to close the gap between them, he was doing C.C. Pyle's bidding. The promoter was in a desperate financial situation, with creditors queuing up to take legal action against him, and his one prospect of raising a decent amount of cash was by filling Wrigley Field on the final day with 10,000 paying customers. But the Los Angeles sporting public would only pay to watch the concluding marathon if they were guaranteed a close race. If the Transcontinental was all over bar the last twenty-six miles, they would stay away. The ultra-distance historian Andy Milroy was a near-neighbour of Peter Gavuzzi's during the latter's final years in the Wiltshire village of Steeple Ashton, and he says that the runner told him unequivocally that Pyle had asked him to slow down. 'Pete said that Pyle had come to him and said "Look, Pete, the prize money for this event is going to depend a lot on the gate receipts for the final day. If you build up a huge margin nobody's going to turn up on that last day. And so nobody's going to get any money. So what you've got to do is ease back and allow Johnny Salo to catch you some more, so it still looks like a very competitive race."' It seems clear that Gavuzzi was asked to do this; and it also seems clear that Pyle's request was reinforced by Arthur Newton.

The mental strain on Gavuzzi must have been immense. He was no longer in control of his own race, and it became clear as he and Salo approached Los Angeles that he had perhaps allowed the Finn to get too close to him. This was how the local paper in San Juan Capistrano reported on the conclusion to the penultimate stage on the road:

> With but two laps to go the 23-year-old native of Southampton, England, leads the runner from Passaic, New Jersey, by just 9 minutes and 56 seconds. And brother the race is on! For 62 miles the leaders ran side by side today. Then suddenly, and without the slightest warning, Salo began to quicken his pace. Faster he ran and still faster, with Gavuzzi striving like the courageous little man that he is to keep pace beside. Salo was tired, yet strong. Gavuzzi was tired and weakened. Salo was the stronger of the two runners. He was moving ahead with every painful stride. Gavuzzi, while not precisely staggering, presented a white face in the twilight and was running with his head down, his eyes to the ground and his feet leaden. But he kept on running.

The reporter clearly understood the implications of what was happening:

> The entire complexion of the race has now changed. Instead of being decided within Wrigley Field Sunday evening, it may be determined between Capistrano and Huntington Park tomorrow. Salo may step right out and kill Gavuzzi's

threat with a terrific pace, a pace which Salo appears to be able to stand, Gavuzzi not. Yet Gavuzzi is so courageous it seems more likely that if he loses at all tomorrow it will be by no more than another ten minutes. Gavuzzi may be recognised by his whiskers and the number 103. He looks like a little old man as he trots along the road, but actually he is 13 years younger than the smooth-faced Finn.

If there was any one day from his more than seven decades of life that the elderly Peter Gavuzzi would have looked back on, and turned over and over in his mind in the solitude of the Wiltshire cottage to which he had retired, it would have been Sunday, 16th June 1929. Together with the remaining band of Bunioneers he woke up that day in the leafy Los Angeles neighbourhood of Huntington Park. Four miles away was Wrigley Field – the baseball stadium that had been opened in 1925 and was named after William Wrigley, the chewing-gum magnate who owned the first club to be based there, the Los Angeles Angels. It was here that the climax to seventy-eight days of running was to be staged, with a classic twenty-six-mile marathon. The runners were all told that because the streets between Huntington Park and Wrigley Field would be so crowded – partly because of interest in the race, partly just because it was a Sunday – those four miles would not be regarded as part of the race. Nobody was to be penalised for getting held up by traffic or inquisitive fans. They were told to get to the stadium as quickly as they could, and that once everyone was there the marathon would start. Peter Gavuzzi still held a ten-minute lead over Johnny Salo, and he would have been entirely confident that this was ample to assure him of overall victory. His year of dedicated training had, it seemed, paid off. The working-class ship's steward from south London was on the verge of becoming a very rich man indeed.

Gavuzzi set off for the stadium protected from the crowds by a phalanx of six fellow runners – 'men at the back who were not in the prize money', as he described them. But they were helpless to protect him from what happened just before they got to Wrigley Field. This is how Gavuzzi himself remembered it almost fifty years later: 'Lots of places in America the train runs right through the town. So as I was coming along there was a train and the gates went down and we were all stopped: unfortunately for me it was one of those long trains with three engines in the front and about two hundred of these oil trucks and an engine behind. It took five or six minutes for it to go by.' This was an unwanted inconvenience, no doubt, but Gavuzzi would have realised that it was precisely because of this sort of eventuality that the journey to the stadium was not to count for the race. Arthur Newton confirms that this is what the runners had been told: 'the official notice had definitely stated that racing would only commence when all the competitors had reached the track in the stadium'.

However, when Gavuzzi finally arrived at Wrigley Field he found that the marathon had been started without him and several others, and that Johnny Salo was already on his third lap. Gavuzzi tried desperately to find out whether or not the journey from Huntington Park had in fact become part of the race and, if so, what had happened to his ten-minute cushion. Had most of it disappeared while he waited for that endless train to pass? No one seemed to know, or at least no one was prepared to tell him. So it was a confused and anxious Gavuzzi who had to take to the track and attempt to catch Salo in front of a packed house of more than 10,000 spectators, who were all cheering the possibility of an unexpected American victory. C.C. Pyle might have got many things wrong during the epic journey across America, but he had certainly got it right on the final night. He had manipulated a stunningly exciting finish. 'No man who witnessed the event,' Newton wrote, 'would have believed that either Salo or Gavuzzi could have managed to keep up the speed they were going, after having run 3,500 miles without a day's rest. Yet they ran, and ran, and still ran, till the whole house was on its feet shouting and hullabalooing.' For a brief spell in the middle of the race Peter Gavuzzi did manage to overtake Salo, but by then it must have become clear to him that his defeat was being stage-managed, that Pyle had decided he did not want him to win. The management had gone back on their word: the miles from Huntington Park *were* to be considered part of the race. 'We had run this entire race of three thousand six hundred and thirty-five miles,' Peter Gavuzzi was to recall, 'and I had lost it by two minutes and forty-seven seconds.'

Arthur Newton was to describe this, disingenuously, as 'a right splendid finish to the greatest athletic event ever staged'. It might have seemed so to the thousands of innocent spectators inside Wrigley Field on that warm June evening, but to those who knew anything about C.C. Pyle – either his character or his finances – the finish was a sham. Harry Berry, the Lancashire writer whose narrative of the two Transcontinentals was published privately in 1990, has no doubt whatever that Gavuzzi was 'robbed' because Pyle needed an American victor. 'Salo was a better property to market,' he says. If this was the case, and it seems extremely difficult to argue that it was not, then Peter Gavuzzi was robbed of $15,000, the difference between the prizes for first and second place. This raises the question of what Arthur Newton thought or did about this. He was, after all, Gavuzzi's partner and so stood to lose financially as well, but he was also the race's 'Technical Adviser'. Where was he on that final day? Surely he would mount a protest against Pyle's duplicity. Far from it. He seems to have done everything he could to avoid a confrontation with the promoter. Gavuzzi always insisted that he wanted to protest, but that Newton argued him out of it. 'I consulted with my partner Mr Newton,' he said in 1976, 'and he was one of those English gentlemen who believes in fair play and being a good loser.' Gavuzzi recalled that he and Newton were cornered by a group of journalists who wanted to know what they were going to do. When he said something about feeling tricked over the status of the stretch from Huntington Park to the stadium, a reporter warned him, 'if you make an announcement that you're not satisfied with the result you'll be branded as a very bad loser'. Newton apparently led Gavuzzi away, saying, 'after all we did get second prize and it's ten thousand dollars and we can come back next year and try it again'. Harry Berry, who is no fan of Newton, sees him as pulling rank on Gavuzzi here – both in terms of class and age – and persuading him that it would somehow be demeaning to make a fuss. 'I think it illustrates the relationship between them, and I think it was something that Peter Gavuzzi regretted all his life.'*

Not that any protest, as it turned out, would have resulted in a larger prize. After the Wrigley Park marathon the runners were all taken back to their hotel in Huntington Park and told that the following day the fifteen prize-winners would be presented with their cheques at the downtown offices of Pyle's

---

* In conversation with the author.

lawyer. From a distance of almost fifty years, Peter Gavuzzi's memory of that fateful morning was crystal-clear. 'All of us went together in the big coach, and we went to Los Angeles to this building and we went up in the lift, I forget how many floors, and we went to this lawyer's office. Then we all sat down and we were chatting and we were happy; it was all over, you know, it's a great relief after a race like this and all that distance. And we were waiting for these cheques. But . . . disaster.' Johnny Salo was first to be summoned into the office; he was with the lawyer for a good fifteen minutes, and Gavuzzi remembered sitting in the lobby expecting a grinning Finn to emerge. Quite the opposite. Salo came out grim-faced. 'I'm sorry Pete,' he said, 'there's no money.' Then Gavuzzi and Newton were asked into the lawyer's office. Pyle, wisely enough, was not present himself. The runners were told that the promoter had 'gone broke' long before the Transcontinental reached Los Angeles, and had been pinning his hopes on the gate money from Wrigley Field. But he had not received a cent of it. The US tax authorities were well aware of his plans, and had sequestered the takings on the night of the final marathon.

Pyle's lawyer told the two Englishmen that they had two options. They could sue Pyle for breach of contract, and they would undoubtedly win the case. Pyle would be sent to prison, where he would have no means of raising the money he owed them. Or they could not sue him, accept a promissory note, and wait for him to come up with their prize. Gavuzzi was to keep the note for the rest of his life, and it is among the papers now in the possession of his grandson Guy at his home near Derby. Gavuzzi and Newton were assured they would be given $750 in cash to pay for their passages back to England, so the promissory note is for $9250, and it specifies that 'until this cheque is cashed there would be 7% interest per annum'. Initially, at least in public, Newton and Gavuzzi insisted that they trusted Pyle to come up with the money. A few days after their meeting with the promoter's lawyer they were both in San Francisco as guests, along with Guisto Umek, of the city's Italian community. 'I'm not worried,' Peter Gavuzzi told a local reporter, 'Pyle paid the runners off last year and I'm sure he'll do so again.' He never did. It would be some years before the two English runners finally gave up on the quest for their money. We know that in the summer of 1933 Gavuzzi was to travel to Chicago from his base in southern Canada for a confrontation with C.C. Pyle, who was at the time maintaining a suite of rooms in one of the city's more expensive hotels. Pyle pleaded temporary poverty, and gave yet more empty assurances. Twenty-five years later Arthur Newton found himself living out his last years on the outskirts of London in something approaching real poverty; and he confided in a letter to a friend that everything about his old age would have been different had he received what he was due from Pyle in 1929.

In early July that year, a fortnight after the controversial Wrigley Field marathon, Pyle let it be known that he 'would never promote another Transcontinental Foot Race'. One can hardly blame him. He was being pursued for money by runners, by vaudeville performers, even by an electrician who claimed he was owed $500 from the 1928 race, and he was a virtual prisoner in his Los Angeles hotel room. 'Harrowing tales were related by participants in C.C. Pyle's "bunion derby" before Labour Commissioner M.E. Richardson yesterday,' reported the LA *Daily News* on 4th July, referring to claims from actors and dancers in the Follies. A fortnight later the same paper turned its attention to the runners. 'Almost a month after the finish of the race, winners complained yesterday to investigators that the prize money had not been paid. At the offices of his attorney Pyle reiterated his determination to pay all he owes.' (The report mentioned that Peter Gavuzzi and George Barratt were still living in a cheap Huntington Park hotel.)

During the first week of August Pyle was obviously fighting for his freedom. The Associated Press reported on 7th August that he had been 'granted a week's respite from wage claims of employees in the bunion derby, which four times within a week nearly landed him in jail. City Prosecutor Lloyd Nix gave Pyle until August 13 to pay $1000 to Cleo Balcom and her orchestra and Paul Hickman, leader of a troupe of actors, or make good on his promise to find employment in the films for the stranded girls.' Pyle pleaded yet again for more time, saying he did not have a 'thin dime'. If he was embarrassed by his inability to meet his responsibilities over the Transcontinental, Pyle, one imagines, would have been more worried by his becoming *persona non grata* in the Los Angeles business community. In late August a group was formed to raise money so that lawyers could be retained to represent the Bunioneers from outside the United States who were still without their prize money. 'The reputation of Los Angeles is at stake,' its spokesman said. 'This city is getting a lot of unfavourable comment in French and Italian newspapers. These papers are hinting that there is no assurance that foreigners entering in the Olympic Games in 1932 will fare any better. This Pyle fiasco is damaging Los Angeles' reputation as a city of good sportsmanship and we are determined that something shall be done about it. We will raise enough money to pay the transportation of all the foreign runners back to their native lands.'

But Arthur Newton and Peter Gavuzzi did not want, yet, to return to Britain. The former had known for several years that he was probably the best ultra-distance runner in the world; he had finally, if reluctantly, accepted his social position as a professional; and he must have felt that he was too old to try and find yet another way of earning a living. The latter had discovered an unexpected and rare ability, and he had personal reasons – his ambivalence towards his wife and child – for wanting to delay his return to Southampton for as long as possible. They had their partnership too, one that had strengthened during the long grind from New York, and they knew that if there was money to be made from professional running, then it was to be made in America. On their visit to San Francisco in July Gavuzzi had been asked about his future plans. He said he wanted to 'make a business of long-distance running'. 'I will run anything from 100 to 10,000 miles. Running isn't such a tough business as one would think. After the first couple of weeks it is just like a day's work in any trade to go out and run 30 or 40 miles.' This was the bravado of a young, confident and extraordinarily tough man. But what he was not to know was that July 1929 was not such a propitious moment to be embarking on any new business. The New York stock-market crash was just three months away.

6

'The Leading Lights of the Paid Brigade'

Newton and Gavuzzi's Professional Partnership

I

'**B**oth Salo and I are keen on making a bit at racing if we can as none of us came out of the Transcontinental race financially strong. I am up here in the Catskills just to keep in training for anything that may turn up.' So wrote Arthur Newton to his old friend Len Dilks in the middle of October 1929. Peter Gavuzzi, he mentioned, had sailed back to England a week previously, and Newton can have had no idea how long he would stay. So for the time being Newton was once again on his own in America. He told Dilks of his hope that he would get some compensation for the accident that had put him out of the Pyle race earlier in the year; he reported that there would definitely not be a third Transcontinental; and he asked, 'what are the chances of a 24 hr. race against horses at your city?'

Newton – one of life's natural organisers – was now looking to mix the roles of competitor and promoter. By the beginning of September it had become clear to those Bunioneers still on the West Coast that they were wasting their time hanging around Los Angeles in the hope that C.C. Pyle would produce their money. He simply did not have any, and summonses and subpoenas were not going to change that. (Pyle was to reinvent himself a few years later and rebuild his business life, but only after he had struggled back to health after suffering a massive stroke in 1930 that left him unable to walk or speak for several months. The stress of the financial and legal position in which he found himself after the second Transcontinental must have contributed to the crisis in his health.) In any case his impecunious runners were far more likely to find some competition on the East rather than the West Coast, so that is where they headed. Newton's first aim was to re-establish contact in New York with Hugo Quist, Pyle's right-hand man, who had first welcomed him to America in 1928. 'For some months I worked with him to learn the ropes,' Newton wrote.

But the first event he and Gavuzzi found themselves in was nothing to do with Quist or any other promoter; it was a result of the civic pride that the small New Jersey town of Passaic took in Johnny Salo. Soon after his victory at Wrigley Field in June, Salo had been offered a job in the local police force, and on 21st September a special fifteen-mile race was organised at the Passaic School Stadium by way of a welcome-home celebration. Only three other runners were invited: Newton, Gavuzzi and the man who had beaten Salo in the first Transcontinental, Andy Payne. Each was guaranteed some money, with $2,000 as first prize. The local paper did its best to talk up the event. 'Rivalry is keen between these four outstanding foot racers who are the greatest distance runners that the present age has produced,' gushed the Passaic *Daily News*. But the race itself disappointed. It was, the paper concluded, 'a contest that failed to provide many thrills: Payne was flat and flabby, Salo also was in poor shape. He knew he had little chance to win but was too proud to leave the race, as Payne did, with so many of his home folks looking on. Gavuzzi could have been in better shape too.' Newton won and alone escaped criticism: 'as fine a piece of running machinery as there is in professional circles'. The sports columnist Arthur G. McMahon, whose articles were syndicated across the US, was impressed too. 'At the age of forty-six Newton is in splendid physical condition,' he wrote, 'a remarkable example of clean living. Newton evidently took the race as a challenge to ability as well as an opportunity to make some money. He is a real English gentleman, scholarly and studious.'*

Only two days after the Passaic fifteen-mile event, Newton and Gavuzzi were in Philadelphia, getting ready for the start of a six-day race. There were five other teams, largely made

---

* Over the next few months Johnny Salo was given special dispensation by the Passaic Police Department to continue his running career, but early in 1930 he was diagnosed with diabetes and his health rapidly deteriorated. He continued to work when he could, and towards the end of that year's baseball season Officer Salo was on crowd duty at the local ball-park when some fans invaded the playing area. He went in after them just as a player threw the ball from the outfield. It hit Salo behind the right ear and felled him. He got up almost immediately and shrugged off all offers of help. Later that day he suddenly collapsed and died. The people of Passaic turned out in their thousands for the funeral of a man Newton described as being 'as inoffensive and generously disposed as anyone you could find'. Peter Gavuzzi, of course, lost the friendship of the one man to whom he could really talk about running across America.

up of former Pyle runners, though Johnny Salo was partnered by Joie Ray. The six-day format had become standard fare for cyclists, and had been particularly successful at Madison Square Garden, but this was not simply a 'pedestrian' equivalent. The promoter Hugo Quist's idea – and this lay behind Newton's bizarre request to Len Dilks mentioned above – was that five teams of men were to race five teams of horses. Milton Crandall, the king of New York's dance marathons, was also involved in organising the event. Given that (not to mention the horses), it is hardly surprising that one local paper dismissed it as 'this latest of freak contests'. But men who were experimenting with a life as professional distance runners had to fall in with what promoters dreamed up, however bizarre or possibly demeaning the contests might be. Newton and Gavuzzi, as star attractions, were offered $500 each to take part.

'Ladies and Gentlemen! Runner No. 3 is the famous Pete Gavuzzi, of Southampton, England. He is known around the world for his great feats upon the track. And while he is running over here in this tremendous endurance contest of man versus beast he has a wife and kiddie back in England whom he has never seen before.' Each runner was introduced as they jogged a lap of the track, and this is what the audience were told about Gavuzzi. During a spell when Newton was doing the running for the team, Gavuzzi got hold of the microphone and issued a corrective: 'He said I hadn't seen my wife and kiddie. I've seen my wife; it's my kiddie I haven't seen. He was born since I came over here.' A good rejoinder in the context no doubt, but not strictly true. We do not know whether Gavuzzi had seen his son or not; we do know that the baby had been born during the John o'Groats to Land's

End training run in the autumn of 1928, some four months before Gavuzzi had arrived in the States for the second Pyle race.

Newton wrote a few pages about the race against horses in his short 1949 book *Races and Training*, and he was mainly concerned to explain why the general public were wrong to have assumed an equine victory. In fact, even though the team of horses was changed halfway through, and then changed back to the original animals, the runners were miles ahead at the end. The reason? Newton had no doubt. 'It was evident that what obsessed the horses was nothing less than sheer boredom: they could not see the object of circling and ever-lastingly circling that limited track. They lost heart completely.' So apparently did the public, and the gate was so small over the last day or two of the 'race' that Hugo Quist called the runners together at the end to plead with them to accept a 25 per cent cut in pay. He had an ally in Arthur Newton. 'I pointed out that as professional runners we were dependent on promoters, and unless we met them reasonably and even generously, we could not expect them to arrange contests for us.' Peter Gavuzzi knew all too well what his partner was talking about.

Newton stayed in or around New York during the winter of 1929–30. He was working on his claim for compensation from his accident in Brazil, Indiana; he was writing, trying to organise his thoughts about training into a publishable book; he was, of course, keeping fit with a daily routine of running fifteen to twenty miles; and he was, as he told Len Dilks, 'in touch with Hugo Quist at all times'. It is from his correspondence with Dilks that we can piece together something of Newton's preoccupations and plans at this stage of his life. Or perhaps, more accurately, we can understand something of how he constructed his dilemmas. He makes frequent mention of setting sail for England and Africa, but it is hard to know if this is what he really wanted or simply what he assumed he was fated to do. Against this, he was obviously keen to explore whatever opportunities might arise in the US or Canada for doing some professional running. But when a race was fixed up, he more often than not expressed the hope that it would be his last.

Two letters to Dilks from January 1930 survive. The first was a strongly worded warning to his friend not to get involved in any way with George Barratt, the driver, cook and general helper whom he and Gavuzzi had employed during the second Transcontinental. Dilks had been contemplating a run to set a professional US record for 100 miles on the road and had obviously sounded out Newton on whether or not to employ Barratt to assist with the attempt. Newton implored him not to, on the grounds that Barratt 'has an unfortunate habit of living upon anyone he can manage to, and it is almost impossible to get rid of him unless you lend him money'. What makes the letter interesting, though, is not what Newton had to say about Barratt, but his obvious discomfort at being seen to criticise someone so strongly. 'Be kind to me and burn this letter when you have read it, as I should not like anyone to find that I had written unkindly about them at any time.' He signed off the letter: 'so much for that; burn it like a good fellow'.

The second letter, barely more than a note, is significant because it provides the first evidence of a professional endurance-athletics business in Canada which was to become important for Newton and Gavuzzi over the next few years.

It was to make it possible for them to run for a living and was to make them, for a brief moment, extremely well known in both Quebec and Ontario. Newton told Dilks about a 200-mile race on snowshoes from Quebec to Montreal that was due to take place at the end of January and gave him the name of its French-Canadian promoter, Armand Vincent. Newton, who regarded snowshoes as 'fiendish affairs', said he would not be taking part himself, but that he would be running in a separate fifteen-mile event to mark the end of the long trek from Quebec. 'With the entry of Arthur Newton,' a local paper crowed, 'Montrealers are assured of seeing the most phenomenal runner, in many respects, that the world has ever known.'

II

Descriptions of that six-day snowshoe event show that it was part of a distinctive sporting culture – one that English-speaking North America knew little about. At a simple level it can be seen as a sporting celebration of Quebeckers' relationship with the unremitting harshness of their winters. The overall distance was 190 miles, to be covered in six daily stages that varied in length from twenty-five to more than fifty miles. The temperatures were often below zero, the roads often deep in drifting snow. Race officials, medical teams and the competitors' trainers followed on sleds pulled by horses or dogs. The attraction for the public was that the athletes were taking on and overcoming the very conditions they had to deal with in everyday life. There was huge press interest in the event, and Édouard Fabre, the forty-four-year-old favourite, had heroic status throughout French Canada. This is how David Blaikie, the historian of Canadian twentieth-century marathon running, describes the atmosphere surrounding the start of the event: 'Crowds cheered the cavalcade out of the city and noisy knots of spectators waited at each hamlet beyond, drawn by the colour and drama of the spectacle. Between settlements families came out from farmhouses to stand at the roadside and shout encouragement. Some offered the racers hot soup and steaming mugs of tea. Others hopped on sleds of their own and rode along, their snorting horses and jangling sleigh bells adding colour to the scene.' When the race finished one day in the small town of Sainte-Anne-de-la-Pérade there were so many people keen to catch a glimpse of the black-clad Fabre that a balcony overlooking the street collapsed. The penultimate stage was more than fifty miles long, and an injured Fabre had to struggle to maintain his overall lead. He did so, and finally arrived at the Montreal Forum, where a special snow-track had been constructed so that the final mile could be run in front of a reportedly ecstatic full house.

Fabre's main rival in the race was Philip Granville, the black Canadian from Hamilton, Ontario, who had become a close friend of both Newton and Gavuzzi during the Transcontinental runs; and Johnny Salo had been invited to compete with Newton in the fifteen-miler. So some of the more prominent among Pyle's Bunioneers were congregating in French Canada in the early months of 1930. They were able to do so because of a decision by two brothers, Sam and Harry Bronfman, to use long-distance endurance-racing as a means of selling their product – whiskey. The sons of Russian Jewish immigrants, the Bronfman brothers had started out in the hotel business, but had quickly realised the commercial potential of the liquor trade with Prohibition in place south of the US border. They had set up a distillery in Montreal in 1925, and in 1928 took over their main rivals, Seagram's. Rumours abounded as to their links with the likes of Al Capone, but within Canada they were known for their involvement with sport and for their philanthropy. All proceeds from the Montreal Forum on 7th February 1930, the day the snowshoe marathon finished, went to a fund for building a Jewish hospital in the city. It was to be sponsorship from the Bronfmans' company, the Distillers Corporation, that was to keep Arthur Newton in Canada and that encouraged him to summon from England his old partner, Peter Gavuzzi.

But there was a larger politics to the emergence of professional endurance-athletics in French Canada in 1930, because it was in the same year that the intensely pro-British politicians of Ontario staged the first ever Empire Games – which were, of course, a strictly amateur event. There was so much imperial propaganda emanating from Britain during the 1920s – most obviously the giant Wembley exhibition of 1924–5 – that it would be natural to think of the Empire Games as an idea hatched in the metropolis. Nothing could be further from the truth. Neither British politicians nor sporting administrators expressed any enthusiasm for the idea; the former were looking for more 'important' expressions of imperial solidarity (ideally military), while the latter saw the event as a possibly dangerous distraction from Olympic preparations. The team that was sent to Canada was far from being the strongest available, and the Prince of Wales famously snubbed the Games by pulling out of a commitment to open them.

The first Empire Games that took place in August 1930 were a product of both Canadian and larger North American politics. The host city was Hamilton, an industrial centre that is closer to the US border at Niagara Falls than it is to Toronto, about forty miles to the north. During the 1920s Hamilton had christened itself the 'Ambitious City', and it was dominated both politically and culturally by a Protestant elite who thought that 'true' Canadian identity was under threat from two sources – creeping Americanisation and the 'disloyalty' of the French speakers of Quebec. Canada had paid hugely, both in resources and in loss of life, during the First World War, and in many parts of the country this had left a legacy of deep resentment. Many saw the conflict as none of their business, as a self-inflicted product of 'European imperialism', and argued that Canada should think of itself as part of 'America' in large terms and not as part of the British Empire. Economically the shift was already taking place. Whereas 75 per cent of foreign capital invested in Canada had come from Britain in 1914, this had declined to 36 per cent by 1930. There were no longer calls, as there had been in the later nineteenth century, for Canada to become part of the US, but there were powerful voices arguing for Canadian independence.

The most committed and strident of these came from the French-speaking province of Quebec. There were few ties, either emotional or economic, between France itself and French Canada, and there was virtually none of the continuing emigration that peopled Canada's cities and plains with the English and the Scots. So most citizens of Quebec thought of themselves as Canadian through and through – as more Canadian than those of their countrymen who identified with a 'mother' country in Europe. 'On the soil of Canada, his only home and country,' wrote Quebec's great political intellectual Henri Bourassa, 'all the national aspirations of the French Canadian are concentrated.' This, needless to say, had made the conscription that was introduced in 1917 a hugely controversial issue in French Canada. The call to serve the British Empire was both resented and ignored.

For several years after the end of the First World War the question of Canada's imperial loyalty was a constant source of anxiety among British politicians. There was even talk of Canadian sympathy for a possible US invasion, and in 1925 the War Office in London sent a mission to the Dominion to see what could be done to counter it. It was led by a Captain T.B. Trappes-Lomax, and one of his conclusions was that Canada was dangerously susceptible to cultural influence from south of the border, because neither cricket nor rugby had taken sufficient hold. He recommended that teams be sent out as a matter of urgency and was confident that they would 'strengthen imperial ties'. In the absence of the great public-school team games, and with both baseball and American football becoming ever more popular in Canada, members of the pro-British elite of Ontario were faced with a sporting dilemma. Their solution was to focus on amateurism, and on encouraging Canadian national pride in success at the Olympic Games. Nowhere was more effort put into this than in Hamilton. In 1926 the city's Olympic Club was formed, and in 1928 it staged all of Canada's track-and-field trials for the Amsterdam Games. Percy Williams, a slight, frail and previously unknown Canadian sprinter, caused a sensation by winning both the 100 and 200 metres in Amsterdam, and he became a national hero overnight. He was presented as all that was best about the country: British, Protestant and amateur. He was injured just before the Empire Games in Hamilton and could not compete, though he was given a place of honour at the opening ceremony.

A few hundred miles away in Montreal and Quebec the

sporting priorities were entirely different. Larry J. Pickering, the historian of Canadian sport in the 1920s, has written that 'the rise in national feeling that was promoted by sport was not experienced by French Canadians to the same degree . . . French Canadians played the purely Canadian sports of [ice] hockey and lacrosse, but most of the Olympic sports were not practised at a high competitive level. During the 1928 Olympics, when Canadian sports nationalism was at its peak, [Montreal's] *Le Devoir* gave minimal coverage to Canada's performance.' It gave even less to the British Empire Games in Hamilton in the summer of 1930, because for the French Canadian press by far the most important sporting event of that summer was the 500-mile 'Peter Dawson' professional marathon from Quebec to Montreal and back – a follow-up to the great snow-shoe race of the previous winter. It was for teams of two runners, and it was for this event that Newton had summoned Gavuzzi from Southampton. Newton, in his surviving writings and correspondence, makes no mention of the Empire Games, even though, as we shall see, the city of Hamilton became for a time extremely important in their lives. He was without a doubt an Empire loyalist and it must have been difficult for him to find himself, because of his professionalism, confined to the sporting ghetto of French Canada, unable to go and socialise with runners from southern Africa or Australia with whom he shared so much in terms of politics and class. For Peter Gavuzzi, on the other hand, Montreal and Quebec would have been far less threatening or alien. He was a working-class professional among others, and he was as at home in French as he was in English. 'Pete is a cocky lad, exuding confidence galore: he is not as modest as his mild-mannered partner,' concluded a local reporter who met the pair when they went for the obligatory pre-race medical in downtown Montreal. His command of the local language must have given Gavuzzi, perhaps for the first time since they had met, a sense that he did not always have to be in Newton's shadow when it came to social and cultural matters.

He certainly was, though, when it came to the 500-mile race itself, because Arthur Newton had been part of the team putting the event together. 'Don't get excited, there is nothing at all certain about this,' he had written to Len Dilks in early March, 'but I have an idea a road race will be put up shortly . . . Would you care to compete, and, if so, what would be the smallest sum you would be prepared to accept? You can tell me this in confidence, and I will see to it that it goes no further . . . You see I know who is considering the event and shall be in a position to say what men had better be asked to compete. Send me an answer at once like a good man.' Three weeks later Newton wrote again. 'Bet you were pleased with the contract! Lucky you got in early, for the late comers are not faring so well by any means.' Finally, on 10th April, he sent Dilks a short note clarifying the situation. 'I may tell you I am in partnership with Hugo Quist: this will explain how it was I was able to get you fixed up so quickly with the Canadian race. You are one of two or three to get moderately well paid.' There can be little doubt that Newton himself and Peter Gavuzzi fell into that particular category.

The Dawson race itself – its name came from the Bronfman brothers' best-selling brand of whiskey – proved almost too easy for them. The daily stages were between fifty and eighty miles, but each runner covered only ten miles or so before handing over to his partner. 'All the best distance runners in the States and Canada were up against us,' Newton wrote, by which he meant that the event brought together, once again, the leading Pyle runners. The favourites were Johnny Salo and Joie Ray, who duly raced away with the first stage. But by keeping to their relentless pre-planned pace, Newton and Gavuzzi found themselves comfortably in the lead after three days. Two days later they found their lead almost embarrassing, and one suspects some furtive discussions took place with Hugo Quist and Armand Vincent as to how the event could at least be made to look more competitive. As with the second Transcontinental, the race was to end with a track marathon, and the Bronfman brothers wanted a full house. This is how Newton later described what he called a 'very awkward proposition': 'Gavuzzi and I now had to learn how to run a race in public not only without racing but with as much actual waste of time as circumstances would permit . . . we had to exercise a lot of caution or the position would have become obvious to the public, and that would have spoilt the race, so we carried on as slowly as we dared.' This involved losing the penultimate stage and making sure the final marathon provided a real spectacle. The Montreal paper *La Patrie* needed no convincing, calling it 'the most sensational marathon that's ever been run in the entire universe'. Arthur Newton was to tell a South African paper in 1956 that he and Gavuzzi had been offered an extra $500 each if they agreed to slow their pace.

After the race Arthur Newton managed to persuade a local reporter that neither he nor Peter Gavuzzi had any idea what their winnings amounted to, which led to a sentimental report of his being an 'amateur at heart'. Perhaps he always remained so, but sentiment was not something that either he or Gavuzzi could afford, and it is precisely from this moment in August 1930 that they set to work with the promoter Armand Vincent to make 'Newton and Gavuzzi' into a marketable brand in Canada. They were the star attraction at a twenty-six-hour men-versus-horses race in Montreal later that month, and then on the 23rd they took part in a thirty-mile track event as part of the annual Canadian National Exhibition in Toronto. This was significant, as it was a first sortie into 'enemy' territory in Ontario, where athletes were meant to be amateur, and preferably middle class and Protestant. As the local *Star* put it, 'the race gave Toronto her first opportunity of looking over the leading professional runners of the world, all the leading lights of the paid brigade being on the job'. No one made more of an impression that Peter Gavuzzi. The race was for teams of two, but Newton was carrying an injury and had to retire with eleven miles still to run. Gavuzzi continued on his own, pressing for victory with 'the stands in uproar every time he passed'.

More significantly it was at the end of August that they made their first appearance as 'personalities' rather than as competitors. A film had been made of the 500-mile relay they had won so convincingly earlier in the summer, and for one Sunday evening Vincent booked the Capitol Cinema in the Quebecois town of Chicoutimi. A little over 100 miles to the north of Quebec City, Chicoutimi, developed as a centre for the wood-pulp industry, represented the heart of working-class French Canada. The film was introduced by Newton and Gavuzzi, who then answered questions about the race, about their careers and about distance running in general. Gavuzzi, one imagines, did most of the talking as he would have had to interpret for his older partner. At the end of the evening it was announced that the following Sunday they would be back in town, this time to challenge ten of the best local runners to a five-mile race at the Chicoutimi stadium, in which they would give their opponents a one-mile start.

Commercial sponsors in Canada were soon to realise the potential of Newton and Gavuzzi – a potential that would be that much the greater if the two men could be portrayed as 'characters' as well as extraordinary athletes. The press settled on some easy clichés. Gavuzzi was the chirpy, cheerful cockney who always dropped his h's and was graced with the most beautiful and effortless running style. Newton was the courteous athletic scholar who always seemed slightly out of place among tough professionals, yet who constantly proved himself the toughest of them all. He was also, the more intelligent press realised, a man with a fascinating and unlikely past. *Time* magazine picked up on this and published a profile of him soon after Newton's and Gavuzzi's victory in the 500-mile Dawson relay. This was the article that Newton, when he eventually saw it, called a 'really glorious column of fiction' because of the way it portrayed his early training regime in Natal. But he was not bothered in the slightest about being painted as an eccentric; what he was concerned about when he wrote to the magazine's sports editor was to correct any impression the article might have given that there had been something vainglorious about his decision to take up serious running:

After the War, at the age of 39, I decided to put up world's records in order that I might make sure that other settlers should get to learn what awaited them in the Union of South Africa. I knew that when the Backveldt was in power I, as an Englishman, had no hope whatever of any compensation for the loss of my farm; but I was, and still

am, anxious to make the affair so public that in future
the government there will find it discreet to act more
wisely with others. I fight for others, not myself.

He mentioned that he was still in close contact with the South
African press, who had not, he insisted, forgotten about him.

Ever since the conclusion of the second Pyle race in June
1929 Arthur Newton, as we have seen, had found it difficult
to talk to anyone from the press without suggesting that he
was on the point of having to return to Africa. But in the
autumn of 1930 that pessimism about what North America
had to offer him as a professional athlete finally lifted. In late
October the Montreal French press announced – with evident
pride – that Newton and Gavuzzi had decided to live in the
city for the foreseeable future, and that they were setting up
a coaching scheme for young local distance runners. 'Our aim
is to create a running club on the line of existing boxing clubs,'
Gavuzzi said. 'We will give talks, hoping that members will
profit from the experience we've gained over long years of
work. We'll organise training programmes, and will go out on
the road giving advice and correcting individual errors.' He
added, doubtless as a provocation to the amateur athletic
authorities in nearby Ontario, that they were confident they
would 'find some runners who'll be able to represent Canada
at the Los Angeles Olympics in 1932'. Arthur Newton might
have been hoping that his pursuit of compensation for his
accident during the second Transcontinental would provide
some capital for their coaching venture; but by the end of
November he knew such hopes were in vain. 'I have only just
returned from Terre Haute in Indiana,' he wrote to Len Dilks
on the 30th, 'where I went to settle that lawsuit with the

Insurance Company. I did not do at all well. I decided with my lawyers' advice to accept $500 rather than continue for several years – and they assured me that that is what would happen – with the case. By the time I had paid all expenses I was some $40 to the good.'

So he and Peter Gavuzzi had to make some money; and in a Canadian winter there was only one sure-fire way for endurance athletes to do that – by racing in snowshoes. Armand Vincent was planning another snowshoe marathon for February 1931, and this time Arthur Newton was not in a position to turn up his nose at it. It goes without saying that his preparation was meticulous, and even before the snows arrived he was to be spotted practising on grass, getting to grips with the novel and uncomfortable sensation of running with what he called a 'pair of double-size tennis racquets' on his feet. The Canadian sports columnist E.W. Ferguson described Newton's preparation as furnishing 'amusing entertainment that amounted to high comedy for scores of Canadian-bred youngsters as he plodded doggedly along, day after day, on snowshoes through the hay'. Privately Newton described the experience as 'beastly', but in public he did his best to be bullish about what he found himself having to do. 'Endurance, stamina and judge of pace are the main factors in such a race,' he told a Montreal reporter, 'and the matter of snowshoes is really of no great importance.' He needed to keep the press on his side because, as he wrote to Len Dilks just before the snow-shoe grind began, 'this country is wonderfully keen on anything in the distance field and the papers help in every way.' More specifically, they helped by sponsoring both Newton and Gavuzzi at various stages of their Canadian adventure.

The race was an individual, not a team, event and the press

built it up as a battle between Canadians and 'strangers', the large majority of whom were Pyle veterans. If learning how to run on snowshoes was one challenge that the 'Transcontinental brigade' had to meet, another and potentially more serious one was learning how to deal with racing for long hours in the freezing conditions of a Canadian February. Mike McNamara, the Australian who had finished the New York to Los Angeles run in seventh place, had been brought up in the heat of Queensland and was taking no chances with the cold of Quebec. 'He has had a sweater and tuque woven in one piece,' it was reported, 'the tuque being so constructed that it covers his face entirely, except for a small aperture over the eyes, and a breathing space. In addition he has had heavy coloured goggles built, which fit closely over the tuque, protecting his eyes from snow-glare and cold or snow at the same time. Specially knitted trunks and underwear, and a huge quantity of socks, complete his equipment. He will carry over twenty pounds of clothing daily in the race.' Not that this elaborate preparation helped McNamara much. The very first stage of the race took place on a sparkling day with temperatures well below zero and, despite his goggles, the Australian suffered such severe temporary snow-blindness that he had to be led for the final four miles. (That the man helping him out was a fellow competitor, Ollie Wantinnen, and that as a result Wantinnen lost several places in the race supports Newton's contention that the best sportsmanship he ever experienced was among professional rather than amateur athletes.)

Just before the race Peter Gavuzzi had written to his brother Charlie in England saying that he did not 'fancy his chances very much' in the race. But, for the snowshoe novices that they were, both he and Arthur Newton performed more than adequately, coming fourth and second respectively. The press commented on the older man's 'masterful race'. The winner was a young Canadian, Frank Hoey, who led from start to finish. The whole event, though, was overshadowed by the sudden death at the roadside of another local competitor, Jean Chouinard. It happened on the fifth day, by which time Chouinard – described as 'the weather-beaten veteran from the snow-swept town of Notre Dame du Nord' – was well established in the '*lanterne rouge*' position. (The 'red lamp' being referred to is that traditionally placed on the back of the final carriage of a train, and has long been used to refer to the back-marker in the Tour de France.) Chouinard was running with another French Canadian, Lionel Colin, and they stopped for a drink in the small town of Point du Lac. The veteran's last words, it was reported, were 'Get one for me too' as his colleague headed for a café. He suddenly collapsed and was carried to a nearby hotel, where he died 'after receiving the last rites from a priest summoned in a hurry'. Almost everyone who finished the week-long race suffered from frostbite to some degree of another. Joie Ray staggered home with 'blood filtering through the bandages on his face', while Arthur Newton wrote that 'bits of my face, neck and throat peeled off just like sunburn'. No wonder he later recalled the race as a 'hideous nightmare'. At least the week left him $700 the richer.

III

Not that the money lasted long. Newton decided to invest it in his first serious effort at promoting and organising an athletic event by himself. The scale of his ambition is revealed by a somewhat dog-eared sheet of paper in the archive at Birmingham University Library. It is a long and eclectic list of expenses, which included telegrams, scoring cards, badges for officials, beer and liquor, silk flags, petrol for cars, boxers, wrestlers, referees, photographs, street-car signs, a doctor and an orchestra.

Only a somewhat unusual event could call for all of these, and what Newton had planned for the weekend of 4th/5th April 1931 in Hamilton, Ontario, was certainly that. He had decided to challenge the world twenty-four-hour record, one that had stood for fifty years. He wanted to stay in Canada for the next 500-mile relay in the summer; but that was six months away, and he needed a project to keep himself fit, motivated and, ideally, solvent. Also the record seemed a natural target for a man so often described as personifying the idea of 'perpetual motion'; and if he was going to try to break it, he needed to do so before he got all that much older. The problem lay in making the attempt sufficiently interesting for the public to be prepared to pay to watch it. Newton decided to make it an invitation-only event, and turned to his old transcontinental friends to make up a select field. Johnny Salo couldn't make it, but Len Dilks, Mike McNamara and Paul Simpson (who had come fifth in the 1929 Pyle race) could, while Hamilton's own Philip Granville was a late addition to the list. 'Although constant rivals,' Newton wrote, 'we were the best of friends at all times, due no doubt to the sharing of troubles in those desperate Transcontinental races.' Dilks and McNamara both had the style and the stamina to provide Newton with competition and company as the hours ticked by; and it was decided to make the day more athletically interesting by advertising the fact that within the long grind Peter Gavuzzi would be setting out to break the world forty-mile record.

Here were the cream of the world's professional distance runners moving down from Quebec to set up shop in Hamilton – less than a year after the Ontario city had hosted the defiantly amateur Empire Games. So it was a hard-headed sort of welcome that Newton and his team received from the Hamilton *Spectator*. 'The value to the city from an advertising point of view is readily apparent, and, like the British Empire Games, will place the Ambitious City's name on millions of lips. These runners are already world-famous men. They are super-men who have a genuine reputation.'

At least Newton and Gavuzzi did; and a week before the twenty-four-hour race they did their best to publicise it by jointly smashing the record for the run from Toronto to Hamilton, a long-standing Canadian classic. The Hamilton *Herald* reported Gavuzzi chatting all the way and occasionally breaking into song. 'I never ran so slowly in my life,' he was reported as saying.

Newton also tried to drum up human interest in the contest by contributing some brief sketches of the competitors for the same paper. On Gavuzzi, for example: 'Quite a travelled man, he speaks three languages fluently – Italian, French and English. His style attracts attention at once: he bounds over the ground with a grace and facility that is almost astonishing. Like many of the other entrants, he is neither a non-smoker nor a teetotaller. Only 25 years old, he has every chance of becoming the greatest distance runner the world has yet known.' On Dilks: 'His metier is long distance work on the road, and he holds the professional title for the hundred-mile mark in the United States. He is quite a big man and yet uses a stride which is much shorter than one would expect, so it will be easy to pick him out in the Arena. A particularly pleasant fellow is Dilks, and so unassuming that one might never learn from him that he had ever done any running unless one happened to ask him something about it.' And on McNamara: 'He hails from Brisbane, Australia. He was a farmer, and doing very nicely, when he sold out to try his luck at the first Transcontinental race. This event did for him what it did for many another – turned him professional. He is quite unusually modest, and more than a bit reserved. Marathon men will be well advised to study his action, if they wish to make themselves good enough to be candidates for their country at the next Olympics.' One must doubt if the Canadian Olympic Committee welcomed such advice from a professional athlete, even one who was described by the Toronto *Star*, the day after the Hamilton twenty-four-hour race, as 'without doubt the greatest living distance runner'.

Whereas the Empire Games had been a rather staid event – a mini-Olympics for the parts of the globe coloured pink – Newton's promotion was an attempt at importing into Canada all the usual hype and extra-athletic extravaganza of a Madison Square Garden endurance contest. Thus the bizarre expenses list. The orchestra was to play non-stop, there was a licensed bar, professional cyclists provided a warm-up act, and boxing and wrestling bouts were to take place inside the track. Special prices and attractions were on offer for any children who were brought along on the Saturday morning. What was on offer, a local journalist suggested, were 'fights, hikes and bikes'. The track had been meticulously prepared and measured, and in athletic terms the day delivered what it had promised – though not precisely by whom. Peter Gavuzzi was on course to set a new record for forty miles when he pulled a muscle and had to retire. As Newton wrote, 'it was a rare thing indeed for Gavuzzi to meet with trouble during a race, but he managed it this time'. Mike McNamara, urged to do so by Newton, changed his race strategy to take on Gavuzzi's job and managed to set a new forty-mile mark himself. This left Newton more or less on his own in seeking to cover 150 miles over the twenty-four hours for a new record. He achieved it, adding a further two miles and 540 yards for good measure. The next day's *Herald* summed up his achievement by saying: 'it takes courage for a man to run twenty-four hours, especially when he knows that, instead of being rewarded for his efforts, he must lose money'. Newton knew the event was a financial disaster because of the rows and rows of empty seats that he saw every time he circled the Hamilton Arena. The public simply failed to respond to what was on offer. Newton, it was suggested, lost somewhere between $800 and $1,000. 'A hundred miles and more is a pretty stiff job,' he reflected later, 'and I did not feel inclined to sponsor another on the chance of recouping my losses.' Three weeks after the Hamilton race he responded wearily to a suggestion by Len Dilks that the group of them try and set some more records. 'We have to try and make our living out of the running,' he wrote, 'and, much as we might like to have a go at various records, we cannot do so unless we are sure we shall not actually lose [money] at it.'

But while the Hamilton public failed to find anything particularly interesting in professional endurance running, the Ontario press was clearly fascinated by Arthur Newton himself. For the *Herald* he was a 'marvel' and a 'wonderful man'. 'To look at or converse with him one would quickly form the opinion that he was first, last and all the time a heavy reader, with not even a single thought for sport. The fact that he admits to having been on this earthly sphere for forty-eight years, perhaps more, would add to the suspicion that he has never been interested in sporting activities. But to see him run gives one an altogether different impression of the man.' The *Herald*'s reporter was insightful enough to recognise Newton as a reader, and those close to him knew of the athlete's devotion to Shakespeare and Beethoven. But he had also, it seems certain, found himself intellectually attracted by the modern literature of psychoanalysis – and it is this that perhaps explains his ability to withstand the unimaginable tedium of something like the Hamilton twenty-four-hour grind. The track used was so tight that it needed thirteen laps to complete a mile, so to set a new record of just over 150 miles Newton circled the arena 1,976 times. There was no scenery to admire, no changing terrain to deal with, no alteration in the light from day to night, no rain or wind to welcome or rail against; there were just the rows of empty seats, the flat light, the occasional word with a fellow competitor, a break every now and then for food or a quick hot bath, and hour after hour the relentless sound of feet beating on wooden boards. The key for an athlete being able to deal with such an event lay, Newton argued, in his ability to 'avoid serious mental tension'; and this could only come from developing an ability *not to think* about what he was doing. This is where the psycho-analytic categories came in. In March 1932 Newton was quoted at length in an article that the *Natal Mercury* published about the best preparations for running the fifty-four miles of the Comrades Marathon:

Your subconscious mind takes the place of a general manager while the active mind is the director, and then there's an ultimate umpire who might answer to the name of 'your personal identity'. Having given instructions the 'ultimate umpire' might be allowed to rest a little and only when his subordinates have got into a tangle should he be allowed to exercise his calm judgement. It means that you should train the subconscious mind to carry on the business of training without constant reference to the 'ultimate umpire' or your personal identity. There should be no mental tension at any time: your mind must be kept as far as possible to a definite and unwavering policy. It is essential that you should be able to run many miles without your supreme mind bothering about it. The work should be attended to by the subconscious mind and although, at times, this may fail, you should be able to benefit by its mistakes and instruct the subconscious mind to behave better in future. In a nutshell, you must train your mind as well as your body.

It seems that Newton's good friend Len Dilks had taken the advice of letting his subconscious do the running somewhat too seriously. At the end of the race in the Hamilton Arena, after he had been locked for hours in a private battle with Philip Granville and had completed 118 miles, he failed on several occasions to respond to signals and messages that the contest had in fact ended. He just went on running as if that was what he was fated to do, and eventually had to be physically stopped and helped away from the track.

Despite the commercial failure of Arthur Newton's Hamilton venture, he and Peter Gavuzzi were on the cusp of becoming 'celebrities' in Canada. Ever since the first Pyle race journalists had made much of their dedication to smoking and, at the beginning of May 1931, a month after the Hamilton marathon, they were sponsored by a tobacco company to try to break their own Toronto to Hamilton record. The first of what were to be many newspaper advertisements over the next few years had them as the faces of Wakefield English Mixture tobacco. 'Like many great athletes,' the text read, 'Newton and Gavuzzi get a lot of satisfaction and relaxation from their pipes. Both smoke that famous tobacco . . .' Once again they ran and finished together, taking half an hour off their previous time, though until Gavuzzi started to feel nervous about aggravating his injury from Hamilton they had honoured their promise to the sponsor to run a real race against each other. The distance was just about the younger man's ideal, and it was one of the clearest signs of Peter Gavuzzi's true class as a runner that he covered the first twenty-six miles and 385 yards of a forty-mile race in five fewer minutes than the winner of that year's Boston Marathon – North America's most prestigious race over the distance.

It was the contrast between the two of them that made Newton and Gavuzzi so attractive to sponsors and sports editors, and they were the centre of attention as French Canada prepared for another Peter Dawson 500 in August 1931. The Montreal press made them overwhelming favourites for the race, and Philip Granville was quoted as saying that he could see no point in taking part if they were in the field. On 21st July the *Herald*'s sports page featured a photo of Newton and Gavuzzi signing to run for a local car dealership, Duval Motors, with an accompanying text that emphasised the differences between them. Newton was described as 'slim and wiry of frame, always smiling cheerfully, he can trot on endlessly and runs with a complete conservation of energy', whereas Gavuzzi was portrayed as 'a speedy and graceful runner who moves along with more action than Newton, much like a good miler'. The Bronfman brothers also used Newton and Gavuzzi to advertise their Peter Dawson whiskey in the build-up to the race. 'CAN YOU BEAT IT?' screamed the newspaper ad. 'These famous athletes share the spotlight with one of the most famous whiskies of the Empire.' So, having encouraged tobacco consumption in Hamilton, Newton and Gavuzzi were putting their names to strong alcohol in Montreal. Doubtless this confirmed the great and good of amateur athletics in their contempt for the professional game.

The race was run in appalling conditions, with torrential rain that left the roads often deep in mud. Newton said afterwards that he had been genuinely worried by competition from a pairing of Mike McNamara and Joie Ray, but once the former developed 'muscle trouble' there was no one to challenge the English favourites. The weather relented on the fifth day, and the *Montreal Herald* reported how 'the old foxes of long-distance' Newton and Gavuzzi 'played along the road'. 'Their lead is secure and they rested during the fifty-six-mile lap. Peter Gavuzzi stopped to gather gooseberries from bushes on the road and hugely enjoyed a beer while running the thirtieth mile. Later Art [*sic*] Newton dropped into a wayside stand for a bottle of pop.' The day of the final marathon saw a 'cold, bitter, depressing and heavy' rain falling relentlessly over Montreal, and fewer than 8,000 spectators turned up at the stadium, barely a quarter of the number who had witnessed the end of the race in 1930. 'The gate receipts don't matter,' said Sam Bronfman in response to a suggestion that the marathon be postponed, 'those boys have planned their race for today.' Newton and Gavuzzi duly picked up their first prize of $3,000, but they would not have been aware, as they returned to their rented rooms in central Montreal, that their brief career as the most famous professional endurance-runners in the world was about to come to an end. The supply of events was on the verge of drying up.

IV

However, the autumn of 1931 saw them able to profit in the immediate slipstream of their success on the roads of Quebec. There were no races in the offing, but instead there was the stage. They had already experimented with a show or two the previous winter, when they had built an evening's entertainment out of their own reminiscences and a film of their first Peter Dawson success. But they were now planning something more than a gap-filler: they were contemplating a new, or at least complementary, career; and they were able to offer audiences a real novelty. This is how Arthur Newton described it in a letter to Len Dilks at the beginning of October: 'Peter and I have had a running platform made which is worked by an electric motor: we run on it for a couple of minutes or so at the theatres after we have shown the film of the last Peter Dawson Relay Race. We'll get a photo of the thing presently, and I'll then be able to send you one along.'

The photo would have been a great help, because it seems probable that Arthur Newton and Peter Gavuzzi were responsible for inventing the very first treadmill for runners. The standard history of a machine now used by millions is that it was first developed after the Second World War as a piece of medical equipment for diagnosing heart and lung problems, and that it was not until the emergence of a 'fitness culture' in the affluent West during the 1960s and 1970s that it moved out of the surgery and into the gym. Certainly the primitive and bulky object that Newton and Gavuzzi hauled from theatre to theatre in rural Quebec in late 1931 (they bought a large second-hand Pontiac for the job, and christened her 'Katie') was regarded as a great curiosity and advertised as something people would not previously have seen. The poster for their week-long engagement at the Arlequin Theatre in Quebec City early in November promised:

Newton and Gavuzzi in Person
The winners of the great 500 mile Montreal–Quebec marathon will give a running exhibition on a specially built machine.

Also on the bill was 'an amateur competition', and this was evidently the high point of the evening, as staying on the treadmill for any length of time was beyond most people's ability. 'The running machine is safe enough,' Newton assured Dilks; 'if the motor stopped suddenly the platform would gently skid itself to a standstill and no-one would be any the worse. One fellow fell off when going at 11 miles an hour; beyond a tiny bit of skin off his forehead he is none the worse. We invite all the amateurs to have a try at all the places we go to, and that's where the fun comes in as the machine is a bit awkward to those unused to it.'

Gavuzzi, one imagines, would have been in his element on evenings like this; but it was his older partner for whom French Canadians seemed to have developed a real affection. Newton was seen as benign, idiosyncratic and brilliant. His age and his singular history marked him out. At the end of August

1931, just as their treadmill show was about to take to the road, Newton was the subject of a piece of humorous hagiography in the *Montrealer* magazine. It was written by one Bill Sellar, who told of his morning routine of leaving his house to walk to the bus stop. 'Every morning at approximately nine o'clock just as I start the long walk I hear the sound of rapid footsteps on the pavement. I no longer have to look behind me. I know who it is.' Newton, of course, out for his required ten- or fifteen-mile daily jog. Sellar said that he tried to run alongside and get into conversation with Newton, but he ran out of breath too soon:

The citizens in and around Pie IX Boulevard have grown attached to him. They probably regulate their clocks, their days, yea even their very lives, according to his schedule. Meeting him I always know exactly how late I shall be for my work, depending of course just where I encounter him. As we run our little interview each day I am highly amused at the ovation accorded this great athlete by such members of his public as happen to live in the immediate vicinity. Men, women, and children, they come to their verandas, their factory windows, to wave a friendly greeting to their guest. With easy English nonchalance and characteristic presence, Newton smiles calmly. Then with something very like an air of noblesse oblige, he waves a bronzed arm casually in their direction. Then they go cheerily back to their knitting, their dish-washing, or yet their factory toils. Newton passes on.

Time certainly was passing on for Arthur Newton – he was forty-eight years old – and he made clear in a letter to Len

Dilks that he saw the stage show as something that might save him from having to compete again in the dire snowshoe event. 'If we can get stage contracts we shall NOT enter the snowshoe race,' he wrote, 'both of us hate snowshoes.' But it seemed that sadly there was not enough stage work. In mid-January 1932 Newton was writing to Dilks again, saying, 'Peter is entering; I am thinking of keeping out of it.' Eventually he decided he had to take part, and found a willing sponsor in a Montreal jeweller. The race itself, which had to be postponed for a week due to a lack of snow, was a tense, closely fought affair, with less than an hour separating the first five competitors; Frank Hoey won again, with Gavuzzi in fifth and Newton in seventh place. They came away with $300 and $200 respectively.

The real significance of the event for Newton and Gavuzzi was that, with the exception of a one-off fifty-mile race in Montreal six months later, this was the last time they would race together. The partnership, although they did not yet know it, was over. Immediately after the snowshoe race Peter Gavuzzi returned to England. His plan, according to Newton, was to try to set a new 100-mile record on the Bath Road and then to return to Canada and continue touring with their stage show. He had evidently decided not to live with his family in Southampton, though whether this was with his wife Nellie's agreement we do not know. This left Newton on his own in Montreal. He was putting the finishing touches to his manuscript on training and desperately trying to find a publisher for it. He was also putting on the occasional solo act on the stage. In April, for instance, he was booked for a whole week at the Academy Cinema in the small Ontario town of Lindsay. The local paper was impressed. 'Arthur Newton's act at the Academy is introduced by a short film after which Newton personally runs on his unique motor-driven running platform. This is a very practical affair, slightly more than seven feet in length and roughly fifteen inches above floor level at its highest point. The speed is even, the canvas running belt travelling at a uniform pace of eight miles an hour, but it is apparently not nearly as simple to remain on the machine for any length of time as one might imagine.' Members of the public fell off both the front and the back, and the first evening's winner only lasted for a minute and a half. The audience 'were kept in a constant state of laughter'.

But Newton had a more serious agenda as well while he was in town. He gave a talk to boys and teachers at the local high school, the Lindsay Collegiate Institute, in which he made a plea for 'sport for sport's sake'. In his speech, according to the local paper, he emphasised 'the necessity of clean living and the building up of a strong body' and 'the benefits to be derived from sports'. The audience was apparently won over by his 'modesty'. But there would appear to be a blatant contradiction here. Newton had become doubly professional. He ran for money, and he was now making money again by turning his running career into a stage show. Yet here he was espousing and propagating the values that amateur sport had seemingly reserved for itself. However, there was no contradiction, and certainly no hypocrisy on Newton's part. He had, as we have seen, been initially embarrassed and possibly ashamed to turn professional in 1928. But, in the context of ever-increasing doubts as to how amateur some amateur athletics was, particularly in the USA, he came to regard professionals as the most honest and the 'cleanest' of all competitors. That professionals were the best 'amateurs' was the central insight of his mature years, and he would devote huge amounts of time, energy and ink to arguing it. It was what estranged him from the governing bodies of British athletics, and it saw him condemned to a position on the margins of athletic history.

It was the camaraderie and culture of mutual help that pervaded the two Pyle races that did most to convince Newton of the moral code of professional runners. This was reinforced by his experience of competing against fellow Transcontinental veterans in the USA and Canada between 1929 and 1932, and was summed up for him by the way they dealt with the particular problems of the Hamilton twenty-four-hour race. The track was tight, with thirteen laps to the mile, and there were men who were aiming at very different records. This made for a lot of overtaking, and having to run consistently wide would have slowed the faster men down. So, as Newton wrote later, an agreement was made. 'Every man willingly agreed to allow the inside of the track to any of the faster merchants when they heard them coming up behind. It is seldom indeed that you see anything of this sort on any track, yet it was carried out both in the spirit and letter throughout this twenty-four hour race from start to finish by every man there.'

In the spring of 1932 the fact that the Los Angeles Olympics were only a few months away gave an urgency to debates about amateurism, especially given the fact that a certain Avery Brundage was climbing the bureaucratic ladder at the AAU, the body that controlled amateur athletics in the USA. Brundage, who would go on to become head of the US Olympic Committee and eventually President of the International Olympic Comittee (IOC) itself, was as passionate about amateurism as he was about right-wing politics, and in the run-up to Los Angeles he had his sights on Paavo Nurmi, the legendary Finn who at the 1924 Games had won the 1,500 and the 5,000 metres on the same day. Nurmi had toured America in 1925 (managed by Newton's sometime business associate Hugo Quist) and had raced in front of huge crowds. He had then focused on Central and Eastern Europe, though 1st August 1931 found him in Glasgow, where 50,000 fans packed the stadium. No one knew for certain whether or not he was being paid appearance money, but after 1925 it became all but impossible to argue that Nurmi was a true amateur. His cause was not helped by the fact that while he was a popular phenomenon, he was not liked either by fellow athletes or by the press. He was no Jim Thorpe. Nurmi was aloof, taciturn, unfriendly and largely friendless. 'What is really wrong with the man?' was Paul Gallico's despairing question after he had tried to interview the Finn in Chicago. So when, in 1932, the Swedish IOC President, J. Sigfrid Edstrom, backed up by Avery Brundage, insisted on Nurmi being barred from the Los Angeles Games on the grounds of having broken Olympic regulations on never accepting payment for running, there was little personal sympathy for him.

At the same time there was far-from-universal agreement with the ideology of hard-core amateurism itself, and one of those to go public in opposition to it was Arthur Newton. In May 1932 the sports editor of the Montreal *Herald*, E.W. Ferguson, wrote a piece on the subject that inspired Newton to send a congratulatory letter to the paper, writing:

Genuine amateurism today is only possible for the comparatively wealthy: the ordinary worker cannot afford the time involved now that records have been put at such a high standard. Consequently nearly all the 'great'

amateurs are to all intents and purposes disguised professionals. To my mind professional athletes today are as
clean as the best amateur sport: the followers just try to
make an honest living at it just as professional clergymen,
barristers, baseball players etc. The time must come when
professional sport will be recognised as on the same
footing as amateur, and articles like the one you wrote
will assist with the good work.

Paavo Nurmi had already arrived in Los Angeles and
was in training for the Olympic marathon when the ban was
announced. He stayed on in the city – though he never went
near the stadium – and would undoubtedly have been visited
by a sympathetic Arthur Newton, had the latter been able to
get there. But Newton, who was keen to catch up with some
old South African friends at the Games, was stopped at the US
border in mid-April 1932 and refused entry into the country.
He was heading from Hamilton to New York, where he hoped
to fix up some theatrical dates for his film-and-treadmill act.
But in the depths of the Depression US immigration officials
were hardly likely to be all that welcoming to foreign workers,
even ones with unique and idiosyncratic acts to sell. Later that
summer, not long before he left North America for the last
time, Newton extended a supportive hand to Paavo Nurmi by
challenging him to a 100-mile road race in Montreal. Nothing
came of it.

Nothing further was to come, either, of the professional
running partnership between Arthur Newton and Peter
Gavuzzi. Their friendship was far from over – indeed, as we
will see, it was to deepen during the hardships and loneliness
that both men were to experience over the next decades – and

both of them were to remain involved with long-distance athletics; but the ever-deepening economic crisis of the 1930s meant that even men such as the Bronfman brothers had to pull out of sponsoring endurance events. There was to be no Peter Dawson 500 in 1932, and that had been Newton and Gavuzzi's 'banker', as far as Canadian races went. Sadly no record survives of their communication with each other that year. We know simply that Gavuzzi arrived back in Canada at some time during the late summer, and that in December Newton finally sailed away from North America – not, as he had often threatened to do, to either England or Africa, but, strangely enough, to France. On 17th December the *Journal du Havre* announced the imminent arrival from Canada, on board the liner *Sarcoxie*, of 'the famous runner Arthur Newton, holder of all the world records between 30 and 100 miles'. He was met at the quayside by his manager, identified as a 'Herr Boesch'.

V

Before the end of the decade France was to become Peter Gavuzzi's home – and during the Second World War his prison – and he stayed there for nearly fifteen years. For Arthur Newton, on the other hand, France was a brief adventure, a detour on his route back to England, to retirement from the road and the track and a commitment to a life of writing. His French was minimal (he admitted in 1928 that it was 'more than very rusty and invariably got tangled with Zulu'), so the idea must have been his manager's. Equally the decision to base themselves in Nice and try to put on Newton's theatrical act there must have been made with an eye to the wealthy British community that wintered on the Côte d'Azur. (Newton himself can only have relished the prospect of a few months in the Mediterranean after three winters of, to him, hateful Canadian cold.) The runner spent Christmas and New Year in Paris, where he was tracked down by a gossip columnist writing for the *Daily Mail*. He reported that Newton had told him that he had 'tried in vain to find a French long-distance champion ready to meet him in a race' and that he would also be looking for a 'worthy opponent' in Italy.

Newton had two things on his mind, and he wanted to use his time in France to prepare for them and increase the likelihood of their success. He wanted to find a publisher for his manuscript on training and running, and he wanted to mark his fiftieth birthday in May 1933 by beating his own record for the 100 miles from Bath to London. But he saw his theatre work as his best chance of earning a regular living, and he realised that the more publicity and praise he could get as both a runner and a writer, the better his chances of getting contracts to appear on stage on both sides of the English Channel. 'I am advised to have another cut at the 100 miles on the Bath Road,' he wrote to his old friend Vic Clapham in Natal towards the end of March, 'it will help me to get started at the theatres. What I am after is work in the vaudeville stage.' The previous month he had been in London, talking to Joe Binks about arrangements for the 100-mile run, and Binks had informed his *News of the World* readers that he had received a visit from 'the world's greatest distance runner', who 'is awaiting a contract to perform on the stage in France, and expects to follow on to England'.

But on 20th May 1933 Arthur Newton did not celebrate his fiftieth birthday while running through the English countryside. He was in Nice, where the previous evening he had made his French stage debut at the town's Nouveau Casino. Advertisements for the show emphasised the novelty of his treadmill – '*la Machine de Course sur Place*' – and the competition to see which member of the audience could last longest on it. The promoter was named as M.A. Boesch, whom Newton had recently sacked as his manager. With, it would seem, extremely good reason, for Boesch (Newton wrote to a friend in Canada) had just 'gambled all my available capital away on the gaming table at Monte Carlo'. By the end of the month Newton was reduced to offering challenges through the pages of the local sporting press. He was prepared, for instance, to offer a twenty-kilometre start to anyone taking him on between Nice and Marseilles for a winner-takes-all 20,000 francs.

Newton's erstwhile manager, it turned out, was as crooked as he was careless with other people's money. He had been placing small advertisements in the Nice press offering handsome rates of return for those who invested in 'his' treadmill act, and was claiming to be the machine's inventor and owner. He was, of course, neither. He also conned two local businessmen into lending him 4,000 and 9,000 francs respectively, using Newton's treadmill as collateral. When the 'Gala evening' on 19th May was over, the Nouveau Casino seized the machine until Boesch paid for the hire of the venue; and when Newton left the Côte d'Azur for England the promoter was being investigated by the police and sued by one of the businessmen he had duped. Arthur Newton, of course, had seen it all before: Herr Boesch must have reminded him of a certain C.C. Pyle.

Newton had felt for years that had it not been for the extreme cold, the snow and the floods, his time from Bath to London in January 1928 would have been considerably better. 'I have never been satisfied with that: everything went wrong,' he told a reporter from the *Bath and Wiltshire Chronicle* just before he made his delayed 'fiftieth birthday' attempt to lower his record on 1st July 1933. Asked how long he had been in training for the run, Newton replied, 'twelve years, I am always in training'. Thinking that this would be his very last competitive run, he took his preparation for it extremely seriously, telling Vic Clapham in Natal 'this was the first time I have had proper and adequate training for a 100 miler'. He stayed with his sister in Gerrards Cross, and then spent several days at various points along the route, reminding himself of its particular challenges and idiosyncrasies. Even though it was four in the morning when he started from the Bear Hotel in Box, there was a crowd of nearly 300 to see him off. In following cars were his nephew, who was responsible for food and drink, an official timekeeper, Joe Binks from the *News of the World*, and the greatest professional runner from an earlier generation, Walter George, for whom Newton had deep admiration. But despite all his preparation for the run Newton was five years older than when he had last done it; and where he had fought with the cold in 1928, 1933 saw him battling against an even more debilitating heat. It was too much for him. With only fifteen miles to go, the combination of a troublesome ankle and suspected mild sunstroke forced Newton to retire. He was more than twenty-three minutes ahead of schedule, and during the run had set a new world professional record for sixty miles on the road. 'This is the first time Newton has failed to finish in a race or beat a record when he has made an attempt,' noted Binks. So sure enough, three weeks later, Newton was back in Box determined to try again. This time he had only travelled thirty miles when his old Achilles problem forced him, once again, to stop.

'We have heard of our fast miles, flying sprints and huge shot-puts, but do they really compare with Newton's magnificent record of running 100 miles on the road in tremendous heat, up and down hills, at over seven miles an hour? Surely it is the running feat of the century.' This again was the loyal, if excitable Joe Binks writing in the *News of the World* on 22nd July 1934, a year to the day since Arthur Newton's second failure to complete the Bath to London run in the summer of '33. Newton was now fifty-one years old, but it seems that he had made up his mind that his extraordinary career must end, as it had started twelve years previously, with his setting a new record. This time he started at 3.45 a.m., determined to cover as much ground as possible before the heat set in. A nervous Binks watched him closely from his following car, almost stepping in near Reading to stop the runner, who had become 'very groggy' and was complaining of stomach pains. But Newton managed to keep going, and when he reached a cheering crowd in Hyde Park he had reduced his own record by fifteen minutes. In his memoirs he disparaged his effort, saying that 'any other man with sufficient training will do quite a lot better'. Joe Binks was kinder. 'At the end,' he wrote, 'Newton darted into the park and sat in a chair. All he asked for were his familiar pipe and coat. Then after being photographed and cheered again, he was driven to his home in Wembley. Newton has run his last race. I am doubtful we shall ever see the like of this marvellous runner again.' He ended his report with a poignant plea for help: 'Newton, I am sorry to say, has struck bad times, through no fault of his own, and is anxious to secure a post.'

VI

We do not know how long it took him to find one, though by the outbreak of war in 1939 Newton had a clerical job with the London County Council. But well before that he had finally found a publisher for his first book. It was called, with admirable simplicity, *Running*, and it came out in London in October 1935. 'One does not expect such a man to be orthodox and he is not,' concluded a critic who reviewed Newton's book for *The Observer*. Its title, and a brief study of its contents, might initially suggest it was an early example of the sort of work now produced in dull profusion by 'sports science' departments in British and American universities – it deals with the familiar territory of training, diet and 'psychology'. But Newton's work is far removed from volumes that simply advise on the optimal preparation of body and mind for athletic struggle, and it is nothing whatever to do with 'winning'. Despite its title, it is a book that is about much more than running; it is about learning how to lead a better, happier and more peaceable life. Its modern equivalent would be a work like Haruki Murakami's *What I Talk About When I Talk About Running*. This is how Newton sets out his intellectual stall near the beginning of the book:

> Decent, sensible running will . . . steadily build up a constitution that will stand you in good stead throughout your life. This adds to your value all round. You become a better man at work because you are healthier and more capable, and for the same reasons you are better able to enjoy all the pleasures that come your way. All this tends to increased happiness not only for yourself, but as a

natural consequence for all those with whom you come in contact.

The consequence of such mass happiness will, Newton suggests, be quite revolutionary. 'When all men have become genuine sportsmen, sundry nastinesses such as wars and litigation will have become obsolete.'

The last thing Newton was interested in was what we have got used to calling 'elite' athletics. He knew he had done remarkable things, but that was not because he himself was in any way remarkable. 'I am just an ordinary average man,' he writes, adding that 'any man, within certain age limits of course, can equal and beat my records'. Equally there was no false modesty when it came to the advice he was dispensing: 'The methods I am advocating in this work are presumably the best and most up to date at the moment, having produced better results than any others.' They were grounded, he argued, in the years of solitary experimentation that his life as a farmer in Harding had allowed. Every last detail of how he lifted his feet, how long a stride he used, the pace at which he ran, the length of his training sessions as well as what he ate and drank were endlessly tinkered with and the results meticulously catalogued. No other athlete, he was convinced, had done as much original research because, out on his land in Natal, he was unencumbered by received wisdom or traditionally accepted methods. He had Africans and wild animals to watch and learn from, not well-schooled runners from Europe or America. The single most important conclusion he came to was that 'the mental will always master the physical, not only in athletics but in everything else as well', and that recognising this opened up 'new ground for training'.

But his notion of mental 'mastery' was a surprising one, and it is best summed up by his insistence that in both training and racing 'there should be no serious mental tension at any time'. He seemed to believe in what we would now call evolutionary psychology, stating that to be human was to partake in an 'interminable struggle for fuller knowledge' and that at some time in the future a state of 'perfect mental health' would be attained. We are not there yet, he was telling his readers, but he insisted that those alive in the earlier twentieth century had the huge privilege and advantage of knowing about the subconscious. Understanding the relationship between the conscious and subconscious mind was, Newton argued, the key to relaxation, well-being and happiness. The conscious mind must not try to do what is best left to the unconscious, he said, not allowing it to do so was the key to the making of a healthy mind. That, in turn, led on to a more satisfying and creative life, because 'the better mental health and development you attain the more capable and efficient will it render its physical counterpart. Make your mind healthy and it will do the rest.'

But how was this theory to be applied to the process and experience of running? The most important thing was that the athlete did not actively think about what he was doing. As we have already seen, in relation to the way he approached the challenge of keeping going for twenty-four hours, Newton argued that the act of running itself must be dealt with by the subconscious mind. If not, he warned, 'were you to keep your conscious attention stretched out over all the details of say twenty miles a day for an indefinite period, it would not be long before you were applying for an introduction to a home for the deranged'. In other words, you run best when not conscious of running; and this means, as long as you have other interests in life, that you will never become bored by running. If you never become bored by it, then you can do more and more of it, so becoming ever healthier and happier and more able to get the most out of other things in life. This was the belief underlying the routine that Arthur Newton developed as his life became that of a professional athlete – running fifteen or twenty miles very early every morning, and then having a full day free to do, or think about, other things. He would have found the obsessive training regimes of most modern sportsmen both mindless and counter-productive. 'A mind built up on many subjects will show a greater capacity for work at any one, when tied down to it, than another which has at all times been anchored to the one in a more or less circumscribed area.' Or, as he also put it, more succinctly, 'I advise the ordinary runner to avoid continual concentration on his exercise or its problems.'

But such a philosophy of running needed its own approach to the process of training, and this is where Newton's solitary experimentation in the hills of southern Natal came in. He had started in 1922, he said, 'in too great a hurry, and got pulled up with a jolt', soon realising that the only thing was to 'train gently and gradually'. This is one of his 'precepts' that he recognised as likely to cause controversy, as it ran counter to the prevailing wisdom that training should be both hard and painful. 'Do not attempt to run too fast,' he says, 'just patter along over the ground, taking much shorter strides than you feel you can easily manage; toddle along comfortably, enjoying the knowledge that you could go faster if there was any need for it.' This intentional slowness of pace was to be matched by extremely short strides – shorter, probably, than

seemed natural. 'The long stride for the long journey is wrong,'
Newton insisted, though he told of a sports editor who came
down on him 'like a cartload of bricks for not lengthening
mine'. Equally he could have mentioned that Peter Gavuzzi,
who had a certain skill over 'the long journey', was renowned
for his long, bounding stride. But Newton could only talk
about himself, and what he had learned on his own, and
the more famous he became, the more people marvelled
at the idiosyncrasy of his style. The shortness of his stride was
one thing, the minimal lift of his feet another. 'When you lift
your foot at the back of a stride, raise it no more than is
necessary for safety. You ought to almost slither your feet over
the ground, going as near to touching it without actually doing
so as you can.' This, he acknowledged, 'requires very considerable practice'. If you practised hard enough you might end up
being able to run without your 'active mind' knowing you
were running at all.

One of the greatest mistakes athletes made, Newton felt,
was to try to train as though they were in a race, to attempt
to predict or re-create conditions of intense competition. This,
to him, was wasted effort. 'Never race until you must' was a
favourite maxim, and in explaining how he had come to this
conclusion he gave away the fact that he was, whatever he
might say, no 'average' athlete. 'Curiously enough, I learnt this
tip more than twenty years earlier in connection with classical
music.' He had spent long evenings at his farm near Harding
sitting at the piano practising Beethoven sonatas, mastering
them because he never felt he needed to play as he would have
to in a concert.

'The mere fact that their adoption resulted in lowering a
whole series of world's records by a greater percentage than

at any other time should be sufficient to prove that, in spite of their unorthodoxy, these new methods must have something very sound about them.' Arthur Newton was not here referring to his idiosyncratic ideas about speed and running style, but to something perhaps even more basic: what someone in training for long-distance events should consume, in terms of food, drink and even tobacco. He recognised that his ideas were 'almost diametrically opposed to the hitherto most cherished regulations'; while the reviewer of his book for the *Manchester Evening News* warned that 'his opinions upon the effects of food and smoking on athletes will cause considerable controversy'. It was in relation to diet that the runner felt he had experimented most in the solitude of Harding. He had, after all, no wife or other companion whose tastes or predilections he had to take into account. 'If I ran farther and faster than others,' he wrote, 'it is only because I had the time and opportunity to learn.'

He tried becoming a vegetarian, which he felt was ethically the right thing to do. But he found he could never quite make the transition from a meat-based diet without his stamina being affected. 'Every time I reduced the meat ration I failed to cover my usual mileage with the same ease.' If an injunction to limit the consumption of meat had become commonplace in training circles during Newton's lifetime, so had a belief that the more fresh fruit runners ate, the better. Newton disagreed. 'Fruit, more particularly the raw article,' he wrote, 'does not seem to me to be the sort of stuff to run on.' He felt it caused too much work for the digestive system, thereby using up too much energy. Again, as always, the most important thing was to avoid stress or mental tension. 'If you want to run well you must feed well and live well,' he said. Denial created tension if it created unhappiness. Instead, 'don't shy at a single thing that you like – pastries, puddings etc., things hitherto absolutely and emphatically taboo: for three months and more, prior to the 1924 fifty mile record [London to Brighton], I was taking pastry either once or twice a day, always after my long run.' The last phrase provides the corrective to any notion that Newton was proposing an 'easy' regime. Everything he recommended or permitted was premised on the athlete's day starting with a gentle twenty-mile run, which should ideally be out of the way by 7a.m. An hour or so later, Newton said, he would always 'devour a proper breakfast'. It was also a regime, it is worth pointing out, that required him to be in bed by eight o'clock at night.

The best example Newton gives of how painstaking his research was concerns alcohol, the substance that he felt had been most 'persistently advertised as being ruinous to athletes'. He was not a teetotaller, and did not want to become one, but said he was quite prepared to renounce alcohol if his own experiments showed him that he should. He accepted that a regular habit of drinking anything but very moderately would make serious training impossible, but he wanted to find out whether a certain amount of alcohol taken during a long race could help him overcome moments of feeling exhausted. While he was preparing for the Comrades Marathon at his farm in Natal he had developed a routine of forty-mile training runs and had found that he was getting deeply tired with about five miles left. So he asked a neighbour to help by giving him a tablespoonful of brandy mixed with water at that particular point of the run. He found it helped. He then doubled the dose, but found that this 'merely added to my distress'. He repeated the experiment, with the same results. This gave him the information he wanted. 'I knew then that when it came to the fifty-four mile race I was training for, I should be desperately "done in" when fifty miles had been covered, so at that point I would arrange for precisely the amount of dope that experience had taught me was beneficial . . . I consider that for a man in a really exhausted state it is undoubtedly a very wise and useful commodity to administer.'

The other form of 'dope' that Arthur Newton controversially refused to condemn was tobacco, and few journalists who wrote about him throughout his career failed to comment on his attachment to his pipe, which was always the first thing he called for at the end of a race. Peter Gavuzzi was equally attached to his, and as we have seen, they advertised tobacco during their professional years in Canada. Between the wars any public consensus as to smoking being bad for people was decades away, and cigarettes retained a cachet of sophistication. But, as Newton well knew, the overwhelming majority of athletic coaches condemned the habit out of hand; so his defence of smoking could not but be seen as a provocation. Again, his reasoning was based on experimentation and the need, above all, to avoid mental stress. When he first started serious training in 1921/2 he decided that he had better renounce his pipe:

I was smokeless for ten days: I have been more sensible ever since. During those few days I learnt two definite facts. I could manage entirely without tobacco were it really necessary: that was one. The other – the craving for it was so insistent that it amounted to a temporary menace to my mental health. Sustained mental disquietude naturally hampered physical training. So I allowed two pipes a day, and these only after I had finished my day's exercise. What a relief! And the running progressed better than ever when the craving for tobacco had been killed.

He did acknowledge, though, that it might be better for people never to develop the craving in the first place. He summed up the dilemma of smoking with the choicest of all Newtonian aphorisms: 'It is like futurism, marriage or lobster salads: very interesting if you're that way inclined, but otherwise best left alone.'

Arthur Newton was never entrusted with a regular position as an athletics coach, and there is no evidence that he ever sought one – though in his last years he gave patient and painstaking advice to individual long-distance runners who came knocking at his door in Middlesex. But he did have one gifted pupil who was able, for a time, to pass on Newtonian precepts and methods to top-class athletes. When *Running* appeared in London's bookshops in the autumn of 1935 Peter Gavuzzi was back where Arthur Newton had last seen him – in French Canada.

7

From Exile in Canada to Internment in Paris

Peter Gavuzzi's French Connection

I

Peter Gavuzzi had returned to French Canada in the summer of 1933, and settled in Montreal. It was obviously the place where he felt most at home. He was evidently not – or at least not yet – cut out to be a husband and father, and preferred the Atlantic to be between himself and his family in Southampton. French Canada was also where he had achieved a genuine, if brief moment of fame as a professional runner – a fame that might, in spite of the Depression, help him find a secure and appropriate way of earning a living. He was fluent in French, though he always spoke it with a strong London accent, and he was still a young man, who must have felt that he had yet to find what he really wanted to do in life. He had, after all, only been twenty-six when he and Newton won their second and final Dawson marathon in 1931.

He turned for help initially to Armand Vincent, the boxing and athletics promoter who had managed the Dawson and snowshoe races for the Bronfman brothers. Vincent had recently started a sports club that was situated in Cap-Saint-Jacques, an extensive nature park bordering the lake in the far north-west of Montreal. The park offered hiking, cycling and, in winter, snowshoe-rambling; and Vincent managed to get Peter Gavuzzi a job with the park authorities rather than in his own club. 'Peter always ran on his duties, never walked,' wrote Elmer Ferguson in the Montreal *Herald*. 'He went trotting about the big grounds, and along the beaches, mile on mile, while checking up at all the points, by day and night. Tireless, graceful, smooth, Pete always ran. That's why he was ranked as one of the all-time great distance runners.'

Armand Vincent was obviously taken by Gavuzzi, wanting to help him personally while also seeing such help as an investment for the future. Gavuzzi was a name that could be useful to him, were the economic situation to change for the better. The two men also shared an interest in professional distance contests, and it seems likely that Gavuzzi's experience of the two Pyle races lay behind a bold but doomed promotion that Vincent organised not long after the Englishman settled in Montreal. Gavuzzi was not himself involved when, early in 1933, as part of his operations at Cap-Saint-Jacques, Vincent had formed the Lakehead Wheeler Bicycle Club, and members made up a team to take part in that year's Montreal Six-Day Cycle Race. This was an established biennial event, but what Vincent then came up with for August that year was completely new. It was advertised as a 'Transcontinental Bicycle Race' that was to have an overall purse of $25,000 and would take in Montreal, Quebec, Winnipeg and Chicago – where it would feature as part of that year's World's Fair. Fifty-four cyclists started out, but within days the field had been radically reduced, which was hardly surprising seeing what was being asked of them; the third stage alone was 229 miles. Perhaps Vincent had fantasies of becoming the C.C. Pyle of Canada, but his attempt at establishing a 'Transcontinental' came to an embarrassing end. The tenth stage, beginning at Sault Saint Marie in Ontario, was to have taken the riders across the border into the USA; but Vincent had evidently failed to do his homework on American immigration procedures. The field arrived at the border and was refused entry into the States. No amount of arguing and pleading by the promoter changed the officials' position, and by the end of the day Vincent had walked away from his own race, refusing to have anything more to do with it. It fell to another manager to quickly recast it as a trans-Canada event, which then wended its anticlimactic way back to Quebec.

But if Armand Vincent's cyclists did not make it to Chicago in the summer of 1933, Peter Gavuzzi did. He was on the track of C.C. Pyle and the money he had been promised in Los Angeles four years previously. The promissory note Pyle had given him was a prized and closely guarded possession, and, with compound interest, was now worth nearly $12,000. The possibility of getting his hands on such a life-changing cheque had been another reason for his deciding to base himself in Canada, yet within easy reach of the USA. Peter Gavuzzi would have known that in 1930 Pyle had suffered a massive stroke that left him unable to speak, walk or use his right arm.*

He would have heard, too, that Pyle had recovered

---

* In his book about Pyle, Jim Reisler describes the fifty-year-old promoter's extraordinary commitment to restoring his mobility. He rented a cottage in the north of Wisconsin, where 'he rigged a pulley to a big tree . . . Hooking a rope to his arm and running it through the pulley, Pyle hired

sufficiently to embark on a new career managing an attraction at the Chicago World's Fair – the 'Believe It or Not Odditorium' that had been developed by Robert Ripley, a neighbour of the Pyles in Santa Rosa, California. This was a particularly sophisticated take on the old idea of a Museum of Curiosities, and Ripley was backed by the press magnate William Randolph Hearst, for whose papers he wrote a hugely popular syndicated column detailing his bizarre discoveries. Pyle – who had himself put on a tame and tacky version of such a show as part of the 1928 Transcontinental – was in his showman element. Each day he proudly introduced what the sports journalist Westwood Pegler described as 'Professor C.C. Pyle's astounding and amazing aggregation of unique educational oddities'. But it was not at the Odditorium that Peter Gavuzzi confronted Pyle, whom he had not seen since their final acrimonious meetings in Los Angeles during the summer of 1929. 'I met Pyle at the Hotel Morrison,' he was to tell the Montreal paper *La Patrie* in May 1935: 'he reassured me that he would pay me one day, insisting that he didn't have a cent, despite the fact that he had a whole suite of rooms at his disposal.'

Gavuzzi was not prepared to leave it there, such was his anger against Pyle. He employed a Montreal lawyer to pursue the possibility of taking the former promoter to court, but to no avail. In August 1934, a year after his fruitless visit to Chicago,

a group of neighbourhood children to pull the rope and give motion to his arm. Over and over the boys pulled, every day for months, and after thousands upon thousands of repetitions, C.C. regained the use of his right arm. Then Pyle had the boys pull his legs up and down in the same way – thousands of times, day after day – and several months later, C.C. was walking.' *Cash and Carry*, p.192.

Gavuzzi's lawyer received a letter from the business reporting agency Dun & Bradstreet, which had been instructed to find out what Pyle's financial position was. Their report made devastating reading for Gavuzzi. 'Pyles [sic] went through bankruptcy in 1933, and there are now alleged to be many unsatisfied judgements reported against him and the concerns with which he has been associated, and the local creditors have been unable to find anything from which collection could be made.' They included an invoice for $2 to cover their work on the case of 'Peter Gavuzzi v. C.C. Pyles'. When Gavuzzi spoke to *La Patrie* in the spring of 1935 he was still fuming at Pyle's betrayal. 'He goes on living in Chicago, and he's the boss of the International Oddities Corporation. They say he's very rich, but it's impossible to make him pay. What could one do to have him locked up?'

II

It says much about the local reputation Gavuzzi had gained in Montreal that *La Patrie* was prepared to devote a four-part series to him; and according to the paper they were responding to public demand for information about 'the small Italian runner who has now settled permanently in our town, where he has many friends and admirers'. Gavuzzi's standing in Montreal was built partly on his famous victories with Arthur Newton in 1930 and 1931, but partly also on his growing stature as a skilled and generous coach. Though the professional circuit had collapsed, Gavuzzi kept himself in training, and also kept himself well informed as to what was going on in local distance running. The bosses of Canadian amateur athletics would, as yet, have nothing to do with any idea of tapping into Gavuzzi's unique skill, so it was in a piecemeal way that he developed a small stable of runners.

They were men who had no means of paying him for coaching them.

It was in 1935 that Gavuzzi started working with two very different young runners from the Montreal area – the tall and taciturn English-speaking Walter Young and the short and garrulous French Canadian Gerard Coté. The former was unemployed, surviving on the dole with a wife and child in the suburb of Verdun. The latter was one of fifteen children born to an impoverished farmer whose land lay near the small town of St Hyacinth to the east of Montreal. Both had discovered running when looking to the boxing ring as an escape route from poverty, and both were noticed by Gavuzzi when they ran in local races. The Englishman's coaching style was strictly participatory; if he recommended something, he would do it himself as well. 'You had to follow him if you wanted to learn something,' Gerard Coté later said of his mentor, 'he was not a fellow to say "Gerry, you're younger than I am, we won't do the same thing." No way! Sometimes I was running with him thirty-five, even forty miles.' That both Young and Coté became athletic heroes in French Canada was because each of them won North America's most prestigious marathon, which was run each spring in Boston. Young did so just once, in 1937, with Gavuzzi at hand, while Coté was to achieve the first of four victories in 1940 after his inspirational coach had left Canada for good.

In his detailed study of Canadian fortunes at Boston, David Blaikie tells the moving story of Walter Young's 1937 victory. He and Gavuzzi had been more or less inseparable in the months before the race, putting in 1,700 miles side by side on the country roads of Quebec. Young had also been obliged to take part in snowshoe races to build up his strength. The event had become a central part of the way the city celebrated Patriot's Day, when Bostonians remember the earliest skirmishes of the War of Independence against the British; but in 1937, with just a week to go to the race, it seemed that Walter Young and Peter Gavuzzi would have to leave town and abandon any attempt at the marathon. They were broke, and the downmarket hostel where they were staying refused them any credit. Walter Young's wife and son needed his benefit payments, and funds promised by members of his local running club had never materialised. His coach, meanwhile, was down to his last two dollars. Second place in a recent race had earned Young a decent watch, the only object of any value that he had with him. Gavuzzi told him to pawn it and then take the bus back to Montreal and see if he could raise some funds. This Young did; the watch got him seven dollars, the fare was six. Meanwhile his coach hitch-hiked to New York where he could stay with Harry Richman, an old friend from the Pyle races. Walter Young got back to Verdun and was lucky to find that the local mayor was in trouble over suspected corruption and keen to identify a popular local cause. Helping Young fitted the bill, and the athlete returned to Boston with $50 in his pocket. The watch was redeemed, and after an epic battle with the favourite, Johnny Kelley (the champion in 1935), the race was won. In all his interviews and speeches after the victory Walter Young gave credit for it to Peter Gavuzzi. The coach's other runner, Gerard Coté, came in seventh.

'Three hours slow is better than two hours fast' was the training mantra for which Gavuzzi became known. He was, of course, simply passing on the habits and insights that Arthur Newton had instilled in him, and he told *La Patrie* in May 1935 that he regarded his former professional partner as 'the best runner there has ever been'. Gavuzzi had now made a name for himself as a coach at a recognised Olympic distance, the marathon, and Canadian athletics was desperate to find events at which it could compete successfully with its assertive southern neighbour. So on the evening of 23rd December 1937, eight months after Walter Young's triumph in Boston, Gavuzzi found himself once again on board an ocean liner. He was not about to cross the Atlantic, and he was not in a steward's uniform: he was in Vancouver about to cross the Pacific, and he was the official marathon coach for the Canadian team heading for the British Empire Games in Australia.

December 29th: Arrived in Honolulu. Marathon team took to the roads and we visited Waikiki beach. Sailed at 4 p.m. the same day.

New Year's Day: Our training is going very well, we are making 20 miles a day. Tonight we are having a Maskerade Ball. The weather is pretty hot. The team consists of 90 members. Competition in deck games started today.

These are the first two entries in Peter Gavuzzi's pocket diary for the year of 1938. No one uses such tiny diaries any more, no larger than four inches by two, with the space each day for a couple of sentences at most. They seem like objects from a less self-concerned, more self-effacing and certainly less prosperous age; and among the personal possessions that Gavuzzi left at his death in 1981 were pocket diaries covering most of what he had done and experienced since that voyage to Australia in the early weeks of 1938. He gives no clue as to why he started keeping a diary; perhaps he just wanted to capture the excitement of his unexpected adventure across the South Seas. The more interesting decision was to go on keeping one when his life became more banal and restricted, when often all he had to report was his loneliness and the emptiness of his days.

Gavuzzi was responsible for a team of three, which included one of the favourites, Walter Young. They trained hard and enjoyed Sydney, where all buses, trams, ferries, sporting events and movie houses were free to those accredited to the Games. The small group went to the fights one night, and spent a day out in the Blue Mountains. The Empire Games opened on 5th February and the marathon was scheduled for the 7th. The coach's diary entry that morning was optimistic. 'All the boys are in good shape. We should get in the first three.' But the race was a huge disappointment, with the three Canadians coming in fifth, sixth and seventh. Young was last of all. But they were still able to celebrate when the Games ended and a group of Sydney-based Canadians threw a party for the team. Afterwards their coach wrote, 'the boys went wild in the village till the early hours of the morning'. As they sailed back, the thirty-three-year-old Italian Englishman may well have felt that he had found a new home and a new role in Canada. He had friends, protégés and athletic officials who seemed to recognise his skills. But when their ship docked near Vancouver on 12th March, he was firmly put in his place. 'We arrived in Victoria this morning. I am in trouble with the immigration people. They are keeping my passport for investigation.' He was, though, allowed to continue his journey to Montreal while his legal status as a Canadian resident was clarified. On 11th April he received formal notification that he had 'entered Canada illegally' and would have to leave. Gavuzzi would not accept the decision. Although the trip to Australia had, he admitted, left him no better off than he had been beforehand, he somehow managed to raise enough money to hire a lawyer to file an appeal to the Immigration Ministry in Ottawa. It worked. On 2nd May he could record, 'I am now a Canadian citizen. No charge or fee. I have my passport back.'

What he did not have was a job. His involvement in the Empire Games had meant having to give up his work in the nature park at Cap-Saint-Jacques; and by the time the problem over his residency status was resolved, Armand Vincent was no longer in town. The promoter was in Europe, hatching grand plans for winter-sports spectaculars that might or might not provide Gavuzzi with future employment. In the meantime he had to earn some money, and there was no sign of any renewed French Canadian interest in professional athletics. The one thing that Gavuzzi had on his CV other than running was catering work, and through his connections at Cap-Saint-Jacques he landed an insecure position at a restaurant that was opening that summer on the shores of the lake. People who walk or snowshoe around the park today are recommended to stop for refreshment at the Chateau Gohier, which is where Peter Gavuzzi first reported for work on 17th June 1938. The imposing stone building was constructed in 1916 and named after Montreal's then-mayor, Edouard Gohier. Gavuzzi never makes it clear in his brief diary entries precisely what his job was, though they suggest that he was some sort of maître d'. What he does make clear, though, is that his pay was a percentage of the takings: no customers, no money.

The restaurant was aimed at Montreal's rich set. A live band played every night, and customers needed a car to get there. These were people who expected to be able to drink, but the manager, a M. Vigneault, had made the fatal mistake of opening before he had a liquor licence. Peter Gavuzzi's diary spells out the consequences.

June 25: A very poor house. Made 65 cents.

June 30: No customers. Nil.

July 5: Just plain rotten business.

July 23: Looks like closing.

Gavuzzi would not have had to pay for his board and lodging, so he was able to get by on very little. But his diary entry for 28th July shows, perhaps somewhat surprisingly, that his own needs were not the only ones he had to meet. He was trying to take some financial responsibility for his nine-year-old son in Southampton. 'Peter money. Can't manage this week,' he wrote rather pathetically. Gavuzzi always kept meticulous accounts – he needed to, for as so often in his life there was very little coming in – and he made a point of noting every time he sent money to his distant wife Nellie. The arrangement was for $5 a week – not an inconsiderable sum in 1938 and Gavuzzi managed to send it on three occasions in July and again on 15th August. After that the transatlantic contributions dried up, because so had Gavuzzi's work at the restaurant. 'The Chateau officially closes tonight with the band leaving,' he wrote in a typically matter-of-fact way on 3rd September. Over the next few weeks – which were made somewhat easier for him financially by being able to keep his room at the Chateau – Gavuzzi put in the occasional shift at another

Cap-Saint-Jacques establishment called the Clubhouse; worked with Walter Young, preparing him for the Canadian Marathon Championships in late October; and even took part in a six-day cycle race in Montreal. But he was really just treading water, waiting for word from Armand Vincent in Europe.

III

In October 1938 Vincent was shuttling between London and Paris, putting the finishing touches to a project of startling scale and ambition. He knew that winter sports had become extremely fashionable in Europe during the 1930s, and he also knew they were extremely expensive. So if large numbers of people who would have liked to ski, skate or toboggan could not do so because they could not afford to go to the mountains, then Vincent would bring the mountains to them. What he was trying to sell in London and Paris was what he called a 'Winter Cavalcade', a mixture of circus acts, novelty events on snow and exhibitions of world-class skiing. For this he needed arenas that could accommodate an artificial mountain that would be covered in 2,500 tons of artificial snow, the focus of which was an almost Olympic-sized ski-jump. And he needed Peter Gavuzzi as a performer – both in snowshoes and as part of the crew for the evening's climactic event, when a giant toboggan was to be hurled through the air from the end of the ski-jump.

One of Peter Gavuzzi's fellow crew members was to be one Chief Poking Fire, and in mid-October Vincent had asked the English runner to go out to the village of Coughnawaga (just south of Montreal) to make sure the Chief signed his contract and that he had an up-to-date passport. Poking Fire, who had spent most of his life with the more mundane name that his parents had given him – John McComber – was a true Native Canadian, or 'Indian' as Peter Gavuzzi put it. He was a Mohawk, part of the romantic notion of an 'Iroquois Nation', and by 1938 he had become something of a celebrity in and around Montreal. Two years previously he had opened 'Chief Poking Fire's Indian Village', a tourist attraction that proved surprisingly successful with both Canadians and visiting Americans. The 'Chief' and his family staged rituals of Mohawk life and sold traditional beadwork. The Village became sufficiently well known for European celebrities performing in Montreal – Maurice Chevalier for example – to make a point of going out to Coughnawaga to be photographed with the Chief and his extravagant head-dress.* 'Have the Indian all settled,' Gavuzzi wrote in his diary on 5th November; and on the 18th they sailed for Liverpool. When the boat train arrived at Euston on the 26th, Arthur Newton was waiting to welcome his old partner back to England.

Gavuzzi was keen to spend some time with his brother Charlie and his new wife, Daisy, and the three of them did some routine sightseeing in a London the athlete had not seen for years. But Armand Vincent was also in town, and there was much that he needed Gavuzzi to do before his 'Winter Cavalcade' opened to the public on 6th December. There were costumes to be fitted; a formal reception at Canada House to attend; a press conference; and, as Gavuzzi noted, 'plenty of rehearsals going on'. Vincent was nothing if not ambitious, and the venue for the Cavalcade was the almost brand-new Earls Court Arena, which had held only two exhibitions since

---

* Poking Fire's descendants kept the Village open until 2001. But now its website says 'closed indefinitely'.

its completion in 1937. The building, which boasted of being Europe's largest indoor space, provided a new chapter in the area's long and colourful history as an entertainment venue. An outdoor space, defined and contained by different railway tracks, had first been used for Buffalo Bill's Wild West Show; and then the 300-foot-high Earls Court Giant Wheel had been put in place in 1896.* It was joined in 1899 by a water chute that was marketed as the biggest of its kind in the world. Temporary exhibitions were also held, but Earls Court was in decline long before the First World War killed off such public frivolity. After 1918 it was used as a camp to house several thousand Belgian refugees, and eventually became a final resting place for unwanted vehicles belonging to the London Omnibus Company. Then, in 1935, a group of businessmen, thinking that London could support an exhibition and performance space that was larger than nearby Olympia, embarked on an architecturally ambitious scheme to build one *over* the maze of railway tracks that characterise Earls Court. It was to seat 23,000 people, none of whom would have a view that was obstructed by a pillar or column, and in the centre of the auditorium was a 60 x 20-metre swimming pool that could be turned into an ice-rink and could also be drained and covered over by a 750-ton electrically operated concrete floor.

The 'Winter Cavalcade' was the first chance the new Earls Court had to show off its potential as a venue for grandiose spectaculars. An alpine mountainscape was constructed, which at the end of the evening turned pink in a sunset set to music from Grieg's *Peer Gynt*. It framed a 100-foot-high

* That means it was two-thirds the height of the London Eye.

ski-run. The BBC was sufficiently impressed to send along its outside broadcast cameras, and at nine-thirty in the evening on 2nd December 1938 the TV schedule promised – 'if conditions permit' – 'Ski Jumping and Ski Racing from the snow-slopes at Exhibition Hall, Earl's Court'. Sadly it has proved impossible to track down a programme for the Cavalcade, but Peter Gavuzzi's papers contain one from the Paris version of the show, which opened in March the following year. With the exception of the French National Ski School, for whom the Paris event provided useful publicity, one imagines that the two shows offered much the same mix of routines and contests. The audience was warmed up by a handful of circus routines, and then the 'winter sports' began. There were exhibitions of downhill technique, team races, slalom against the clock for both men and women, skiing set to music and ski-jumping. Peter Gavuzzi and Chief Poking Fire were named as taking part in two 'Canadian' events – an obstacle race in snowshoes and the giant toboggan jump. Earls Court claimed that 'in spite of the looming war, 350,000 people came to see the show'; but, initially at least, Gavuzzi was less than impressed with audience numbers. 'We opened with only half a house,' he noted on 6th December. The next day 'the house is still poor although here they say it is good', and he added that 'our own act is well liked and we are getting our laughs'. On Christmas Eve he was still bemoaning the small houses, yet the Calvalcade continued its run until 25th January.

There is no way of knowing what Peter Gavuzzi and his wife Nellie thought of each other at this stage of their relationship. While there is no evidence in the winter of 1938 of the mixture of hostility and indifference that would eventually lead them to divorce, they were initially very uncertain as to whether or not to spend much time together. Gavuzzi had been in the country for nearly three weeks before Nellie and the ten-year-old Peter visited him in London. They stayed for just two days. 'Both looking well; Peter is quite a big boy' was the extent of Gavuzzi's reflections on the visit. But obviously something good happened between them because on 9th January Nellie and Peter were back in London and they stayed until the 27th, when Gavuzzi had to leave for France. None of them would have known it, but Gavuzzi was not to set foot again in England for more than thirteen years; he would see no more of his son's growing up; and by the time of his eventual return his wife would have divorced him.

The next few months were to be frustrating, disappointing and disillusioning for Peter Gavuzzi. The Paris 'Winter Cavalcade', which opened on 23rd March 1939, was a flop. Perhaps the end-of-winter timing was wrong; perhaps anxiety about the probable imminence of war kept people at home; perhaps, as Gavuzzi himself thought, the venue was at fault. He described the Palais des Sports as a 'cheap dump'. The show managed to limp through to its scheduled close on 2nd April, leaving all those who had taken part uncertain as to whether or not they would be paid. Gavuzzi himself had marginal financial security, in that he had been put on Armand Vincent's payroll just before the Paris show opened. From a small office in the French capital he set about helping the promoter to set up some planned ice-hockey events; but the project fell through. Their other idea was to find a professional long-distance race for Gavuzzi to compete in, which led to his making a terse diary entry on 11th April: 'Will get a salary, but I must pay it back if Vincent organises a race for me. In other words I am borrowing this money.' Even that proved difficult, and by 23rd April Gavuzzi confided to his little book that 'it looks like I must have a bust-up with Vincent'.

In an increasingly desperate search for a sponsor, the promoter contacted the French headquarters of the Coca-Cola company to underwrite a Nice to Paris race. They flirted with the idea, and then said no. Vincent then approached the mayor (some might say the 'Boss') of Nice, Jean Médecin, who asked him and Gavuzzi to come and see him; but their trip to the Côte d'Azur was a wasted one. Finally Vincent tried the pastis kings of Marseilles, the Ricard family. 'We are getting a little closer to a decision, but what it will be I don't know,' wrote Gavuzzi on 1st June. He did not have long to wait. 'Definitely no race,' he recorded two days later, adding pathetically, 'what's going to happen now I don't know'.

When it came to the way he earned his living, Peter Gavuzzi was an unusual mixture of individualism and passivity. He had a taste for adventure and for difficulty; he loved to travel; he was unafraid of solitude; yet from 1928 until his retirement he never really made a decision as to what he wanted to do. That he needed other people to make the important decisions for him is summed up by his diary entry for 6th June 1939: 'just waiting around for something to happen'. He had no idea how to make something happen for himself, so he had no option but to accept the work that those he looked up to and depended upon found for him. In the early 1930s the role had been taken by Arthur Newton – and it would be again in the 1950s. But as France was gripped by the ever-increasing certainty of war in the summer of 1939, it was to Armand Vincent that Gavuzzi turned. When he finally had to accept that there was no money available for 'long grinds' in France, the Canadian promoter also had to accept that he could no longer keep Gavuzzi on his payroll. He had to find someone else to employ him, and he turned to the richest, most influential family he knew – the press barons of Montreal, the Berthiaumes.

IV

'I am leaving for Mr Berthiaume's country house. I am supposed to get work from him,' wrote Peter Gavuzzi on 10th June; 'I am wondering how it will all turn out.' The Berthiaumes owned Montreal's leading French-language daily, *La Presse*, from 1906 until 1955; and in the early 1930s the paper had enthusiastically supported (and extensively reported) the long-distance events that had made Newton's and Gavuzzi's names in Quebec. Eugene Berthiaume worked closely with Armand Vincent, and, when asked if he might have something that Gavuzzi could do, was undoubtedly pleased to be able to offer a helping hand to an athlete he had greatly admired: and on 14th June 1939 Gavuzzi travelled with Madame Berthiaume to the family's country house deep in the countryside of south-east Normandy, about sixty miles from Paris. Here there would be no newspaper headlines for Peter Gavuzzi, no starring roles in London productions; he was employed as the Berthiaumes' gardener and handyman, and the first day he spent in what was to be his 'home' until 1952 was devoted to weeding.

The garden Gavuzzi found himself working in – and working hard enough for him to complain within days of the blisters on his hands – belongs to a house called Le Moulinet. It is a mile or so outside the now-prosperous small town of Pacy-sur-Eure, not far from Vernon on the banks of the

Seine – which is the centre of the thriving tourist industry surrounding Claude Monet's house and garden at nearby Giverny. The road from Pacy to Le Moulinet now passes through an estate of modest modern houses, but when Gavuzzi first came to the area the isolation that he often felt at the house was understandable. Le Moulinet lies at the end of a quarter-mile drive, hidden from the road by high poplars. The white-painted and red-shuttered house dates from the eighteenth century and is clearly an amalgam of three separate buildings: the old mill at one end; then the central residence; and at the other end a small cottage-type extension, with its own entrance, that was intended for the 'staff'. This is where Peter Gavuzzi had his room. The buildings form something of an L-shape, containing a gravelled courtyard that faces a stream. The water that once turned the mill wheel comes from a specially cut diversion of the River Eure. The garden that Gavuzzi worked so hard on, year after year, has now largely reverted to pasture, and Le Moulinet has an air of long-faded glory.

The summer of 1939 was for Peter Gavuzzi a summer of hard physical labour. He weeded and mowed; he dug a 'trout ditch'; and he carted and spread 150 barrowloads of gravel for the courtyard at Le Moulinet. But at least the Berthiaumes treated him as something other than just a workman; Gavuzzi's diary mentions being taken on a family Sunday outing to Rouen, playing billiards with 'Mr B' and going canoeing on the river with his employer's niece. Waiting for war, though, was what that summer was really about. On 1st September Gavuzzi wrote of Pacy becoming empty of younger men as they all left for the army; and two days later – when England declared war on Germany – he wrote simply, 'I am leaving for

Paris to join up.' 'Left Pacy for Paris to visit Consulate,' he continued the next day; 'I registered myself. Paris is nearly empty of people, who walk around carrying gas masks with them. There are signs all along the houses telling that they have a cellar for so many people. Yes sirree, the war is on.' But Peter Gavuzzi was not to take an active part in the Second World War. He was young enough, he was certainly fit enough and there seems no doubt that he was willing enough. But he needed to do more than simply register himself with the British authorities in Paris. He needed to take the initiative himself to find a way of getting across the Channel. But he did not. His passivity took over, and before long he was trapped in northern France.

Over the winter and spring of 1939–40 his diary entries were minimal and banal. He mentions a few domestic events at Le Moulinet and that some passing British soldiers were billeted at the house. He mentions Madame Berthiaume's bad moods and his own 'blues'. He says nothing more about getting involved in the war himself. But by early June 1940 Gavuzzi's dull malaise has been replaced by fear. Eugene Berthiaume had decamped with his family to the safety of Toulouse, leaving his English handyman in charge of Le Moulinet. On the 7th Vernon, eight miles away, was bombed by German planes; three days later Pacy was hit. 'People in a panic, everybody is leaving. I don't know what to do,' Gavuzzi confided to his diary. The aerial bombardment was in support of German troops who were attempting to cross the Seine, and once they did, the handful of residents who remained in the farms and hamlets around Le Moulinet knew it would not be long before they would be on their doorsteps. 'Just a few of us are left, and we hide in cellars all day like rats,' wrote Gavuzzi on the

15th, by which time he was sheltering at the farm of some elderly neighbours. 'You can imagine the panic of these old people. If it wasn't for the crying of the old women my nerves would stand up much better, but I am becoming a little bad-tempered and I have to speak roughly to them to keep quiet.' The roads were full of desperate people, carrying their most precious possessions as best they could, fleeing to the west and south. Many of them looted as they went, and Le Moulinet did not escape: Gavuzzi was to find it stripped of silverware, linen and food.

His fear was compounded by the fact that he had no idea how the Germans would treat him if they found out he was British. But he could pass himself off as French easily enough, of course, and the German officers who requisitioned Le Moulinet on 19th June seemed to have no suspicions about him. They were too busy, from what Gavuzzi wrote, attacking the contents of the Berthiaume cellar. They stayed long enough to celebrate the capitulation of the French government, but then they moved on. 'I'm sorry to see them leave,' Gavuzzi wrote, 'because they were a nice bunch of fellows, they gave us food and drink, and me tobacco, they were very nice with the property. I'm getting gifts from them all, some gave me coffee, tobacco, sardines, soap etc.' They had also allowed him to keep his old room. He mentions receiving a letter from Nellie in Southampton, enclosing a photo of his now eleven-year-old son, and perhaps it was this that tipped off the Germans who were occupying Pacy. On 27th July 'the German commander came and asked me for my passport. I was made a civil prisoner, owing to my being a British born subject. I was taken to the Mairie and questioned. They have given me a room there.' He was then moved to a nearby farm together with some French prisoners. He mentions how pleasant his German guards were and how 'all doors are left unlocked so that if I wished to do a bunk it would be very simple. But just how far would I get? No, I will remain here and see what happens.' What happened was that things got more serious.

August 13: All British born subjects are to be taken and put in Concentration Camps. I wonder if this will be my lot. I hope not.

August 20: Things are tightening up here. The grub is not very good, and very little we get, no beverage other than water. Now my room is locked. It looks bad, what next?

August 26: Still no news. Every day seems like a week.

On 6th September the waiting came to an end. Gavuzzi was in a group of fifteen prisoners who were transferred to a camp not far from Le Mans. It felt like a 'strange country,' he wrote, as there were inmates from Morocco, Algeria, Tunisia and Poland as well as others from Britain. Dysentery rampaged through the camp, and 'sleeping in the straw we are all getting lice'. Then, on 19th October, Gavuzzi was taken on what would be his last journey for nearly four years. He and other British prisoners boarded a goods train and, over a day and a night, travelled back east the way he had come from Pacy; and then on, finally, to the northern suburbs of Paris. Their destination was La Grande Caserne at Saint-Denis, a camp dedicated to the internment of British civilians and those from the British Empire.

V

The camp was located roughly where the iconic Stade de France now stands. It had been intended to house 1,200 men, but for much of its existence the camp contained at least 2,300. 'It was a self-contained little city,' wrote a Canadian journalist, Maurice Desjardins, who visited La Caserne at the end of August 1944 just after the Germans had abandoned it, 'with a cinema, barbers, tailors, a restaurant and a library.' Another journalist, Cyril Upton of the London *Times*, told Desjardins that conditions in the camp had been hellish, and that only Red Cross food parcels had prevented widespread starvation. One long-term detainee was the racehorse trainer William Webb, who for years had run a successful stables in Normandy. He was sixty-three when he first arrived at La Caserne in July 1940, and he kept a detailed diary during his years in the camp, the manuscript of which is now in the archives of the Imperial War Museum in London. He wrote in small school exercise books that he kept hidden in his straw mattress, and arranged for them to be smuggled out of the camp in bags of dirty laundry. Sadly his diaries for 1943 and 1944 were destroyed in a fire, so what remains are what he called his 'Internment Camp Journals' up to 31st December 1942.

His portrait is of a community riven by petty jealousies and class antagonisms; 'there is a sort of "cold" between so many men in here,' he wrote. This was just what the German command intended, no doubt, when they decided to appoint a management committee from among the internees – and change its personnel whenever they felt like it. 'Another clear-out of all our officials, decision by Kommandant,' Webb wrote on 2nd August 1941; 'what will this new lot do?' He thought it unlikely that anyone could 'manage to run this camp without first of all looking after himself and his clique', and thought it better 'for it to be run by the Germans themselves'. By the following February Webb was evidently in a state of fury at what he thought was a homosexual clique running the camp in their own interests. 'A lot of men are fed up with that wormy underneath serpent Adair, with his un-English dirty tricks, but he does as he likes. I know that he has his "acolytes" who come into the camp in hiding. No, give me Germans any day rather than such proud, scenty, stuck-up swines. He really thinks he's somebody in here, but all of us are fed up of being bossed about by these stuck-up prostitutes. Top class greasy nutty lot.'

William Webb was in the privileged position of having two grown-up children in Paris. They had French papers, having been born and brought up in the country, so were not themselves at risk of internment, and they regularly visited their father bringing what they could in terms of food. Sometimes what they brought can only have made Webb an object of envy and resentment for fellow internees. 'March 12: Rosie brought me a large bowl of boiled beef and carrots, ham, rice pudding, eggs, half a bottle of cherry brandy, new shirts and lots of nuts and some oranges. God bless those dear children.' His German captors knew full well how important both visits and food parcels were to the internees, and restricting or suspending them was their usual response to any breaking of camp rules. So someone like Webb had little sympathy for the few who tried to escape, or for a certain Niedergall who got sufficiently drunk one evening to start singing 'God Save the King' to a group of German officers whom he then told repeatedly to 'fuck off'. Webb quickly became maudlin and pessimistic when he was deprived of family visits. He

(*Above*) Newton and Gavuzzi
sign a sponsorship deal with a car
company in Montreal. They also helped
sell tobacco and whisky.

(*Right*) By 1931 Newton
and Gavuzzi invariably
started long distance relays
as the favourites.

Above) Professional long distance relay races had a huge following in French Canada in the early 1930s, and they made the Newton/Gavuzzi partnership both feared and revered.

(*Above*) Newton hands over to Gavuzzi during a relay. They changed after each ten miles.

bove) Newton persuaded a group of 'Bunioneers' – those who had run in the Transcontinentals – to compete in a 24-hour race in Hamilton in 1931.

(*Above*) French Canada's passion for long distance events meant snowshoes had to be used in winter. Newton referred to them as 'fiendish affairs'.

(*Left*) Gavuzzi was no keen on snowshoes, but he could still show his customary grace when wearing them.

(*Left*) A studio portrait of the professional pair – now famous enough in Canada to appear in theatres with their own show.

(*Below*) A rare sighting of the pair at an athletics meeting in suits and ties. Note Newton's lifelong commitment to tobacco.

(*Above*) Newton with a young South African runner outside his house in Ruislip in 1937. It became a home from home for distance athletes seeking bed and breakfast and expert advice.

(*Left*) Gavuzzi's attempt at a new career that did not quite take off. He's in a show with his colleague Chief Poking Fire at Earl's Court on Christmas 1938.

(*Above*) Gavuzzi hated being interned at Saint Denis from 1941 to 1944. But he loved his job as the camp's sports supremo.

(*Right*) A close finish at one of the sports days organised by Gavuzzi at Saint Denis.

(*Above*) Gavuzzi's diary mentions how back-breaking it was to lay all the gravel for the courtyard of 'Le Moulinet' in Normandy.

(*Left*) Newton, in formal coaching clothes, oversees a training run for three South African runners in Ruislip, 1953.

(*Right*) Gavuzzi developed his own reputation as a coach.

(*Above*) Newton with an old friend in South Africa in 1957, two years before his death. He dreaded the trip, but loved it when he got there.

fretted guiltily about his wife, herself interned in a camp for women near Besançon, and felt that the wholesome life they had created together had somehow been defiled by the war. 'I do miss my family and my poor old home,' he wrote on 18th March 1941; 'I dread the thought of seeing it neglected, with grass weeds growing everywhere. To think they took our big brown safe containing the children's stamp books, little treasures, silver etc. Today I feel I am done for. I did my best for my children, tried to make them happy and with an assured future. Now, where's a man's life's work gone to? Ruin.' On the anniversary of being separated from his wife he wrote of his captivity as 'in a small way a form of death'. As winter approached, Webb wondered: 'How many poor souls in here are doomed never to meet freely with their loved ones again? A lot of us will "pop off" this winter. I will do my best to hang onto the reins and not let go.' He was part of a group that played bridge almost every afternoon; he was involved with the camp's Anglican church; he attended regular German-language lessons; and increasingly he found an outlet for his anxiety and boredom in the burgeoning sports culture of the camp; and for this he had Peter Gavuzzi to thank.

In both material and personal terms Gavuzzi would seem to have been in a far worse position than Webb. He had neither friends nor family to visit him, and he had no private money to augment the basic allowance all internees were given by the British authorities. We only have his diaries from when he arrived at La Caserne in October 1940 until the end of the following year – quite possibly he learned that it was unwise to be seen to be keeping one. Yet, for all the deprivations he suffered, there's no doubt that Peter Gavuzzi was a happier man when he was interned than he had been at Le Moulinet, and happier than he would be when he returned to Pacy-sur-Eure in 1944. He was neither bored nor – except during his first weeks in the camp – lonely. Some of his first diary entries after his arrival at Saint-Denis reveal an intense jealousy of those who could look forward to their designated 'visitor days'; but this soon passed. La Caserne had a system (the brainchild of a local French charity) that provided internees who had no one to visit them with what were called 'godmothers' – '*marraines*' in French. These were local women who were prepared to devote half an hour or so each week to talking with and getting to know a particular inmate of the camp, and Peter Gavuzzi became deeply fond of his. She was called Jeannette Veaudeau and she lived in nearby Neuilly sur Seine. Sometimes she came on her own, sometimes with her parents. Gavuzzi never gave any indication as to her age or looks or what they talked about, but there is no doubt that his diary entry for 4th July 1941 was a heartfelt one. 'Saw my marraine. She gave me some bad news. She is going to work and will be unable to visit me again.'*

But by this time Gavuzzi not only had friends within the camp, he also had a role – one that was far better attuned to his skills and interests than that of handyman to the privileged. 'I have been given orders to start training the young men for light athletics,' he wrote on 7th March. The management committee had evidently found out about what Gavuzzi had achieved in the past, and realised that he could provide something to counter the internees' worst enemy – boredom. Initially it went well: 'the class is getting bigger every day, and

---

* William Webb noted in his journal on 23rd July 1942 that 'A very young coloured man was married in camp with his pretty young "godmother".'

the boys are doing fine,' he noted down on 12th March. But within a month it was all over: 'My running class has petered out to nothing.' Perhaps the problem was that it was a *class*, because when, the following month, Gavuzzi was asked to put on an athletics *meeting*, the response within the camp was very different. He chose the distances, marked out the track and selected the fields. 'Everybody here is still talking of the races,' he wrote in his diary on 23rd June about the meeting the previous day; and it was followed by another on 12th July. Gavuzzi himself won the mile in a time of just under five and a half minutes. That this would have involved six laps of the track that he had himself constructed we know from a letter he wrote to Arthur Newton in 1946, when he was struggling to get back into serious training:

Whilst I was interned I developed trouble in the calf of my left leg. I put it down to the small track I had built so I could organise athletics, 6 to the mile: quite alright if you were doing a mile or two, but for the likes of me who wouldn't be satisfied unless I put in a good hour this continual sharp turn played havoc with my left leg. I then went the other way round, but I had to continually dodge the internees who were walking round, and this jumping about did not suit me at all, so I decided to organise walking races so I could let me [*sic*] steam off some way.

William Webb never mentions meeting Peter Gavuzzi in person: the rigid class divisions within La Caserne no doubt saw to that. But his diary records his admiration for what the athlete achieved with his 'sports days'.

July 12, 1941: In the evening athletic sports . . . These are a credit to the organisers. Mr Guvanni [*sic*] is a world champion over 3000 and 2000 metres, and in 1929 he ran across America, over 3,000 miles.

September 5: Watched cricket match; men seem to be going after all manner of sports, also saw some boxing. Two men even went too far, it was awfully rough.

February 15, 1942: A five mile walk was held this afternoon, only four starters . . . Gaduzzi [*sic*]* finished tired in third.

April 6: Easter Monday, with lots of sports arranged, weather permitting.

It seems that Peter Gavuzzi found willing sporting collaborators among a group of about fifty Canadian Catholic priests who were also interned at La Caserne. William Webb became an admirer:

February 7, 1942: Watched Canadians playing hockey. They got permission to flood the court so they could play hockey matches and do some skating. What a good sport, quick on the feet, clever game.

March 22 : Canadian priests are building a second tennis court. They seem to be preparing for a long stay.

* It is unlikely that William Webb himself got Gavuzzi's name so scrambled. The culprit was almost certainly his son, who typed up the journals after the war and had to deal with his father's extremely difficult handwriting.

They were obviously also skilled at football, another sport Gavuzzi helped to organise. His diary entry for 12th April simply says, 'The Cup Final was won by the priests.'

But sport cannot have been easy for men surviving on such limited and unpredictable diets. When the Canadian Maurice Desjardins visited the camp on 28th August 1944 – and he says he was the first Allied war correspondent to do so – it was Peter Gavuzzi who showed him round. Desjardins remarked on the athlete's extreme thinness, guessing that he weighed no more than 104 pounds. He also reported that Gavuzzi 'was the camp's chief gardener, and plots which he cultivated around six long huts provided vegetables for the Canadians'. Gavuzzi's diary for 1941 does not hide the aspects of camp life that he found most difficult. There was the gross overcrowding, the inadequate food, the tensions between men that often led to violent fights; and always the petty retributions and punishments imposed by the German guards. He was frustrated that it was so hard to get letters in and out, and he worried about Nellie and Peter in Southampton. He was also at times very concerned about his own health. It was in his Saint-Denis diaries that he started mentioning the bladder problems that were to dog and embarrass him for the rest of his life, and which would eventually kill him – 'The old trouble' he euphemistically called them. But despite all this, his diary entries often contained the word 'happy'. Perhaps the most telling entry of all, given his persistent post-war dissatisfaction, was that for 9th August – after he'd organised another successful day of athletic competition: 'I wish I could do this in civvy life.'

VI

Peter Gavuzzi had one possession during his years of internment that gave him particular pleasure and comfort: his copy
of Arthur Newton's *Running in Three Continents*, which had
been published in 1940 just before his arrest in Pacy. The
volume was in his Wiltshire cottage when he died, and it is
stamped inside the front cover with his prisoner number from
La Caserne – 1610. When he had been back at Le Moulinet
for several years, and had still not seen his old friend and
partner since before the war, he received a letter from Newton
mentioning an almost-completed new book. Gavuzzi wrote
back: 'Well, I'll be glad when your next book appears. I've read
Running in Three Continents so many times I know it by heart.
Whenever I feel kind of lonesome out comes the book, and
once more I'm back with all those grand men and all those
different laps with so many memories.' A year later, in
November 1949, Gavuzzi responded in almost identical fashion
to news that the book had just been published in London:
'I'm looking forward to getting your new book. I've read
Running in Three Continents a score of times, it always gives
such a pleasure in bringing me back to those glorious times.'
If he really did reach for the book whenever he felt 'kind of
lonesome', then his copy of Newton's memoir would have had
extremely heavy use; because from the moment Gavuzzi
arrived back at the Berthiaume family estate of Le Moulinet
in the early autumn of 1944 his dominant mood was one of
emptiness and uselessness. As Europe celebrated the end of
war in May 1945 he confided to his diary: 'I wish I could be
united with all my people, as it is I find myself once again
lonesome. I wonder in this life if I will ever find happiness. I
seem to be in the wrong places at the times I should be

somewhere else. Oh well, I was born unlucky so why grouse.'
When the people of Pacy put on a street party, he could only
write that 'being all alone I haven't been able to enjoy myself
very much. But still it may come some other time.' On
Christmas Day 1945 he was invited for lunch by some neighbours; but he cannot have been all that good company: 'This
Christmas was perhaps the quietest one in my life. No decor-
ations, no Christmas tree and no pudding. I hope my next
Christmas will be spent with my own people.' By June the
next year nothing had changed. 'It's the loneliness here which
gets me.'

Gavuzzi could easily have arranged to be repatriated back
to England after his liberation from the camp at Saint-Denis.
He chose not to be. The reason he gave was the security of
his employment with the Berthiaumes. 25th August was the
first anniversary of his release from La Caserne. 'What a joy
and great relief to feel free once more,' he wrote. 'Well since
then I have been here at Pacy, working hard trying to re-establish
myself. I suppose I ought to have gone home to England. But
then I decided one certain job was better than looking for
one.' A year later he expanded on this in a letter to Newton,
explaining the lengths he had gone to in 1939 to protect Le
Moulinet and its valuables and then to put the property back
in shape after the war. 'I mention all this as you will then be
able to judge why I decided to remain in Pacy rather than
be repatriated to England. I then stayed on here alone on a
very small wage, about £5 a month. I took this small wage in
the hope that when they came back they would give me an
indemnity of sorts for all that I had done, but it all turned
out very differently.' He said that the Berthiaumes – who had
spent most of the war in Montreal – were divorcing, and that

Le Moulinet was now in the hands of Madame, with whom Gavuzzi never had an easy relationship. She refused him any extra money. 'To come back to England is all very well,' he concluded, 'but what kind of a billet can a man like me find. I have no trade.' Newton replied, suggesting, it appears, that Gavuzzi could find work on a smallholding or a poultry farm. Gavuzzi's response was flat and unconvincing: 'Like you my brother insists on my packing up and coming to England. You are of course both quite right, and I suppose in the end I will do that.'

But one suspects that Peter Gavuzzi still wanted open water between himself and Nellie – even if the Channel in 1945 was less reassuring than the Atlantic had been twelve years previously. He still sent money to Southampton when he could, but the way he acknowledged his son's birthday in his diary was cursory and increasingly resentful:

Sept 30, 1945: Peter's birthday today. I wonder if he gave a little thought to me. I guess not. I sent him a card.

Sept. 30, 1946: It's Peter's birthday today. I haven't sent him a card as it never gets any appreciation. He must be 17 years old.

In fact he was eighteen. Between these two birthdays there had been a bizarre and entirely unexpected development in the relationship between Mr and Mrs Gavuzzi. Peter's diary entry for 18th October 1945 reads: 'Today Nellie wrote and agreed to live with me here in France. Now I suppose I'm going to be swimming in a lot of government red tape to try and get her here.' He had never suggested the possibility of this before, even to his diary. But it was serious enough for him to make the journey to the nearby administrative centre of Evreux to ask the Prefecture of Police what he had to do in relation to Nellie's residence in France. He reported that he was told it was up to her to apply for a visa with the French authorities in Britain; and that was the last mention he made of his wife coming to live with him. They did not see each other again before Nellie divorced him in early 1951.

Peter Gavuzzi lived unhappily at Le Moulinet for more than seven years after his release from La Caserne. We know the bare bones of how he passed the time and of his moods from his diaries, but we also have a series of the letters that he wrote to Arthur Newton. Some of them run to several pages, and they are the most sustained pieces of writing we have from Gavuzzi. Perhaps they are the most sustained pieces of writing he ever did. The handwriting is careful and there are no corrections or crossings-out, as though he made a fair copy from earlier drafts. They all start 'Dear Mr Newton'. It is obvious what the correspondence meant to Gavuzzi from the way he started some of the letters; Newton's replies were Gavuzzi's lifeline to a wider world – of both memory and promise – and he was very upset when they were not forth-coming. 'I know you are awfully busy, so don't mind me if I remind you that I was the last to correspond.' (5th September 1946). 'I take it that you are awfully busy as I haven't heard from you since I last wrote' (16th December 1946). 'You're long overdue with your most welcome letter . . .' (20th February 1948). 'I was getting worried not hearing from you, that's why I wrote.' (2nd March, 1948). 'It seems to me such a long time since I heard from you (20th May 1949). It is a mystery that Gavuzzi did not keep any of Newton's letters to him. We can surmise a little of what they contained from Gavuzzi's responses, and Newton was obviously quite open about the two things that depressed him: his failing eyesight and his poverty. Gavuzzi was solicitous about the former and said he knew all too well about the latter. He told Newton a little about his problems with his employers, and hinted at his loneliness in what he called his 'little tin pot village'; but he never revealed the depths of the despair that filled his diaries.

The subject that took up most of the letters was the one that always connected them across the great divides of age and class – running. In the spring of 1947 Peter Gavuzzi decided he wanted to race again. 'I'm up at about 3.00 a.m., have a good breakfast, let the chickens out and feed them, and then I hit the road for 12 hours,' he informed Newton on 29th March, 'I get back about 4.00 p.m., have something to eat and then do all my chores, and also my garden. Bed at 9.00 p.m., up again at 3.00. You've guessed it, I'm training.' There was no professional distance running in France, but there was a thriving culture of competitive road-walking. There was a national federation, a network of clubs and an iconic national event: a non-stop 500-kilometre walk from Paris to Strasbourg. It was this that attracted Gavuzzi, but to become eligible he had to join a club and achieve qualifying times in events up to 200 kilometres. There was one problem: the sport was amateur. 'You will no doubt be wondering what I am doing concerning myself in an amateur event,' he wrote to Newton:

Well in the first place I don't see that they can object to my trying just because I've been a pro runner, after all it is some 12 to 15 years since we competed last for cash. But I suppose you will say what's it going to get you? Well

I do strongly believe that this is an amateur event camou-
flaged and that the winner gets a substantial sum of
money. I can't see men doing the amount of training
which such an event demands doing it for love. As you
may know, here in France most athletes are all of the
working class.

Peter Gavuzzi felt at home among them, and was soon travelling with his local team Stade Porte Normande to places like
Rouen and Dieppe for weekend races. It did not take him long
to get personal proof of how 'amateur' the sport really was,
and to tell Newton about it: 'As you finish a race an envelope
is handed to you, and in it you find your money. I received
two, one for 12th place, 250 francs, and the other for first place
veteran, in all 350 francs. This of course is small fry, but it
runs in thousands in the big events.' While Arthur Newton's
anger at the deceptions of 'shamateurism' was real enough, it
was nothing compared to the visceral hatred that Peter Gavuzzi
had for the system. Gavuzzi responded to it as a working-class
athlete of stunning ability, who would not have been able to
run at all if he had not been paid for winning: 'I could go on
writing pages on why money must be paid to men who train
and do long journeys, but they insist on saying they are
amateurs. Oh well, I'll go on with it as I want a lot more data,
then I'll bust 'em good and true, if I have to spend the rest
of my days at this matter.' In February 1948 he excitedly told
Newton of another breach of amateur rules that he had
noticed. He had been following that year's Winter Olympics
in St Moritz and came across two skiers whose names seemed
familiar. One was an Englishman, Peter Boumphrey, the other
a Swiss called Carl Molidor. He remembered their names

because they had both taken part, and been paid to take part, in the 'Winter Cavalcade' at Earls Court and Paris in 1939. Boumphrey was neither here nor there, Gavuzzi argued, as he never had any hope of a medal, but Molidor had won Olympic silver. 'Can you beat that, if this man had of won he would have been heralded as an Olympic gold medallist, and he would have been in the record books. Yet he was performing with me and a whole bunch of professionals in Paris just before the war. Aren't you glad that one day all this monkey business will end and these supposed higher-ups will have all this sort of thing to answer to.'

Arthur Newton disapproved of his former partner's attempt to resurrect an athletic career, especially in a purportedly amateur context that would not provide much of an income. 'You are of course quite right in saying that I should forget competitive racing and get onto some work with pay,' Gavuzzi wrote to him. But long-distance running was the only thing in his life that had made him feel good about himself, and in 1947 he was not quite ready to renounce it. There was his plan of entering the Paris to Strasbourg event; there was an idea of finding a French opponent for a one-off race from the Mediterranean to Paris; and he also thought of offering to do 'long journeys' as commercial advertising. Ideally, too, he wanted Newton involved. 'We're still and always will be partners,' he wrote to his mentor in June 1947, 'instead of my running partner you'll become my manager.' We do not know how Newton responded to the idea. But within a year Gavuzzi had had to give up his athletic fantasies. In the summer of 1948 Le Moulinet was finally sold, to a member of the Rothschild banking family, and Gavuzzi found that he was expected to do a full-time job. 'I suppose it's curtains for good,' he wrote to Newton. 'I've had a good time and enjoyed every minute of it, but now I must look ahead to more serious things.'

Gavuzzi's new employer had ambitious plans for Le Moulinet as an elegant weekend retreat that could be used all year round. He extended the garden further and further into the surrounding fields, and Gavuzzi found himself spending day after relentless day pushing a lawnmower. 'This boss of mine is just plumb crazy on lawns,' he complained to Newton, adding that he could not understand why someone so rich could not invest in a motor mower. In winter his problem was a new central-heating system that Gavuzzi found so complicated that he had to go on a course to learn how to maintain it. But it was not really the work that made Gavuzzi so unhappy with his new employers, it was the way they treated him. He had been close to the Berthiaume family; now he was just a worker, who often found himself criticised and shouted at. 'This job is now becoming unbearable,' he wrote in his diary. 'This place is becoming intolerable. I'm like a stranger.'

VII

'I'm afraid that my visit to England will not materialise for a few years yet,' Peter Gavuzzi wrote to Arthur Newton on 8th November 1949. 'You see I get two weeks holiday a year and those two weeks I owe to my old mother who is 75. Till she lives I shall always go to her for my holiday, also my brother manages to have his holidays at the same time, so it's a family reunion once a year.' Re-establishing contact with his mother and with his extended family in Piedmont was without doubt the best thing to have happened to Gavuzzi since his release from the internment camp. He and his brother Charlie – who had been working for more than fifteen years at an Italian restaurant in Soho – arrived in Turin by train on 4th June 1949 and went straight to the old Gavuzzi stronghold of Montecello. It was, he calculated, the first such family gathering for twenty-three years – since before he had gone to America to run for C.C. Pyle. He met aunts, uncles and cousins; and for the first time his sisters' children. 'My dear old lady, well she's distinctly getting old now, but she's a champion at eating ice cream,' he wrote. And he visited the grave of his father, who had died (without Gavuzzi knowing until months later) in March 1945.

There were of course two members of the extended family who were not in Piedmont that summer: Nellie Gavuzzi and her twenty-one-year-old son, Peter. There seems to have been virtually no contact between Gavuzzi and his wife and son after the bizarre moment in the autumn of 1945 when it was suddenly on the cards that Nellie would move to France. Gavuzzi's diary provides no clue as to why this never happened, and his Southampton family seems subsequently to have faded from his mind. He mentions writing to Nellie in November 1946 and again in May 1947; then nothing at all for more than three and a half years. There is no way of knowing whether he was either surprised or distressed to receive a letter from his wife's solicitor on 13th January 1951 informing him that Nellie wanted a divorce. Gavuzzi certainly was not going to fight it, and he immediately sought help from both his brother and his employer in getting the necessary paperwork prepared. A Rothschild solicitor was put on the case, and within a fortnight Gavuzzi's response to Nellie's action was lodged with the High Court in Nottingham. The law for once moved quickly. The case was heard on 6th March and on the 15th

Gavuzzi made the following matter-of-fact entry in his diary: 'Peter wrote me a nasty letter. Nellie won her divorce. I'm working with Martin on the fence.' After this his diary was silent on the subject of his wife and son – other than a mention on 24th August that year that he had received a demand for maintenance from Nellie's solicitor. 'Let's see what happens' was Gavuzzi's comment.

Peter and Nellie had been married for more than twenty-one years, yet the time they actually spent together can be counted in months. Gavuzzi's son died in 1985 at the age of fifty-seven, so we cannot know what he said in his 'nasty' letter of March 1951. But there was to be a rapprochement of sorts, and Gavuzzi at least had the pleasure in his final years of getting to know his three grandchildren. Given the way he had treated his son in the young Peter's childhood, he was a lucky man. Nellie could have used desertion as grounds for the divorce; she could also have used adultery, because since the summer of 1950 Peter Gavuzzi had been having an affair with a young woman in Pacy-sur-Eure. Her name was Mimi, and she was the daughter of the Martin with whom Gavuzzi was fencing on the day he heard that he was no longer a married man. He never mentions Mimi's age, but she was probably in her late teens or early twenties. She had yet to go out to work, and was responsible at home for her younger siblings. So the forty-five-year-old Gavuzzi was twice her age, which explains both why the relationship was a fraught and fragile one and why Mimi's parents were so opposed to it. There is no indication that Gavuzzi had had a sustained sexual relationship with anyone for many years, and being with Mimi was also a counter to the anger and resentment that dominated his working life during the final phase of his time at Le

Moulinet. His diary first mentions Mimi on 8th May 1950, when they go for a walk and 'pick some lilacs'. On 5th June, a Sunday, Gavuzzi takes advantage of his employers being out for the day: 'X for the first time,' his diary records, like that of a teenager. But their subsequent intermittent sex life was undermined by the heavy drinking to which Gavuzzi had resorted as a way of dealing with the constant rows he was having with his employer:

September 1: I had a nice evening with m.m., but no use. I had a bit too much booze.

September 2: We had a try, but I failed.

The uncertainties of his relationship with Mimi mirrored Gavuzzi's anxiety and ambivalence about his life at Le Moulinet itself. In May 1951, a few days after yet another confrontation with his employer, he confided to his diary for the first time that he wanted to leave, though whether to England or Italy he did not know. He also wrote that his relationship 'can now be almost certainly written off as a bad affair'. Mimi had had a flirtation with a young man of her own age, and had flaunted him in front of Gavuzzi. Yet in September her older lover was still saying to himself, 'I wish I could get rid of my feelings for m.m. but I can't.'*

* The fact that neither Newton nor Gavuzzi established a successful long-term relationship with a woman, and spent so much time with each other, will no doubt cause some to question whether or not they were gay. There is no evidence at all that they felt sexually attracted to each other, and in so far as we know anything about Gavuzzi's private life, it was resolutely, if unsatisfactorily, heterosexual. We know even less about

Peter Gavuzzi's habitual passivity had trapped him in a situation he disliked and felt humiliated by. But, as always, it was someone else who pushed and cajoled him into doing something about it. 'I'm a bit scared of all this change,' he wrote pathetically in his diary in mid-September 1951, having given in his notice at Le Moulinet, 'but I took the advice of others, now I must face it.' Arthur Newton had for years been pressing his old running partner to return to England and find a satisfying job before it was too late. That August, encouraged by both his now-elderly mentor and his brother Charlie, Gavuzzi had taken his two weeks' holiday in England; and he went almost straight from Victoria station to Newton's house in Ruislip. The two men had not seen each other for eleven years, since Gavuzzi had performed in the 'Winter Cavalcade' at Earls Court in early 1939. 'He is getting very old and has very little sight left,' Gavuzzi wrote ingenuously in his diary that evening, 'we had a nice chat on sports.'

Athletics, needless to say, took up a considerable amount of Gavuzzi's stay. He went to a meeting at White City, and accompanied Newton along the route of the London to Brighton road race that had been specially revived – thanks largely to Newton's own work – as part of the Festival of Britain celebrations. On a day of persistent rain Newton was also plotting Gavuzzi's future, and made sure that he

---

Newton's. He mentions a brief engagement in Natal, but subsequent to that would appear to have led a largely asexual, perhaps celibate, life. It is of course possible that he hid a gay sexuality, just as it is possible that he suppressed its expression. What seems more to the point is that their shared addiction to solitude militated against their establishing lasting sexual partnerships.

introduced him to the race organiser, Ernest Neville. Neville was sympathetic to Newton's athletic ideas and, as Secretary of Surbiton Town Sports Club, was perhaps, Newton thought, in a position to find Gavuzzi some sympathetic work. On 24th September, while Gavuzzi was seeing out his notice period at Le Moulinet, Neville wrote encouragingly to Newton: 're. Peter Gavuzzi. Shall be very glad to meet him again and will certainly arrange something. Tell him to write me fully about himself and his family, and requirements re. job and I will see what I can do for him.'

In May the following year Neville wrote again to Newton reassuring him that 'I have put out feelers in several directions re. Gavuzzi and hope they will bear fruit.' By this time Peter Gavuzzi had been back in England for several months. He had found a menial job as a kitchen porter at a US air-force base near Ruislip and was renting a nearby bedsit. He was forty-six years old. He made no attempt to contact his son. He wrote in his diary of his contentment.

8

The Scribe of Cottingham Chase

Newton and British Athletic Politics

I

On 2nd December 1950 *Athletics Weekly*, the mouthpiece of the AAA, the Amateur Athletic Association, published a letter that began: 'Please Mr Editor, may we have a little less Arthur Newton? Every athletics periodical, weekly or monthly, one picks up to read contains an article by Arthur Newton, usually criticising something or somebody, or someone is replying to Arthur Newton, or Arthur Newton is answering somebody who has replied to Arthur Newton, and . . . it gets a little wearing.' The letter had come from Terence Lloyd-Johnson, and Newton would undoubtedly have known that the man he had come to annoy so much was something of a star in that resolutely unfashionable, yet surprisingly popular athletic discipline of road-walking. Lloyd-Johnson had won the bronze medal in the fifty-kilometre walk at the London Olympics in 1948; and while Arthur Newton could never quite hide his disdain for the discipline, he could only have admired

Lloyd-Johnston as someone who could handle 'long journeys' and who had won his medal a few months after his forty-eighth birthday.

Lloyd-Johnson, it is fair to say, had a point. Newton's age – he was sixty-seven in 1950 – and his dreadfully limited eyesight meant that any active hands-on role in athletics had been out of the question for some time; and his having been a professional meant that any involvement in the administration of the sport was impossible. But athletics was what Arthur Newton knew, and he remained convinced that he had a responsibility to pass on his knowledge to the next generation. He had no doubt that he had done extraordinary things, and from an early point in his running career he had wanted to explain how he had done them and suggest that his achievements exposed the mistakes and fallacies of mainstream approaches to training and racing. The only way he could do this, once he had settled back in Britain, was by writing; and for more than a decade, from the early 1940s onwards, what he understood as his real work was done sitting at a typewriter in his small semi-detached house in Ruislip, at no. 9 Cottingham Chase. Over that period Newton published as much athletics journalism as anyone else in Britain (if not more), which is deeply ironic, given that one of the busiest agencies of the AAA was the somewhat sinisterly titled 'Permission to Write, Broadcast or Lecture Committee', which tirelessly policed the press to make sure that no amateur athlete was earning a penny from writing about the sport without due authority. It angered Newton that he was not allowed to coach or help in athletic administration. He found it demeaning, given what he had achieved. But his professionalism gave him the freedom to say and publish what he wanted – including his frequent accusation that those who ran amateur athletics, both in Britain and elsewhere, were rank hypocrites. Like any jobbing journalist, Newton understood the value of recycling his material and of hiding himself behind different bylines, so it is hardly surprising that by 1950 Terence Lloyd-Johnson came to feel that he had read enough Newton.

Arthur Newton's favourite nom de plume was 'On the Shelf', and he first used it in the August/September issue of *World Sports* in 1943 for an article on an issue that was particularly close to his heart – the distinction between amateurs and professionals. 'We have, one and all,' he stated, 'been brought up from our earliest childhood to look askance at professional sport . . . we have been taught to consider that once a man embraces professionalism he throws overboard all that is good in amateurism and his work ceases to be "sport". Yet this theory hasn't a leg to stand on. Because you apply a different adjective to a man it doesn't in any way alter the man himself, and if he was a "clean" sportsman as an amateur he will be exactly the same as a professional.' Newton's piece was intended as a contribution to a debate that was just beginning to get under way concerning how different British sports could best be revived once the war was over; and it is an indication of how rapidly and deeply the experience of war had challenged and undermined old class certainties that even the editor of *Wisden* could refer to amateurs in 1943 as 'survivors of an almost lost society, of an age that's almost gone'. This was a sentiment with which Arthur Newton – proud amateur though he had once been – was in complete agreement; and he argued that British athletics was shooting itself in the foot by barring professionals from working as coaches, whether in schools or clubs. He insisted that athletics be seen as a 'science' in its infancy, which needed the input of those who devoted themselves to its study. 'Would our young men and women expect to be given lectures on medical efficiency by doctors who had spent no more than their spare time for a few years in their youth at medicine or surgery?' Aspiring athletes, he concluded, 'are worthy of more than this'.

World Sports was a typical product of wartime austerity, printed on cheap paper and devoid of photographs; and Newton, it seems, kept it going, sometimes contributing one-third of all the copy. Many an issue carried articles under his own name *and* by 'On the Shelf'. But *World Sports* was no struggling commercial venture. It billed itself as 'The Official Magazine of the British Olympic Association, the Women's Amateur Athletic Association, the Amateur Fencing Association, the Amateur Gymnastics Association, and the National Health Culture Association'. So Newton, perhaps the best-known professional runner in the country, found himself as the lifeblood of the amateur sporting establishment's house organ. It was a position he used to push his own idiosyncratic ideas on how athletes should train, and to pour scorn on other – more mainstream – approaches. Newton's hobby-horses had not changed since his first articles for the South African and Rhodesian press in the later 1920s, and his opponents came to disparage them as his 'theories'. They included his views on diet, on always running at an even pace, on never trying to 'race' in training, on recognising the primacy of mind over body, on ignoring one's opponents when racing, and on training all year round and not just for a 'season'. They also included discourses on such specialist subjects as how far the body should lean forward when running, whether sweaters or tracksuits were better and whether or not a pre-race massage was beneficial. To a non-athlete, many of these concerns appear so minor and arcane that Newton's constant repetition of them comes to seem almost liturgical. And one suspects that the authors of a guide to training for road-running that was published a few years after his death had Newton in mind when they warned their readers that 'Intrusion into the highly individualistic field of long distance training, in which the devoted enthusiast delights in arguing his pet theories for hours at a time, could easily court ridicule.'

II

On 19th October 1946 the postman delivered a letter to no. 9 Cottingham Chase informing Arthur Newton that he could have an unexpected and no doubt unwelcome lie-in the following weekend. It came from his old friend and ally at the *News of the World*, Joe Binks. 'Don't bother to hurry up next Saturday,' Binks wrote, 'as I find those beautiful AAA officials will not allow a professional to officiate. Colossal humbug. I hear Finchley Harriers got into trouble once through having your name in their programme. They are lunatics.' The 'lunatics' of the Amateur Athletic Association had tolerated Newton while the war was on. He had been useful in keeping some sort of athletics journalism alive, and the dissemination of his quirky and unorthodox 'theories' had seemed harmless enough. But all this changed with peace, with preparations for the London Olympics and with reassertion of control over the sport in Britain by the AAA, whose own magazine, *Athletics*, was back in production by the end of 1945.

The AAA's patron was the King; it's vice-patrons included the likes of Field Marshal Alexander of Tunis and the Bishop of Rochester: its president was Lord Burghley, the former

Olympic hurdler; its offices were in Chancery Lane; Oxford and Cambridge Universities sent their own representatives to its meetings. The notion of the Establishment could have been invented to describe the AAA. Yet, in the aftermath of the Second World War, this was a worried and fearful institution. It was the body that had defined what it was to be an amateur and had passed the definition on to the rest of the world; but much of the world, from the USA to the Soviet Union, was beginning to ask pertinent questions about it and to develop practices that seemed tailor-made to undermine it. Amateurism itself was at risk, and the Association had to be vigilant. When it published its Annual Report for 1946 it welcomed the decision of the IAAF, the International Amateur Athletic Federation, to move its headquarters to London and appoint Lord Burghley as its President, but it warned that the Federation 'has many delicate and difficult tasks in front of it, [and] perhaps the most outstanding problem is that of the Amateur Status Rules'.

The big challenges for the AAA in relation to this, over the next few years, were to be demands for 'broken-time' payments for elite competitors (that is, compensation for the wages lost when they were competing rather than working), the growing ability of star athletes to make money from journalism, broadcasting or advertising, and the need for increasingly professional coaching. In the meantime there were any number of possible infractions of amateur rules to investigate; and during the late 1940s and early 1950s the AAA, it seems fair to say, went about sniffing out professionals in just the way that Senator McCarthy and his friends in the USA were sniffing out Communists. In April 1946 the General Committee was informed that 'the amateur status of an athlete employed as a masseur by a hospital was confirmed'; and in May – not long after it had been announced that London was to host the 1948 Olympics – it had to assess an offer from Butlins Holiday Camps to help the national effort by employing leading athletes 'for the purpose of training in connection with the Olympic Games, and to assist with the organisation of physical recreation facilities'. No way, the AAA said, ruling that 'any athlete so appointed would lose his amateur status'.

The imminent Olympics put the AAA in a difficult position. On the one hand, it knew that the Games presented an extraordinary and unprecedented opportunity for their sport to capture the public imagination, and that it therefore had the responsibility of ensuring that Britain did not, as seemed all too possible, end up with embarrassingly few medals. On the other hand, it had to make sure that the search for excellence did not lead to compromises with true amateurism. The Association decided that it had to bite one bullet of professionalism by creating the post of full-time national coach, choosing the hurdler Geoff Dyson to fill the role. He started work in February 1947, and an illustration of the strange dilemmas thrown up by the amateur code was the subsequent arrival at AAA headquarters of letters from worried athletes asking whether they might compromise their own amateur status by taking part in training runs with the (professional) national coach. Just before Dyson started work the Association decreed that he 'may not give private lessons, nor write articles for the press, books, or pamphlets, or broadcast'.

Geoff Dyson was to become a much-respected – and eventually much-published – figure, and he was to have courteous exchanges on training matters with Arthur Newton in the early 1950s. He was also careful to keep his mouth firmly shut on matters of athletics politics. Within the AAA the most prominent voice was probably that of Harold Abrahams (the Olympic 100-metre champion in 1924), but his desire to protect his media career with both *The Sunday Times* and the BBC meant that his public contributions on issues of controversy were notable largely for their blandness. But there was one man who was more than happy to go to war on behalf of amateurism and that was P.W. Green, the editor of *Athletics*. It was a monthly until January 1950 when it became *Athletics Weekly*, adopting at the same time the subtitle 'The Official Organ of Athletics in Great Britain'. Not that Green had ever seen it as anything else. His first target was the Soviet Union and its widely suspected system of state support for elite sportsmen; and when it was mooted in March 1946 that 'Russians' might take part in the London Olympics, Green wrote that they would have to 'conform' to amateur rules, adding that he doubted 'whether they will be amenable to this'. He would have none of the official explanation that the money received by Soviet athletes was not payment, but 'acknowledgement of their contribution to national life', and he was back on the subject in September that year, with an uncompromising editorial: 'The news of the payment of large sums of money to the successful athletes of the USSR makes the recent European Championships rather a farce . . . We should be the first to welcome the Russians to international competition, but they must conform to the regulations which are the desires of the majority.'

P.W. Green was both fascinated and exasperated by the scribe of Cottingham Chase; and among Newton's papers is a long letter, dated 18th November 1946, in which the editor took Newton to task for his views on the most difficult political issue facing athletics. It reads as a rejection of a piece Newton had submitted, and Green did not mince his words:

> This amateur and professional business is not just silly nonsense . . . I have nothing against a man because he was a pro. But I know what I'm talking about when I say that when money comes in sport flies out of the window. 99% of pro running is sprinting and any pro sprinter will tell you that it is all a big wrangle from start to finish. It is a case of trying to beat the book . . . Ever heard of a 'light sting' or a 'heavy sting'? These are the terms for dosing a runner with brandy or cognac, or caffeine or strychnine. I have an article in front of me about pro running in Australia. Reeks with it. That's what I don't want to see in athletics. It's only the money which does it, and no amount of whitewashing will make it clean.

Others, it seems, were certainly anticipating a Newton piece on the subject. Wilfred Richards – a friend and future collaborator in Manchester – had written to him in September saying 'I have been expecting a topical article in *Athletics* from you . . . The continental people seem to be hovering between amateurism and all-out professionalism; the Russians apparently pay sums of money quite openly to their stars . . . We, of course, maintain our strict amateur bias. But can we continue this way if almost all the other nations are prepared to relax their rules?'

Precisely the same question, of course, echoed around the AAA's offices in Chancery Lane, where it was couched in terms of whether 'broken-time' payments were justifiable. The question had to be answered, because there were beginning to be suggestions that athletics was about to take the route that rugby football had taken in the 1890s, with the creation of a separate breakaway organisation that tolerated a measure of professionalism. An AAA committee, led by Harold Abrahams, was appointed to come up with recommendations; and when it reported in October 1947 its proposals – which the AAA immediately accepted – were at one and the same time ground-breaking and extremely cautious. For the first time the principle of 'broken-time' payments was accepted; but an individual athlete could only claim for actual days of travel or competition (so not for training), could claim for no more than twenty-eight days in a year and would receive a maximum of £1 per day. The AAA also insisted that it retained the right to 'investigate' every claim made. Harold Abrahams knew that any AAA tinkering with 'pure' amateurism would cause ripples throughout the international athletic and Olympic communities, and in the autumn of 1948 (in the wake of London's successful 'austerity' Olympics) he argued the case for 'the British proposal' in the pages of *World Sports*. It was, he claimed, a pragmatic intervention into a debate that was all too often bedevilled by sentiment, nostalgia and much sitting on high horses. 'It would be highly desirable,' he suggested, 'to draft rules without using the word "amateur" . . . real progress will only be made if the problem is regarded not as an attempt to achieve a kind of perfect conception of how ideal amateurs should behave, but simply what rules are necessary to control satisfactorily international athletic competitions between athletes who are not professionals.' And such control 'is to be achieved not by stringing together high-faluting phrases, but by sensibly drafted regulations, directed towards the real problem and not handicapped unduly by traditional voices from the past'.

III

The pragmatism of Harold Abrahams's approach to broken-time payments perhaps served to prevent any amateur/professional schism in British athletics at an institutional level. But many, especially in the north of England and Scotland, resented what they experienced as the arrogance and authoritarianism of the Amateur Athletic Association; and they mistrusted a body that had quite so many men with titles in its leadership, and quite so many who had been educated at public schools and at Oxford or Cambridge. In its rules the AAA had jettisoned its original nineteenth-century insistence that amateurism excluded the 'artisan' or the 'labourer'; but it was a moot point as to whether it had in its spirit. So it was a significant moment when, in May 1947, a new athletics magazine came off the presses. It was called the *Athletic Review*; it was edited and printed in Manchester; and it proudly described itself as the Official Organ of the Northern Counties Athletic Association. (In fact, it had initially been intended to call it *The Northern Athlete*.) An article in its second issue made it clear that the magazine had different priorities, a different political stance and spoke to a different audience from *Athletics Weekly*. In his piece 'What is Professionalism; to pay or not to pay?', V.S.D. McKernan argued that:

> any test of public opinion should include what might be called 'working mens' clubs like Sutton, Salford and Hallamshire. Clubs such as these have supplied this country with more internationals than any one university

– and internationals who, more often than not, have had to do a hard day's work before representing their country. It is more than likely that [such men] would welcome some form of compensation. It is a question which all who have the welfare of athletics at heart would do well to bear in mind . . . Compensation for a [particular day], or very occasionally a particular week, of sport is hardly likely to keep an athlete for a year.

The reference to 'any one university' was a pointed one, as there was undoubtedly resentment at the amount of coverage and support being given to a gilded generation of Oxbridge athletes represented by Roger Bannister and Chris Chataway.

Athletics Weekly, with its northern working-class bias, was to become the journalistic home and platform for that prolific southern middle-class gentleman Arthur Newton. Its editor, the Manchester businessman and coach Wilfred Richards, had written to Newton asking him to become 'a regular contributor' and offering him space for a monthly piece of about 600 words. 'We certainly won't worry if your article is controversial,' he added in a pointed reference to P.W. Green's efforts to distance himself from Newtonian arguments. For Newton, the working-class professional par excellence was of course Peter Gavuzzi, and he paid an annual subscription on his old partner's behalf. For Gavuzzi, the magazine's arrival each month was a moment of rare excitement in his gloomy exile at Le Moulinet. 'I want to thank you very much for your generous gesture in paying my sub,' he was to write in one of his regular letters to Cottingham Chase. He was replying to one in which Newton had evidently mentioned his anger at having his pension taxed, and Gavuzzi went on, 'but it mustn't go on like this, you have enough trouble with the spendulicks [*sic*] (in your language, financial affairs)'.

Disaffected though he was from the mainstream of British athletics, Newton hedged his bets over the next couple of years and continued to contribute articles to both Green's magazine and Richards's. He nakedly recycled the same material, and for a time his editors enjoyed the polemics. But before long they picked up that many of their readers had had enough. Wilfred Richards spent part of his Christmas Day in 1950 composing a long and delicate letter to his most regular contributor, struggling to find the right words so as to avoid hurting Newton's feelings too deeply. 'There is just one thing I feel may have been overlooked by you,' he began. 'In most of your writings you deplore the backwardness of Britain in the science of athletics, and I wonder whether this is quite as justified at the present time as it was a few years ago . . . Many readers, particularly the younger ones, may get the impression that you would scrap practically all the present-day coaches and their ideas. I don't want readers to think that Arthur Newton is only concerned with pulling to pieces.' The following year P.W. Green made effectively the same point. 'Send another article by all means,' he wrote, 'but I should very much like you to write in a different way – more of a constructive nature than "having a go" at accepted practices. I am not exaggerating when I say many readers are tired of the latter.' Green suggested that Newton pen 'some reminiscences of your races in a breezy style'. He might as well have suggested that he take up sprinting.

Ever short of money and in search of other sources of income, Newton had summarised his main ideas on training in a short book that appeared in the autumn of 1947. He called it *Commonsense Athletic*, and he published it himself from

Cottingham Chase. We have no idea how many copies he sold, but the fact that Newtonian 'theory' was now available in concentrated form between the covers of a single volume meant that criticism of it could be more focused and stringent. When P.W. Green reviewed it, he said he thought its idiosyncrasy made it unsuitable for 'reading by our younger athletes'. Newton, in response, said Green's review showed that 'he has not begun to understand my attitude to athletics'. Their relationship was strong enough to survive this spat, but almost two years later, in October 1950, Green contacted Newton to warn him that he was about to publish a lengthy critique of *Commonsense Athletics* that he insisted had appeared 'entirely unsolicited' from a researcher at Edinburgh University. This was a D.V. Ellis, who described his field of research as 'evolution and physiology'; and the fascination of his piece lies in seeing someone finally taking Newton on at his own game – that is, mixing mundane training recommendations with both lofty statements about human evolution and sharp denunciations of British athletics' ruling elite.

Ellis cleared the ground for his critique by separating the recounting of 'facts' in Newton's book from the exposition of 'theories'. With the former, he had no problem, but for the latter he had only snooty academic disdain. 'The majority appear to be based on a knowledge of Zoology and Physiology gained from a rapid perusal of *The Kiddies Bumper Book of Natural Science* or a similar type of work.' Newton had certainly made himself vulnerable to academic criticism by describing his writings as contributions to the 'science' of athletics; but when Ellis claimed that 'statistics' showed there to be 'little relationship between athletic ability and good health', he revealed how far he missed the point of Newton's argument about fitness and well-being. But if Ellis could restrain his tone when complaining of the book's 'insufficient basis of scientific knowledge', he strayed close to abuse when he came to Newton's chapter on professionalism. He called it 'useless', detecting in it 'a perverted form of inverted snobbery'; and he cautioned any professionals to keep away from specialised field events because they 'require considerable intelligence, and professionals as a class have a lower intelligence than the first-rate amateurs'.

It was hardly surprising that Arthur Newton, in his largely good-humoured and courteous reply to Ellis's critique, took evident umbrage at this last remark. He asked for the evidence for such a preposterous claim, given that 'probably 90% or more of the world's progress and scientific knowledge have been due to professionals'; and he expressed his regret that Ellis was not, in his view, capable of the 'reasoned and clear thinking on this subject' that was so needed. The controversy did not end there, with correspondents to *Athletics Weekly* weighing in on both Ellis's and Newton's side. Eventually P.W. Green decided that enough was enough, and refused to publish yet another missive from Cottingham Chase. 'It is time to let sleeping dogs lie,' he wrote to Newton. In that case, the elderly athlete replied, he would never again submit his work to Green's magazine. It was the beginning of the end for Newton's career as an athletics journalist, because that same year the new proprietors of *World Sports* informed him that they would not be needing him in the future. For much of 1951 Newton continued to supply short pieces to the *Athletic Review*, where his good friend William Clark was now editor. But he had nothing new to say. In so far as he had been waging a war against the AAA – over the acceptance of professionalism and the principles of training – he had lost. But Cottingham Chase, a quiet street of pebble-dashed and net-curtained houses, was never going to be a match for Chancery Lane.

IV

Ironically, just as Arthur Newton became absent from British athletic journalism the AAA was becoming more and more obsessed with the seeming threat posed to the amateur order by leading athletes writing for the press or broadcasting for the BBC. The 'Permission to Write, Broadcast or Lecture Committee' met throughout the latter part of 1951, agonising over how to square amateurism with the need to create as much publicity as possible for a sport whose popularity was being challenged by resurgent post-war football and cricket. Not since the 'broken-time' issue had the Association found anything quite so difficult. The Committee finally reported in February 1952. Accepting in principle that an athlete could write or broadcast for a fee *with the AAA's permission* was easy enough. What was tricky was coming up with a set of guidelines for how and why such permission might be given. They make amusing and enlightening reading. An athlete had first to make an application. The AAA had then to ask itself the question 'Is the athlete capable of directly producing articles?' If they thought not, and that any pieces signed by him or her were likely to have been ghost-written, then permission would be denied. Permission was only to be granted for twelve months at a time: and 'the general way in which an athlete given permission to write uses that privilege will naturally be considered when a renewal of permission is sought'. Note that word 'privilege'. Any athlete/journalist would know the AAA was looking over his or her shoulder all the time. This was censorship by threat.

For Arthur Newton the new rules were further confirmation of his long-held view that the instinct of the AAA's hierarchy was to humiliate athletes, to treat dedicated grown-ups as children whose every move needed to be monitored. Nowhere was this clearer, it seems fair to say, than in the working of the AAA's 'To and From Abroad Committee'. Its job was to either approve or reject requests from overseas that a British athlete take part in an event, or requests from British clubs wanting to welcome a foreign athlete. In the Committee's minutes, 'permission denied' comes up far more often than 'permission granted'; and what many competitors felt about this – but could not express at the time – comes through clearly in the furious autobiography of the great middle-distance runner Gordon Pirie, published in 1961 after his retirement: 'Over and over again in many countries I have been asked "Why didn't you accept an invitation to race in our country?" Over and over again I have felt humiliated by having to reply, "I'm very sorry, but I didn't know you had invited me."' The AAA simply had not bothered to inform him. Pirie says he never wanted to be paid for running or for winning, but he did want to be able to control his own career and profit from his rare ability through sponsorship or advertising or the press. 'I have always believed,' he wrote, 'that if a man or a woman is prepared to be dedicated to athletics the sport should in some way provide him or her with a reasonable living free of humiliating patronage.' But the reality, he insisted, was that the AAA treated him and his fellow athletes as 'performing monkeys'. There is no record of Gordon Pirie and Arthur Newton ever meeting, but had they done so, they would have found much to talk about.

Newton would, though, have been familiar with the sad

story of McDonald Bailey – Britain's and Europe's leading sprinter in the late 1940s and early 1950s. Born in Trinidad, he served in the RAF during the war and then decided to stay on in England. He reached the final of the 100 metres at the 1948 Olympics in London, and then won bronze at Helsinki four years later. Between 1951 and 1956 he was joint holder of the world record at the distance; and for seven consecutive years he won the sprint double at the AAA Championships that were held before capacity crowds at White City. He was an iconic figure at a time when there were very few significant black people in British society. But to the bosses at Chancery Lane he was first and foremost a troublemaker. 'For some reason the AAA has never been very helpful to Bailey,' wrote the senior and well-respected athletics doctor, C.R. Woodard, in the August 1950 issue of *Athletics Review*. Earlier that summer Woodard (who happened to one of the few people sufficiently close to Newton to address his letters to 'Dear old Arthur') had been appointed Official Doctor for the British Games, and had witnessed the tensions between the sprinter and officialdom, who refused to allow Bailey to warm up before races as he wished. 'When an athlete is in the class of a McDonald Bailey it isn't fair that he should be treated as an average runner: Mac is a highly sensitive and temperamental creature,' Woodard suggested, before going on to hazard a guess as to why the sprinter achieved his best times overseas: 'he never runs with the same relaxation and ease here as he does elsewhere'. Bailey did not do well, it seems, under the censorious gaze of the AAA. Woodard also mentions that Bailey suffered the same insult that Gordon Pirie was to complain about – he had been invited to run in Europe, but Chancery Lane never bothered to pass on the letters. The great contemporary marathon runner Jim Peters mentioned a few years later that 'Mac' 'seemed often to be in trouble with the AAA about this time' – a reference no doubt to the sprinter's loss of amateur status in 1953.

What happened was this. The programme for that year's Oxford and Cambridge Athletic Sports Meeting in March carried an advertisement for 'Lilywhite's Comet Starting-Block, made to the requirements of E. McDonald Bailey Ltd. Similar to the type used in the Olympic Games 1952.' The Southern Committee of the AAA was outraged, and immediately summoned one of the best sprinters in the world to a disciplinary hearing. Their judgement was as unequivocal as it was pompous. 'You have infringed the Amateur Definition set out in AAA Law 2 (1), and have therefore lost your amateur status.' His banishment was *sine die*. There would be no way back into the amateur fold. But McDonald Bailey – a true star at a time when athletics had a mass following among the British public – refused to accept that his career could be ended by a handful of provincial administrators, and he appealed to the AAA in London. He won, with the Association's Appeals Committee deciding there was no proof that Bailey himself had authorised the advertisement. Despite this, the incident brought his illustrious athletic career to an end, because Bailey decided he could no longer tolerate being subject to the censure and punishment of such people. Later that summer he accepted a contract with Leigh, the Lancashire rugby league club. He knew he was finally burning his amateur athletic boats. In his first game for Leigh he was badly injured. He never played again, nor did he ever run again competitively.

After his falling-out with P.W. Green, Arthur Newton had

very little contact with the 'official' world of British amateur athletics. He had brief and courteous meetings with Geoff Dyson and with D.N.J. Cullum, head of the AAA's Coaching Committee, both of whom had the grace to acknowledge the wisdom of some of the ideas that had been emanating from Cottingham Chase over the previous decade. But all athletic eyes in 1951 and 1952 were on Helsinki and the next Olympic Games, and Newton's 'theories' seemed deeply irrelevant to most people in the sport. Fortunately there were few who were as dismissive as George Brogden, an honorary AAA jumping coach, who wrote in May 1952 that while 'Mr Newton's theory [that time spent away from the main exercise is time wasted] may possibly be correctly applied to long-distance runners ... the moronic mentality of marathon men must not be allowed to develop in other spheres'. Newton, he said, was 'trying to return to the old days when athletes didn't have the know-how, and couldn't think beyond the obvious'. But perhaps Newton's most direct impact on the mainstream of athletics came from his influence over a coach who thought so far beyond the obvious that many regarded him as deranged.

V

One can only hope that Arthur Newton, who had little more than a year to live, was aware of what was happening at an athletics meeting at the Morton Stadium in Dublin on 6th August 1958. That afternoon a lean young Australian, Herb Elliott, just twenty years old, broke the world record for the mile. Later the same month, in Gothenburg, he was to break that for the 1,500 metres. He had been coached – intensively, idiosyncratically and almost secretly – by a strange visionary called Percy Cerutty; and back in September 1949, towards the beginning of their friendship, Cerutty had insisted in a letter to Cottingham Chase that 'had I never heard of Arthur Newton I might easily have still been an invalid, a no-hoper, unknown'.

'I am convinced that movement is life – activity in the human being regenerates, makes for life. That ease, rest, relaxation, unless well earned, is the way to a painful finish . . . The possibility of regeneration and the certainty of being able to enjoy life to the full, as a man should, is open to everyone. But the way is not easy. It is hard. Only those of courage would attempt it. But the reward is certain.' This was Cerutty – whose name, he insisted, was to be pronounced as 'Sincerity, but without the sin' – in a radio talk he gave in his home city of Melbourne in 1946, when he was just beginning to acquire a local reputation, both as a distance runner and as a coach. He had been born in 1895 (making him twelve years younger than Newton) into a troubled middle-class Victorian family, and he was only four years old when his mother walked out on her alcoholic husband. She had six children to support, and Percy had to leave school when he was twelve to start working. He eventually embarked on a career in the Post Office. He dabbled in athletics for a local club, but was a frail and anxious young man, subject to frequent and vicious migraines. When conscription came, controversially, to Australia in 1916, Cerutty was deemed unfit for military service. He married, but neither domestic nor work life seemed to hold enough meaning for him, and long periods of depression eventually led to a major breakdown in 1939. It was the making of him, and he was later to characterise the anguish that he experienced as 'the only time any man ever really grapples with the fundamentals of life'.

Cerutty told Arthur Newton ten years after his breakdown

that he came out of it intent on embarking on a 'crusade to show men how to live with zest'. He said three books had inspired him to think that a new and different way of life was possible. The first was Alexis Carrel's *Man, the Unknown,* which had first appeared in France in 1935, quickly becoming a best-seller. Carrel was a brilliant biologist and surgeon who also held uncomfortable views about eugenics. He believed in the perfectibility of the human race, but only in so far as the criminal, the inadequate and the insane were progressively eliminated from the collective gene-pool. He was to be a loyal, and well-rewarded, servant of the Vichy regime. But in his comments on the book, which he regularly recommended to others, Cerutty makes no mention of this aspect of Carrel's thinking, describing *Man, the Unknown* as a mystical text that extolled the spiritual benefits of an ascetic lifestyle. The second book that 'saved' him, Cerutty said, was *Physical Strength and How I Acquired It* by the Estonian wrestling champion Georg Hackenschmidt. The sport had been hugely popular in both Europe and the USA before the First World War, and Hackenschmidt became perhaps the best-known and richest professional sportsman in the world. But to him physical strength was nothing in itself; it was a means to understanding the capabilities of the mind as well as the body, and the following passage suggests why Cerutty was so fascinated by the wrestler: 'The knowledge of one's strength entails a real mastery over oneself; it breeds energy and courage, helps one over the most difficult tasks in life, and procures contentment and true enjoyment of living.' Hackenschmidt devoted the latter part of his long life to writing strange philosophical tomes with titles like *Attitudes and their Relations to Human Manifestations* and *Man and Cosmic Antagonism to Mind and*

Spirit. Cerutty remarked in 1949 that 'some of the people I am in touch with cannot make head or tail of Hack's books, [but] I think I can grasp what he is after'. Arthur Newton thought he could too, and he became not just a fan, but a firm friend of Hackenschmidt's when the Estonian lived out his final years in south London. The third book that set Percy Cerutty on his 'crusade' was Newton's own *Running*.

The training regime Cerutty developed at Portsea on an isolated stretch of the Victorian coast south of Melbourne became famous for his relentless use of the area's high sand dunes, making Herb Elliott run up them time after time to strengthen his legs. But the coach once said to his star pupil, 'I'm not interested in athletics, I'm only interested in achievement,' and Cerutty also made him read Plato and the Bible. It must have been soon after he gave up his Post Office job in 1946 and bought the land at Portsea that Cerutty first contacted Newton, and by the next year they had become regular correspondents. Cerutty's early letters (perhaps when he was searching for common ground with the older man) make much of his contempt for the amateur bosses of Australian athletics, whom he dismissed as the 'smug superior'. 'They hounded me and insulted me,' he wrote to Cottingham Chase, 'when it was announced that I was going to accept fees for teaching. I was ordered out of one of our bigger club-rooms. Out here to be a professional is only second to being a criminal, a pariah. The very name carries a stigma as if unclean.' He dismissed the amateurism so admired in Australia as something 'possible only to wealthy men's sons'. So far he would have had Newton nodding in agreement, but Cerutty made a further political step for which the older man never indicated any sympathy. 'It seems to me that the country that has the most sensible attitude to the matter is Russia,' he wrote in 1948, 'they, at least, appear to think that the acceptance of a sum of money for an outstanding performance does not convert a man into something less than a man and a citizen.' Three years later, when it was announced that the Soviet Union was to take part in the 1952 Olympics, Cerutty was jubilant. 'I am at heart as much a revolutionary as any Russian prior to their revolution . . . Within ten years their athletes will hold most of the world's records. They have the realistic approach. We have the humbug and old school tie attitude. Russia is the one country, as far as I can see, where a man like myself would be taken seriously.'

'Your letters open up so many facets on training and life that it would take a book to reply to them,' he told Newton in April 1950. The two men realised they shared something extremely rare – a commitment to finding out what the mental and spiritual effects of relentless, usually solitary, daily physical effort were. They were experimenters, who had to accept that they lived on the margins of society because they had not done what was expected of them. This is what Cerutty had recognised in the author of *Running*. 'To know truth and live with truth, even about athletics, one must forego the ordinary world,' he wrote to his mentor in November 1951: 'One must be prepared to do what you did. Give up one's life to it if necessary. One cannot serve God (truth, reality) and mammon (worldly success, greed). There is not one man in 10,000 has even a glimmer about these things. I speak to you in all humbleness since I believe you grasped all these principles. Sacrifice is the keyword. Effort, killing effort, the road.' Newton, in turn, said that he would not dream of writing to many people as he wrote to Cerutty because 'the great majority of men haven't time (they don't spend enough time alone for such a purpose) to do much constructive thinking and consequently they are apt to regard those who do as queer. But of course this doesn't worry either of us.'

It was a huge moment for both of them, then, when Percy Cerutty knocked on the door of no. 9 Cottingham Chase in the autumn of 1952. He was on his way back to Australia from the Helsinki Olympic Games, where one of his stable of athletes, John Landy, had competed in both the 1,500 and 5,000 metres. The manager of the Australian Olympic team had wanted Cerutty to be on hand, given that Landy was only twenty-two years old, but of course the coach's professionalism was a problem. A compromise was eventually reached. Cerutty's expenses would be covered, but he had to accept that he could not be an accredited member of the party, could not travel with them and could not stay in the Olympic village. Not that Cerutty seemed to mind. 'The sham-amateurs are greatly afraid I may stain their lilywhite amateur purity by wanting official recognition in the team, a blazer etc. and all those useless trappings so beloved by little men and so ignored by the bigger,' he had written to Newton that March. Cerutty had been contributing occasional articles to *Athletics Review* since 1949, and when he visited Ruislip he was introduced to its editor, William Clark. Arthur Newton made a point of inviting Peter Gavuzzi to the meeting as well. As his boat crossed the Mediterranean in November, en route to the Suez Canal and the Indian Ocean, Cerutty addressed a heartfelt thank-you letter to Newton: 'It does surpass my most rhetorical efforts to adequately state the indebtedness and gratitude that I owe you. The discussions we had must lead to a broader understanding, and the opportunity to meet men like Gavuzzi and Clark was far more than I ever merited.' Newton had cause to be grateful in return, because Percy Cerutty's remarkable achievements as a coach of middle-distance runners gave the lie to any accusation that Newton's 'theories' were only applicable to long-distance men.

It had been his extraordinary achievements over long distances on the road, of course, that had shaped Arthur Newton's bizarre and unique athletic life; and, to his great delight and pleasure, he had been able, by the autumn of 1952, to rekindle his involvement with road-running. This was to allow him, in old age, to re-establish contact with South Africa and work once again with Peter Gavuzzi.

9

Old Age, Poverty and Recognition

Newton and Gauvzzi's Final Laps

I

'Can we get accommodation for five chaps and what will the board and lodging cost? Is the food position fairly easy or must we have food parcels sent over? Meat is our main item, also fresh vegetables.' The worried man whose letter arrived at no. 9 Cottingham Chase in late January 1953 was Wally Hayward, South Africa's best-known long-distance runner. He was forty-four years old, and he had won the classic Comrades race between Durban and Pietermaritzburg in both 1950 and 1951, setting a new record on both occasions. He took a year off from the race to compete in the Olympic marathon at Helsinki in 1952, finishing tenth behind the phenomenon of Emil Zátopek, and he was to win the Comrades again in 1953 and 1954. Hayward was the best known among a group of South African road-runners with whom Arthur Newton had been in touch over the previous few months, encouraging them to come to England to give a boost to his favourite branch of athletics – one whose revival in the land of his birth was to be his last great sporting cause.

Newton wanted Hayward and his colleagues to take part in the London to Brighton road race, England's answer to the Comrades. It had, of course, been on the Brighton road in 1924 that Newton had first announced himself to a startled British public; and in 1937 he had helped a brilliant South African of a later generation, Hardy Ballington, to beat his own course record. But the race had been one of the many sporting victims of the Second World War, and road-running itself at any distance greater than twenty-six miles suffered from not being canonised by the Olympic movement. Then, in 1951, Newton was asked by his friend Ernest Neville of the Surbiton Sports Club if he would lend his support to an attempt at reviving the London to Brighton as part of that year's Festival of Britain. Newton was keen and immediately tried to get his old collaborator Joe Binks at the *News of the World* involved, writing to ask if the paper would sponsor the event. Binks, though, had his doubts about the quality of any field of British runners. 'To put on such a race with no knowledge of decent form amongst the entry might be asking for a washout affair,' he responded, '52 miles is a long way with no Newtons or Ballingtons about.'

The *News Chronicle* stepped in as sponsors, and the race took place – with sufficient success, despite appalling weather, for Ernest Neville to suggest the formation of a Road Runners Club dedicated to making it an annual event. The run was advertised as a strictly amateur affair, but Neville was well aware of the particular cachet of Newton's name in relation to the Brighton road and suggested that an 'Arthur Newton Trophy' be established as the winner's prize. So a request went out for contributions, and during the summer of 1952 the cheques and postal orders flooded in from around the world. 'Such a noble cause,' wrote Newton and Gavuzzi's old friend Jacques Girling from Hamilton, Ontario, enclosing one Canadian dollar; Bill Payne, Newton's closest friend in Natal, sent five shillings, while Joe Binks doubled this, saying, 'I just like the idea of this appeal, it will please Arthur very much I am sure.' Undoubtedly it did, but it would also have embarrassed him. At the prize-giving ceremony after the race in September 1952 Newton 'had little to say, except thank you', according to a report in *Athletics Review*, while the victorious Derek Reynolds of Blackheath Harriers 'said he could only say how proud he was to win [the trophy] because he owed his win to the man whose name it carried'. Among Newton's papers is a letter to him from Derek Reynolds dated 12th July 1953. It touches briefly on the imminent arrival of Wally Hayward and his South African colleagues, but then Reynolds goes on the ask for 'a few words of advice'. He says it has been some time since he's raced but he intends to compete in the South London Harriers thirty-miler. 'Should I do the full distance before the race?' he asks. 'Should I lengthen the evening run from the office of 9 miles to 20 and run 30 to 35 each weekend? Can you give me some idea of what I should do from now until the week of the race?' This is a perfect example of the sort of letter that arrived week after week at Cottingham Chase. It was how Newton, barred from being seen to coach amateur athletes, actually did so.

The formal log of 'English Native Records' maintained by the AAA recognised no distance longer than the Olympic marathon; but very occasionally achievements outside the normal canon of events were 'noted' or 'confirmed'. Arthur

Newton's 1928 run from Bath to London had, for instance, been 'noted'; and in January 1953 Derek Reynolds's times for both forty and fifty miles were confirmed by the Association's Records Committee. They were achieved by the same run, at the Motspur Park stadium on 13th December 1952; and in all probability they would not have been recognised by the AAA had they been achieved on the road. The great and good of Chancery Lane were obviously confused by road-running and did not know whether to welcome or mistrust its revival in the early 1950s. It was not, like cross-country, part of the accepted calendar and culture of amateur athletics, and it had been closely associated in the past with professional pedestrianism. Wally Hayward's record run over the London to Brighton distance in September 1953 was 'noted', and when the British runner Tom Richards set an even better time two years later his achievement was acknowledged as a 'Noteworthy Performance'. But at the same General Committee meeting a proposal to 'introduce other road-running records' was defeated. It was to be almost a decade after its creation before the existence of the Road Runners Club was acknowledged by the AAA, and then only in the context of a warning. Its Annual Report for 1960 mentioned that the RRC had been organising a 'very successful' London to Brighton race since 1952, but then went on: 'A problem this year has been the growing interest in "Long Distance Marches". Many of these have been publicity stunts with money prizes and several athletes – both runners and walkers – have lost their amateur status. Clubs are asked to remind their members that the fact of entering an event of this type, even if the individual does not actually start, will cause the athlete to be disqualified in events held under AAA rules.'

In 1953 the Road Runners Club had been well aware of the public-relations impact of having a group of high-profile South Africans make such a long trip for the sake of the Brighton race. 'You will probably not be surprised to hear that I have been inundated with queries,' James Audsley, the RRC's press officer and a freelance athletics journalist, wrote to Newton at the end of August. 'Their presence gives us a wonderful opportunity for building up press and public interest in distance running. Queries have reached me from Dixon's Agency, Reuters, South African Morning Newspapers, and the Press Association.' The previous month Derek Reynolds had contacted Newton to say that the BBC was interested in the South Africans appearing on the *In Town Tonight* programme. But the men from Johannesburg were wary of too much fuss being made of their presence in England. 'It would be a pleasure to go running with them, as long as they don't ask us to attend any party or dances where it concerns late nights – I don't drink any alcohol. Please don't think we are snobs, but I feel we are going over to do a job of work and not have a holiday.' So wrote Wally Hayward to Arthur Newton in June 1953 after the latter had passed on an invitation from Belgrave Harriers; and unfortunately others in South Africa agreed that his trip to England – which was to result in new records for the Bath to London 100 miles and for twenty-four hours on the track, as well as the Brighton race – smacked too much of 'work'. Hayward had struggled to raise money for the trip and had accepted small private donations. It did not matter how small they were, according to the South African Athletics and Cycling Association, the donations meant that Hayward was accepting money to be able to run and that made him, in their eyes, a professional: in 1954 they duly banned him. His amateur status was only restored in 1974, when he was sixty-six years old. Not that the AAA had any doubts about Hayward when their official timekeepers were among those who assembled at the Bear Inn in the village of Box near Bath in the early hours of 24th October 1953. It was the traditional starting point for the 100-mile course, and while they had no suspicions over Hayward himself, they found themselves in what must have felt uncomfortable proximity to some diehard professionals. There was Newton, of course, and among the support team who had slept at the Inn the night before was Peter Gavuzzi.

As we have seen in relation to his years at Le Moulinet, Gavuzzi's diary entries were often bland and infuriatingly brief. But we have also seen that they could, at times, be revealing and honest. In any case, they are all we have for piecing together a narrative for the daily life of a private and reclusive working-class man. So it is infuriating that among the boxes of papers he left at his death, and which are now kept by his grandson Guy, there are no diaries for the period 1952 to 1960. Whether they were lost or he decided not to keep up the habit, we do not know. All we can say for certain is that his life seemed to be taken up with just three things – his work, and his friendships with his brother Charlie and with Arthur Newton. The latter undoubtedly did what he could to involve Gavuzzi in his social and athletic life. Theirs was a deep bond, forged during those extraordinary years in the USA and Canada. We have seen that Gavuzzi was on hand when Percy Cerutty visited Ruislip in the autumn of 1952, and that summer the two former partners had gone on a cycling holiday together. 'Don't try and overdo it,' a friend had advised Newton.

Arthur Newton also did what he could to publicise Gavuzzi's athletic achievements. In the early summer of 1953 he had been asked by the RRC's press officer James Audsley, who was also a freelance athletics journalist, to collaborate on a piece for the *Eagle Sports Annual* – a publication that, with its carefully crafted mixture of adventure, science, sport and patriotism, was beginning to establish itself as an almost obligatory Christmas present for boys of a certain age. The *Annual* had wanted a feature on the Pyle Transcontinental races, and on 23rd June Audsley sent Newton the (undoubtedly ghosted) galley proofs, with an accompanying note. 'You will recall that the editor wanted it told in the first person by a "known" athlete who had taken part. He would, of course, have been well satisfied had you appeared as the narrator of the whole story: but I know that you wanted Peter Gavuzzi to join in, and I myself was only too pleased to bring in such a successful and interesting all-round sportsman, about whom far too little is known by the public.' He wrote again six weeks later expressing regret at missing Gavuzzi, who had just left on holiday. 'Like you,' he told Newton, 'I agree that he deserves much more prominence and praise in print than he has yet received, and that he could render a great deal of useful service to sport if brought back into the swim. Gavuzzi is, I am sure, a man with so many tales to tell that the very least a writer can offer to do is help him to tell them and add a few that are about, rather than supplied by, him.' In his final years Gavuzzi was indeed to become, as we shall see, a sought-after teller of tales. The *Eagle Sports Annual* never published the article on the Transcontinentals, but James Audsley was as good as his word in trying to push Peter Gavuzzi's name. When it was announced in March 1954 that the British champion Jim Peters was to enter the Boston Marathon that year, a debate started in the athletic press as to who should go along as his manager. Audsley had no doubt whom the AAA should choose. 'As for the best man for the job,' he wrote in a newspaper column, 'I am as certain that I can name him as I am that he will not be selected. The man best fitted on every count . . . is undoubtedly Peter Gavuzzi, that great runner who 25 years ago this month completed what was probably the greatest run ever achieved by a British athlete.' Audsley was right. Gavuzzi was not selected, and he never held any official position in British athletics.

II

'I'm not really looking forward to this trip,' Arthur Newton told a reporter from his local Ruislip paper in the spring of 1956: 'I'm too old for all this travel and I hate crowds.' The latter had always been the case, and the old runner also had a point about the travel. He was now in his seventies, and he was not referring to travelling down to the West Country or even to crossing the Channel. He was referring to an invitation that he had, after much thought and hesitation, accepted – to make a final visit to southern Africa. The invitation was from the South African Marathon Runners' Club, which had raised the necessary money by asking for contributions from the athletics communities of both the Union and Rhodesia. They knew that Newton was both frail and virtually blind, and that if they wanted him to make the trip they had to act quickly. Their invitation was reported in the *Johannesburg Star* in June 1955. So was Newton's initial response. 'I understand I am to be a guest of honour at a banquet, that they want to name the next Comrades the "Arthur Newton Marathon", and that I will have to give lectures. I feel honoured and very touched indeed at this kind and wonderful invitation, and it's nice to know that I'm still remembered out there. But I feel embarrassed about it all.'

It was fitting that his final adventure should be a return to the scene of his first; and in a way he had long been preparing himself for South Africa, while at home in Cottingham Chase. For several months before his departure in April 1956 no. 9 had grown accustomed to the clipped vowels and guttural consonants of Natal, the Transvaal and Rhodesia. The Comrades founder, Vic Clapham, and his wife had stayed for six weeks; then Alan Gillespie, an athlete from Rhodesia, had stayed; so had a Major Watkins, a friend of Newton's from the Bulawayo police; and then the rising long-distance star from Johannesburg, Jackie Mekler, had checked in. He was to stay for several months, and he provided a touching account of daily life chez Newton that Rob Hadgraft included in his biography *Tea with Mr Newton*:

They were very happy days. Whenever visitors arrived he used to shout 'Slave!' and I would have to go and make tea. He really enjoyed that . . . He used to accompany us on long runs on his bike, and he knew all the lovely country roads around places like Burnham Beeches, Beaconsfield and Chalfont St Peter . . . He used to get correspondence daily from around the world and would reply promptly always. He was a keen stamp collector and loved classical music, especially piano concertos. He introduced me to his favourites, the Grieg and Schumann concertos, that he played every time I sat down to a meal . . . He believed that running should be as natural and regular as eating and sleeping. He would help anyone he could and was genuinely pleased to help others break his own records. He was way ahead of his time and proud to be a professional.

It was as though Newton had finally found a family; and his acceptance of the invitation to South Africa was as much his way of thanking them as theirs of honouring him. But he was quite right to be wary of what was being asked of him. Among his papers are three typewritten, coffee-stained sheets itemising his planned itinerary in Africa. He was to be there for just over three months, dividing the time equally between the Transvaal, Southern Rhodesia and Natal. Of nearly 100 days, only six had no planned engagement. The prospect before him was one of press conferences, banquets, receptions, speaking engagements, meetings, concerts, school visits, weddings and, of course, athletic events at which he would be the guest of honour. But even on this valedictory tour Newton's professionalism followed him like an unwanted shadow. At one of the first banquets given for him, by the South African Athletic Council in Johannesburg on 6th April, the chairman said that 'the fine gesture of the Marathon Runners' Club in inviting Arthur Newton, a professional, out to South Africa as their guest was an example of sports broadmindedness which could well be followed by other bodies'. But it was not followed, sadly, by the South African Amateur Athletic Association. Each year the Marathon Club staged a 'torch relay race' between Johannesburg and the nearby town of Springs, and they wanted Newton to take part – to make a brief cere-monial cameo. But no. He was a professional; so if he ran, the South African AAA said, every other participant would lose his amateur status. They somehow managed to outdo even the British AAA in their zeal for amateur purity.

Newton's second month, May, was spent in Natal. This was the real homecoming. In Pietermaritzburg there was a lecture and dinner at Hilton College, where he had taught in his early twenties; there was morning tea with the mayor, there was a cross-country race to start, a visit to a new dam, and two other schools to visit. There was also – probably most important for Newton himself – an evening at 'Gunga Din Shellhole'. 'Moth Arthur Newton, the famous long-distance runner, who has been overseas for a number of years and is now back in SA, will be visiting Gunga Din Shellhole on Friday 4th May,' wrote the editor of *The Mothball*, 'a Monthly Digest of Moth Affairs'. To be a 'Moth' was to be a member of the Memorable Order of Tin Hats, a successor organisation in South Africa to the Comrades of the Great War, and its local clubs were known as 'Shellholes'. Moths committed themselves to three things: True Comradeship, Mutual Help and Sound Memory. It was at this meeting in May 1956 that Bill Payne, Newton's neighbour from his farming days near Harding, gave a moving speech (quoted in Chapter 1) remembering Newton as a 'useful musician and a philosopher' as well as a 'cross-country runner with a brittle sense of humour'.

Then it was on to Durban, where he stayed with Hardy Ballington, the runner he had helped on the Brighton Road in 1937, and where he was subjected to an altogether more formal programme. There was a civic welcome by the mayor, a dinner for 150 local athletes at a top hotel, a lecture to give at Durban High School, an address to another Shellhole, and a cocktail party in his honour at the Durban Press Club. Everywhere he went Newton was asked how and why he had first started running on the Harding farm, and he was also happy to talk about the Pyle races in the States. But he would not stray onto the political terrain of what had been known as the 'Newton Case'. He couldn't even bring himself to visit his old farm. He was driven down to Harding from Durban. While there he attended a civic tree-planting ceremony in his honour and gave a speech to local school children. A day had been set aside for him to visit his old farm, but he could not do it. 'I don't want to see it,' he told a Pretoria newspaper. 'I put in a lot of hard work on that place before I had to sell it. No, I don't want to see it again.' Among the memories he did not want to rekindle was, no doubt, that of a reluctantly terminated engagement.

The last picture we have of Newton is in an article about him published by his local Ruislip paper in the summer of 1957. 'He Hates Walking, But He Starts At Four' was the headline:

Although 74-year-old Arthur Newton 'hates walking' he leaves his bed just after 4 a.m. every day to take an 8–10 mile walk. Why so early? Mr Newton's sight is bad and he finds by going early there are not so many cars on the road. And anyway, he likes to get back for the 7 a.m. news. Provided that some of his many athletic friends are not visiting him he goes to bed soon after 8 p.m. Mr Newton started his 80-mile-a-week schedule in 1956 when he found he couldn't run so easily. While he walks he thinks. Says pipe-sucking Mr Newton, 'I have quite a lot of problems.'

His health suddenly deteriorated in the summer of 1959 and, following a minor stroke, he died in Hillingdon Hospital on 7th September. Three days later he was cremated in Ruislip. Arthur Newton's will was made public in February 1960. He did not, it hardly needs saying, die a rich man. His estate was worth less than £2,500, and most of that represented the value of his house. Specific legacies were to his neighbours in Cottingham Chase, the Burtons, who for many years had provided extra beds whenever necessary for visiting athletes when no. 9 was full. He left Mr Burton £25 and his wife 'any foodstuffs in the house or house linen they require'. To his youngest brother Bernard he bequeathed his stamp collection and his gold watch; to William Clark, the editor of *Athletic Review*, he left 'all my books, mss, unsold books, photographs and diaries'; and to Peter G. Gavuzzi, 'my former business partner', he left the one thing the recipient would most treasure: 'my largest scrapbook'. It is a huge volume of press cuttings covering their adventures in the States and in Canada.

III

Peter Gavuzzi started keeping a diary again in 1959, but with one exception all the entries for that year simply recorded his betting life. The exception was a two-word entry for 7th September. It read: 'Newton's death'. He could find nothing else to say about it. For the next several years, until the autumn of 1968, the diaries record a humdrum and predictable life. He works as a school cleaner and caretaker in Uxbridge, employed by Middlesex County Council. He lives alone in different bedsits, and most weeks he seems to lose more money than he wins on the horses. It seems to be his one passion, and just as he did with his depression at Le Moulinet, he 'hides' his losses by recording them in French. '*Perd au chevaux, quatre livres*' is the entry for 19th July 1960. The only social events he mentions are visits to or from his brother Charlie, who still lives in Brixton. Each summer, at first by motorbike and then by train, he heads west on holiday. He goes first to Steeple Ashton in Wiltshire to stay with a friend called Ned Whiting. Whiting had a smallholding, with horses; he also had a relative or friend by the name of Joan, with whom it is likely Gavuzzi had a brief affair. In 1962, for instance, he spent four days in Steeple Ashton and for each of them he put an X in his diary after mentioning going out with Joan – just as he did with Mimi in France. He then habitually went on to the Isle of Wight, to stay with a friend called Ben Sharpe for what was left of his annual leave.

But there was one important change in 1962. Gavuzzi had always put the addresses of those closest to him inside the front cover of his little diaries – for years they had been his brother's and Newton's – and that year, for the first time, he included his son Peter's address in Derby. He also listed his three grandchildren's birthdays. (Though he evidently did not refer to it sufficiently often, as his diary entry for 16th February reads: 'Guy's birthday. I was late with card and Dinky Toys.') That August his son and his family joined Gavuzzi for the Isle of Wight section of his holiday, and from the next year he included a visit to Chaddesden, near Derby, in his holiday routine. Given that Gavuzzi's son died in 1985, and no letters between the two Peters survive, we can only speculate as to how they managed to build any trust between them, since Gavuzzi had given up on being an involved father long before Nellie divorced him in 1951. Certainly his son told his own children little about their paternal grandfather, and it was by chance that one of them, Guy, came to know that he had been a runner who had achieved extraordinary things. He was in his late teens, Guy Gavuzzi remembers, when he called on his grandfather in Steeple Ashton and happened to pick up an athletics magazine that had been left on the coffee table. It contained an article entitled 'The Great Gavuzzi'. It was the first he knew of it.

Arthur Newton's death broke Gavuzzi's most important link to the world of athletics, and to road-running in particular. Few competitors would have made their way to his bedsit in the way that they had gravitated to Cottingham Chase. But there are certain clues in his diaries that suggest he kept in touch with at least some of Newton's circle. In September 1960 he 'assisted' Jackie Mekler when the Johannesburg athlete set a new record for the London to Brighton run. In January 1966 he noted the death, aged ninety-one, of Joe Binks; and in February 1968 he recorded that of Georg Hackenschmidt. But the most poignant indication of the hold that his former mentor and partner still had on him came a few months later, on 17th June. 'Another try for a room in Cottingham Chase. All full.'

In the summer of 1968 Peter Gavuzzi was two years away from being able to take some sort of pension and retire – to Wiltshire, he hoped. He was sixty-three years old, he was largely on his own in life, and it was more than forty years since he had achieved the only remarkable things he had ever done. The few people who knew and cared about them were either dead or living in South Africa or Australia. He was fated, it seemed, to end up as at best a footnote in an obscure branch of athletics whose story nobody, in any case, was telling. But the final twelve years of Peter Gavuzzi's life, up to his death in 1981, were not to be ones of slow and obscure decline. They were to be years in which he was finally, and surprisingly, discovered, recognised and honoured.

The process began when a letter arrived at his Ruislip bedsit in early September 1968, just after he had returned from his annual trip to Steeple Ashton. The writer was Bruce Tulloh, one of Britain's most successful distance runners of the 1960s (he had been European 5,000 metres champion in 1962) and he wanted to pick Gavuzzi's brains. 'I met Pete Gavuzzi first while I was watching the London to Brighton race,' Tulloh wrote in his 1970 memoir *Four Million Footsteps*; 'when he heard what I was planning he invited me back to his bed-sitter in Ruislip. It was in a dim suburban area, in a group of dull houses, where I found the abode of this amazing man.' Tulloh, needing a fresh challenge after retiring from the track, had decided to try and set a new record for running across America; and, as he recognised immediately, there was only one person in the country who could tell him what it was like. 'He [Gavuzzi] was very keen to talk about it, and it was an amazing story. We think we're quite good runners nowadays, but the fact that people could run that distance day after day on poor roads without decent shoes, was quite amazing. His story was very inspiring. I thought if people could cope with that, then I can certainly cope with doing it under modern conditions.'*

Tulloh was able to fund his attempt at a transcontinental record through deals with *The Observer* and Thames Television, to both of which he would be providing regular material. He must also have told people at Thames about Gavuzzi and the Pyle races, because in early February 1969 the TV company

---

* In conversation with the author.

got in touch with the elderly athlete in Ruislip. Gavuzzi's diary entries, in response, became more forthcoming than they had been for several years:

February 8: Met Miss Gambles from Thames Tele. We had lunch and talked a lot on Pyle races. To do with Tulloh's races [*sic*] in America. Nothing settled.

February 9: Lots of home-work on the Pyle race. May have to make a recording with Thames.

February 18: Today I went to Thames Television studios in Kingsway to do a film recording of the Pyle race. Quite an ordeal. Lasted two hours.

February 28: No results of my recording with Thames yet.

March 8: No news yet on my TV recording.

When Bruce Tulloh began his epic run on 21st April, Gavuzzi had still heard nothing from Thames Talevision. But among the papers he left in his Wiltshire cottage at his death are newspaper cuttings showing that he followed Tulloh's progress day by day:

June 18: Today Tulloh finished his run across America. 2,860 miles, 64 days.

July 1: My interview about Tulloh went on. OK.

Gavuzzi's interview was finally broadcast on the same day

as the formal Investiture of the Prince of Wales, which the elderly runner would doubtless have watched on television – beyond the world of athletics, his political opinions were consistently royalist and conservative. But Bruce Tulloh was not left with the impression of a meek or deferential man. 'Peter Gavuzzi was very pleased to talk to someone who knew what running meant, who could appreciate the nature of his feat. He had a great deal of self-respect. He was very proud of being a working-class lad who'd achieved great things.' He had indeed, but the sadness of Gavuzzi's life is that his great achievements – his runs across America – were products of his early twenties, and that for more than fifty years nothing else came close to matching them.

'Well here's my last lap. Seven weeks to go,' wrote Gavuzzi in his diary on 10th August 1970; and on 25th September he could record that it had been his 'last day as a working man', and that the staff at the school he had been looking after had presented him with a pipe, a pipe-stand and some tobacco. It was the gift that people always seemed to give him. He had already found a small cottage to rent in Steeple Ashton – part of a whitewashed Victorian terrace near the crest of a long hill, with open fields on the other side of the road, giving broad views down towards Trowbridge. His last diary is a small red notebook that covers the period from summer 1972 until his death in January 1981. Where in London he had obsessively noted down his life in the betting shop, here, in the countryside, his diary was very largely a record of his walks and his occasional runs. He set himself daily or weekly targets, and whether or not he could meet them came to be indicative of his general state of health. His ability to take physical exercise was also, in true Newtonian fashion, the key to his sense of well-being: and his long-standing anxiety over his recurring urinary problems was never far away:

November 1974: I will close this mileage diary, with no long walks, a little leg worry.

April 1975: No walking. Had infected water trouble.

May 1976: This has been a good month for me. I'm walking real good.

October 1977: I can go out nearly every day. I'm feeling really fit.

June 1979: I have decided to give up jogging, too much strain on the old legs.

Not long after Peter Gavuzzi settled in Steeple Ashton, Andy Milroy – one of the world's leading authorities on ultra-distance running – came to live just down the road in Trowbridge. Milroy has published widely on the sport's history, especially online, and is the international co-ordinator of the Association of Road Racing Statisticians. Once he found out who he had as a near-neighbour he took to walking over to Steeple Ashton to spend afternoons with Gavuzzi; and it was the elderly athlete who did most of the talking, grateful once again to have a knowledgeable and appreciative audience. Milroy thinks that he was able to coax some long-repressed and uncomfortable feelings from Gavuzzi about his loss of the 1929 Pyle race and what this had meant for the rest of his life: 'He was very bitter that he had been robbed of recognition in terms of winning the 1929 race. That was something he was very concerned about. He felt he should have won the race, and that if he'd won it would have made him feel more complete. The fact that he didn't win the race meant that somehow he hadn't achieved what he was capable of doing, and he'd been stopped from doing that.' Milroy says Gavuzzi told him that C.C. Pyle had specifically asked him to slow down over the final stages of the 1929 run so as to create more excitement and entice a larger gate to see the denouement at Wrigley Field; and when Milroy asked him why he agreed to it, Gavuzzi said simply that, as a professional runner, he had no option but to do what the promoter wanted.

The Lancashire-based sports writer Harry Berry takes a very different view of this defining moment in Gavuzzi's life. Berry contacted Gavuzzi in the mid-1970s asking if he would collaborate on a book about the two Pyle races. Gavuzzi was thrilled: at last there seemed a possibility that his story would be told, and he put whatever materials he had at Berry's disposal. The writer – whose detailed day-by-day narrative of the Transcontinentals was eventually published privately in 1990 – came to have a deep respect and affection for Gavuzzi; but he developed a different and critical view of Arthur Newton: 'Newton was a very difficult man. He was very thorough, an egotist, very dogmatic. He'd had very troubled relationships with native Africans, he was a man who was seldom wrong in his own eyes, believed he was the best runner who'd ever been born, and he was a prickly man.' As we have seen, Newton was often an obstinate obsessive. He certainly regarded most black Africans with disdain, and he never had any doubt that his achievements on the road were extraordinary. But we have also seen that he could express great generosity towards others – Gavuzzi included – and Harry Berry's condemnation of him is echoed by few others. Berry is convinced that Newton bossed Gavuzzi around at crucial moments in their partnership, nowhere more so than at the end of the 1929 race. The latter, he is convinced, wanted to stand up to Pyle as he and Salo were approaching Los Angeles; just as he also wanted to protest at the way he was robbed of victory at the Wrigley Field marathon. But Newton, Berry argues, persuaded his partner not to do so: 'Peter Gavuzzi would have challenged it, but for the fact that Arthur Newton told him that Englishmen don't challenge decisions. Newton was steeped in the old British colonialism and the way we held our heads up high even in adversity, and he thought it was demeaning to have to challenge that.' Gavuzzi certainly regretted being cheated out of receiving a potentially life-changing cheque in 1929, and, as we have seen, he tried for years to get Pyle to pay up. But there is no evidence that he ever blamed Newton for the disappointment or suspected that his partner was somehow doing Pyle's dirty work for him. Harry Berry, it seems fair to suggest from the language he uses, came to harbour a certain antagonism towards Newton because he saw him, perhaps too uncritically, as representative of a white colonial ruling elite.

In September 1978 Peter Gavuzzi wrote to John Jewell, a leading figure in the Road Runners Club (who had himself interviewed Gavuzzi at length for the Club's magazine in 1976) with an update on Harry Berry's project. 'Berry who is writing my book [sic] on the Pyle race has just completed the last chapter. He's sent me the manuscript and I found it very good. He has done a great deal of research work, and found quite a few of the men still alive, all around 80 to 95 years.' The well-known Devonshire publishers David and Charles were fascinated by the story Berry had to tell and expressed a firm interest in the book. But they were less than convinced by his style and held back from offering a contract. Then in the spring of 1980 the editor who had initially been responsible for the manuscript, Geoffrey Household, mentioned Peter Gavuzzi and the Pyle races to an old friend of his, Will Wyatt, a senior (and sports-mad) producer in the documentary department at BBC television. Household also, evidently, spelled out his reservations about Harry Berry's manuscript. Wyatt went down to Steeple Ashton to see Gavuzzi and was sufficiently fascinated to return as soon as he could – this time with a tape recorder. He interviewed the elderly athlete at length. On 13th May he wrote Gavuzzi a gracious letter, thanking him for his patience in going over the 1928 and 1929 races again, and adding, 'I am keen to do something, but I am not sure what. When the tapes have been transcribed I will go through them and get in touch with you again to let you know what is on my mind.'

Three months later, in August, Gavuzzi received some clarification from Geoffrey Household, who wrote to say that Will Wyatt would be making a programme about the races, and 'may want himself to rewrite Mr Berry's book'. But his confidence about a possible television project was misplaced. In late November Wyatt himself got back in touch with Gavuzzi. 'I have been trying to arrange the possibility of making a documentary film about you and your great runs,' he wrote, 'but I am not sure there is the money around here at the moment. But in any case I would like to go ahead and write a book about the "Bunion Derbies".' Wyatt was to go on to become Managing Director of BBC Television, and the demands of his career made sure that the book never appeared.

Neither did the film. If the BBC lacked the money, Peter Gavuzzi lacked the time. Wyatt's letter had reached him in hospital in Bath. He was dying of prostate cancer.

Gavuzzi had had problems with what he always referred to as his 'water works' ever since his internment at La Caserne during the war; but it was only in June 1980 that he found out how serious his condition had become. His diary entry for that month linked his own distressing problem with the relentless rain that fell on England throughout that summer: 'My water works went wrong and I went to see the doctor. It wasn't what I thought, that my water was infected, it's much worse. I'm now incontinent, the old man's complaint. So I'm stuck with it now. Weather has been just awful. Rain and winds.' 'I'm doing very little walking, but I must keep going,' he added defiantly. July brought no relief, either inside or out: 'There is little summer weather. We're getting too much rain. I'm miserable with my water works. Bed wetting is a problem.' In September there was even worse news – a definite diagnosis of cancer. 'Things are very bad for me,' he summed up at the end of the month. 'The doctor came and I was sent to St Martin's hospital. I had an operation on my prostate gland. I was 14 days in hospital. I'm very weak. I lost 1½ stones in weight. I came back to the cottage on the 19th. I'm having a job managing, but I'll make it.' He was told he needed what he called 'radium treatment': there were to be twenty sessions, and they would be carried out in Bristol. This was too far from Steeple Ashton for Gavuzzi to be able to get there and back in a day; and, in any case, he had no one to drive him. So on 2nd December he was moved into Combe Park Hospital in Bath. His diary suggests that he never quite accepted how serious his condition was. 'This morning I was sick,' he wrote on 4th December, 'but I don't think it was anything to do with the treatment. It was a strong cup of tea what upset my stomach.' The same day brought a letter from his son in Derby, saying that he hoped to get down to the West Country. He never did, and the saddest aspect of Gavuzzi's diary for his month of radio-therapy in December 1980 is his constant expression of lone-liness. On more than one occasion he mentions being left alone at weekends, while others undergoing the same treat-ment were allowed home. His only visitor was a neighbour from Steeple Ashton called Brian, who came with his son on Christmas Day. 'I'm feeling the effects of this treatment,' Gavuzzi admitted on 29th December. His final diary entry was for 2nd January 1981. 'My last ride to Bristol for treat-ment, then home.' It was to be his last ride home as well. Three days later Peter Gavuzzi was dead.

He did not live to read a book or hear a radio broadcast or see a film about what he and Arthur Newton had achieved together. But in his last years Peter Gavuzzi did experience the interest and the admiration of others – Bruce Tulloh, Harry Berry, Will Wyatt – who recognised his rare qualities and who hoped to communicate them to a wider world. His near-neighbour Andy Milroy, though, was able to show Gavuzzi one surprising piece of public recognition. It was an entry in a book of no little significance to an athlete. Despite the fact that Gavuzzi had come second, Milroy had been able to persuade the editors of the *Guinness Book of Records* to include him. The category was 'Longest Running Race' – the 1929 Transcontinental. After giving the details of Johnny Salo's run, the entry goes on: 'His elapsed time of 525 hours, 57 minutes and 20 seconds (giving a mean speed of 11.21 kilometres or

6.97 miles per hour) left him only 2 minutes and 43 seconds ahead of Englishman Peter "Pietro" Gavuzzi.'

'I don't think he ever valued himself as highly as he should have done,' Milroy says, 'and I think that probably made him feel a lot better.' His last memory of Gavuzzi is of the old athlete 'sitting in his armchair, with his legs crossed, his pipe stuck in the corner of his mouth, just very quiet and very peaceful'. On 13th January Will Wyatt sat down and wrote a letter of condolence to Peter Gavuzzi the younger: 'I was very sorry to hear of the death of your father. I only met him twice but I spent many hours with him on each occasion and became very fond of him. He was delightfully helpful, generous and straightforward to me. I enjoyed his company enormously and he was full of fun. I do hope that he did not suffer, and that he left this life with the dignity and courage he showed while he was alive.'

Peter Gavuzzi is buried in the churchyard of the fine medieval parish church of St Mary the Virgin at Steeple Ashton. His simple headstone describes him as 'A Great Marathon Runner', adding the lines: 'I have fought the good fight, I have finished the race.' Perhaps a more apt and individual epitaph would be what Arthur Newton said of his old friend and partner: 'He was a permanently good-natured man, as are all who are in splendid physical trim.'

IV

Newton and Gavuzzi were unlikely but genuine friends and they formed an unlikely partnership. They differed in almost every possible way – in class background, in age, in education, in what they read and the music they listened to, in their interest in women, in their ability with words, in their social

331

confidence – yet they shared something that they shared with no one else, and it made them deeply at ease in each other's company. In one sense what they shared was an ambivalence about Britain. In their different ways they came across as very English, certainly to people meeting them for the first time. Newton was easily taken for a 'Victorian gentleman', Gavuzzi for a 'cockney lad'. They both loved the English countryside and were uncritical of British social and political institutions – with the exception, of course, of the Amateur Athletic Association. But they both became who they were elsewhere; and they were both more valued elsewhere.

Gavuzzi, of course, was the child of immigrants. He grew up in a Mediterranean household and, at least as long as his mother was alive, could refer to Piedmont as 'home'. It seems apt that his first proper job was on boats that took him away across the seas; and he was to spend his most active decades in places that required him to speak French. Having a wife and son in England only made him more reluctant to return across the Channel or the Atlantic. Newton had grown into a man by leaving England (and his censorious father) behind. He had gone to a place where ironically he was doubly English – by being neither black nor Dutch – and the campaign he mounted against the Afrikaner-dominated government of South Africa was in the name of future British settlers. But it came to be England-in-Africa that he identified with, not England itself; and once he had settled in Ruislip his support for the likes of Ballington, Hayward and Mekler confirmed his identification with southern Africans – white ones, it has to be said. He was at ease with them. There seems something expatriate about his life in Cottingham Chase; and when Gavuzzi eventually came back to England to lead his rather meagre and marginal life as a school caretaker, he found his richest human sustenance in Newton's household of outsiders and foreigners. Neither of them was embedded or rooted in English life. Their rejection by the AAA stood for more than an exclusion from athletics.

This is to link Newton and Gavuzzi in terms of something that they both lacked. But they also, of course, carried with them something that was unique, that no one else in the whole country had experienced – their participation in the Pyle races of 1928 and 1929. These, and the subsequent years of hand-to-mouth professional running in Canada, provided them with layer upon layer of memory, anecdote and shared respect. One can imagine them returning time after time to that moment in 1928 when they met unexpectedly in what Gavuzzi called the 'Jungle' of Arizona, and realised they were alone and lost in the vastness of the American West. Or one can imagine how a sharp winter morning in Middlesex would turn their minds back to the unimaginable cold of the Quebec, across which they had stomped on snowshoes. The 'Transcontinentals', the 'Bunioneers', were a race apart; and Newton and Gavuzzi were the only ones in Britain. It was this, also, that ensured an equality in their relationship. Newton had been the favourite in 1928, the star attraction: he was the multiple world-record holder and C.C. Pyle's right-hand man. But it had been the young, unknown Gavuzzi who had led the race for weeks, and who had enthralled Newton with the power and grace of his running. In 1929 it was Gavuzzi who became the star, who was the rightful winner of the world's hardest race. How one ran was, for Newton, a metaphor for how one approached life; and he never lost a profound respect for Peter Gavuzzi. Where others might have seen a cheerful but nondescript and unsuccessful man, Newton saw a hero. He knew Gavuzzi in a way that nobody else did.

Their genius linked them, and it isolated them, because their genius was for a sort of running that the 'official' world of athletics did not recognise. This world had been created in the Victorian public schools, and had then been institution-alised by their great admirer Pierre de Coubertin, the leading force behind the establishment of the modern Olympic Games. Regular competition at national and international level led unavoidably to the creation of a canon of events for which records could be set and progressively bettered. The canon drew its inspiration from ancient Greece, so no race longer than the marathon could be considered. Any definition is also an exclusion and a limitation; and any definition produces institutions that see their job as protecting and preserving it. 'Athletics' came to be what the AAA and the IOC decided it was, just as they determined who could or could not compete. But there were many people whose skills and instincts lay outside the canon of permitted events – and none were more excluded than those for whom twenty-six miles was too short a distance to interest them. 'Each person, particularly distance runners,' says Andy Milroy, 'has got a particular distance they're really good at. If they're lucky it will be the marathon. But if it's longer than the marathon they'll get less notice: and if it's something that's very long and that's difficult to put on then you're in a tough spot.' Peter Gavuzzi, it is worth remembering, had been described by Arthur Newton as someone who got into his stride 'after a thousand miles or so'; which was why, Milroy says, he was so intent on getting the *Guinness Book of Records* to recognise Gavuzzi's 1929 run. 'His success was in long sustained racing over a stage race. That's where he used his brain, that's where he was strategically very good. And he never had another opportunity to run that sort of distance.'

Gavuzzi and Newton lived the frustration of having a rare and extraordinary skill for which there was no longer a market. They can best be seen as the last of the 'pedestrians', the professional foot-racers who had so enthralled the crowds of late eighteenth- and early nineteenth-century England – men like Captain Barclay, who at Newmarket in the summer of 1809 ran a mile every hour for a thousand hours; or like George Wilson, who in 1815 ran fifty miles a day for twenty days at Blackheath. The crowds who came to see Wilson were so huge that they frightened the authorities into insisting that he stopped. Given that tens of thousands flocked to Hyde Park to welcome Arthur Newton at the end of his record-breaking 100-mile run from Bath in January 1928, C.C. Pyle's vision of a Tour de France-type event on foot does not seem entirely fanciful. But it would only have been of interest to professional runners, and in twentieth-century Britain they were no longer deemed worthy of public recognition. They would have got neither sponsorship nor press coverage.

Since Newton and Gavuzzi's running days amateurism has died an inevitable death, and elite athletes in Britain have become civil servants, paid by the state to break records and win medals for the good and glory of the nation. They are cosseted and monitored and tested; how they use their time is overseen and checked; what they eat and drink is carefully selected. They travel with entourages of physiotherapists, masseurs, podiatrists, psychiatrists and dietitians. Even those who have never been near an illegal performance-enhancing substance are somehow products of a system, not quite themselves in the raw. Men like Newton and Gavuzzi most certainly were, and Peter Radford – Olympic sprinter and historian of the great age of British pedestrianism – thinks we should honour them all the more for that: 'What we see in these athletes is a particularly tough, self-centred, problem-solving athlete. They're not doing it because of the publicity, the fifteen minutes of fame, they're doing it because they find in it something irresistible that helps them express themselves. And they become immeasurably strong because they've done it themselves. They've solved every problem, they've made every decision, it is theirs, they own it.' Radford thinks we should pay particular attention to what Peter Gavuzzi was taking on, as a twenty-two-year-old with no experience of distance running, when he set off from Los Angeles in March 1928. 'If you imagine him standing on that starting line, there were no contingencies, there was no medical team, you can bet your bottom dollar there were no fancy sleeping arrangements. He didn't have any of that. For us to comprehend how a man on his own can prepare himself and take on a task like that without any safety nets of any sort . . . This man is monumentally strong, and not just a sporting hero but a hero in terms of human endeavour.'

In 1996 the Japanese novelist Haruki Murakami (for whom running every day is, he says, 'a lifeline') entered the famous Lake Saroma ultra-marathon in Hokkaido in the country's far north. For some time Murakami had made sure that he ran one full competitive marathon each year, but this, at sixty-two miles, was almost two and half times the distance. In his memoir/meditation about his obsession, *What I Talk About When I Talk About Running*, which was published in England in 2009, he says that 'no normal person would ever do anything so foolhardy'; and the day obviously had a profound effect on him:

> When I look back on that race I can see that it had a lot of meaning for me as a runner. I don't know what sort of general significance running sixty-two miles by yourself has, but as an action that deviates from the ordinary yet doesn't violate basic values, you'd expect it to afford you a special sort of self-awareness. It should add a few new elements to your inventory in understanding who you are . . . For better or worse, this happened to me and I was transformed.

After 26.2 miles there was a white line across the road and a sign to tell the runners they had reached the marathon mark, and Murakami experienced 'a slight shiver' passing through him as he crossed it. After thirty-four miles he changed his clothes and had to put on a larger pair of shoes as his feet had become so swollen. The next fifteen miles were the worst. He says he felt 'like a piece of beef being run slowly through a meat grinder', and 'like a car trying to go up a slope with the parking brake on'. The temptation to rest, or to walk for a bit, was intense; but he resisted, and then 'around the forty-seventh mile I felt like I'd passed through something'. He had reached a state of exhaustion that somehow liberated him, and he knew then that he would finish the race. 'After that,' he writes in a passage that could have been penned by Arthur Newton, 'I didn't have to think any more. Or, more precisely, there wasn't the need to try to consciously think about not thinking. All I had to do was go with the flow and I would get there automatically.' By the end of the race he had so accepted his exhaustion that he felt 'there was nothing more I could ask of the world'.

This, ultimately, was what underlay the friendship between Arthur Newton and Peter Gavuzzi. There was, of course, mutual admiration and trust; there was the excitement of adventure and risk; there was their needing each other to earn a living; but most important was their mutual recognition of the other as someone who only felt fully alive when running, ideally alone, over very great distances. It was the solitude of their running that brought them together. Newton theorised at length about the links between running and feeling truly oneself. Gavuzzi simply said that his ability to run huge distances enabled him to think that he was 'somebody in the world'. It came to the same thing. Neither could stop running for his life.

A Note on Sources

Running for Their Lives is based, most importantly, on the personal papers of Arthur Newton and Peter Gavuzzi. Of Newton's four published books, *Running in Three Continents* (1940) and *Races and Training* (1949) provide invaluable auto-biographical material (though they must at times be taken with a pinch of salt), while his idiosyncratic ideas about athletics were spelt out in *Running* (1935) and *Commonsense Athletics* (1947). His prolific athletic journalism was also consulted.

Fortunately Newton's search for athletic fame in the interests of publicising his grievance against the South African government led to his keeping voluminous scrapbooks of cuttings from the Natal press. These were the basis for my account of the 'Newton Case'. Even more valuable was the volume Newton described in his will as 'my largest scrapbook', the one that he left to Gavuzzi. This contains hundreds of cuttings from the American press about the two Pyle races of 1928 and 1929.

It was in relation to Newton's life in South Africa and Rhodesia that I needed most help from the secondary literature. Of particular value have been Leonard Thompson,

A History of South Africa (New Haven, Connecticut, 2000); Shula Marks, *Reluctant Rebellion: Disturbances in Natal 1906–8* (Oxford, 1970); Robert Holland, 'The British Empire and the Great War, 1914–1918', in Judith M. Brown and Wm Roger Louis (eds), *The Oxford History of the British Empire: The Twentieth Century* (Oxford, 1999); T. Dunbar Moodie, *The Rise of Afrikanerdom* (Los Angeles, 1975); Francis Wilson, 'Farming', in Monica Wilson and Leonard Thompson (eds), *The Oxford History of South Africa*, Vol. II (Oxford, 1971); and Robert E. Baldwin, *Economic Development and Export Growth, Northern Rhodesia 1920–1960* (Berkeley, California, 1966).

For C.C. Pyle as a pioneering sports promoter I learned most from Jim Reisler, *Cash and Carry; the Spectacular Rise and Hard Fall of C.C. Pyle* (Jefferson, North Carolina, 2009); John M. Carroll, *Red Grange and the Rise of Modern Football* (Champaign, Illinois, 2004); and Larry Engelmann, *The Goddess and the American Girl* (Oxford, 1988). I also consulted Ira Morton (ed.), *The Red Grange Story* (Champaign, Illinois, 1988); and Bill Crawford, *All American – The Rise and Fall of Jim Thorpe* (Chichester, 2005).

For the cultural context of the two Transcontinental Races there was Kevin Starr, *Material Dreams; Southern California Through the 1920s* (Oxford, 1990); Burton W. Peretti, *Nighclub City – Politics and Amusement in Manhattan* (Philadelphia, Pennsylvania, 2007); Peter B. Dedek, *Hip to the Trip – A Cultural History of Route 66* (Albuquerque, New Mexico, 2007); and Carol Martin; *Dance Marathons – Performing American Culture of the 1920s and 1930s* (Jackson, Mississippi, 1994).

Two engaging narrative accounts of the 1928 Transcontinental appeared after I had started my research: Geoff Williams, *C.C. Pyle's Amazing Foot Race* (Emmaus, Pennsylvania, 2007) and

Charles B. Kastner, *Bunion Derby* (Albuquerque, New Mexico, 2007). Neither has much on Newton or Gavuzzi, but I gleaned fascinating detail from them both about other competitors and about daily life on the road for the 'Bunioneers'. The pioneering Transcontinental narrative was the one published privately by Harry Berry in 1990, *From LA to New York, from New York to LA*, and I depended on its matchless race statistics.

For the political and cultural background to Newton and Gavuzzi's time in French Canada I turned to R.F. Holland, *Britain and the Commonwealth Alliance 1918–1939* (Cambridge, 1981); Henri Bourassa, *The French Canadians in the British Empire* (Montreal, 1902); Ramsay Cook (ed.), *French-Canadian Nationalism* (Toronto, 1978); John C. Weaver, *Hamilton – An Illustrated History* (Toronto, 1982); Bruce Kidd, *The Struggle for Canadian Sport* (Toronto, 1996); and B.J.C. McKercher and L. Aronsen (eds), *The North Atlantic Triangle; Anglo-American-Canadian Relations 1902–1956* (Toronto, 1996). For Gavuzzi's achievements as a trainer of Canadian marathon runners. I depended on David Blackie, *Boston - the Canadian Story* (Ottowa, 1984).

To flesh out Peter Gavuzzi's time in the Saint-Denis camp I was grateful for William Webb's *Internment Camp Journals, July 1940–December 1942*, which are held in the archives of the Imperial War Museum in London. There is also some material about the camp in W. Wynne Mason, *Official History of New Zealand in the Second World War: Prisoners of War* (Wellington, 1954).

To understand why Arthur Newton was so angry with the Amateur Athletic Association in the 1940s and early 1950s I consulted the minutes of its General Committee and reports of its Permission to Write, Broadcast or Lecture Committee. These are in the AAA archive, which is held in the Special Collections of Birmingham University Library. Also useful was Gordon Pirie's autobiography, *Running Wild* (London, 1961). For those interested in learning more about Percy Cerutty, the book to consult is Graem Sims, *Why Die? The Extraordinary Percy Cerutty* (Long Island City, New York, 2004).

Running for Their Lives is a book about two remarkable men who happened to express themselves by running. It is not a contribution to athletics history – something I am not qualified to make. For those who want an evaluation of Arthur Newton as an athlete in relation to others, and full descriptions of his most important runs, I warmly recommend Rob Hadgraft's *Tea with Mr Newton* (Rayleigh, Essex, 2009). It valuably complements my own work.

Acknowledgements

For the past ten years or so I have tried to keep the last Saturday in October free, as that is when the annual 'Historians and Sport' conference takes place at De Montfort University in Leicester. This admirable event is organised by the International Centre for Sports History and Culture, and *Running for Their Lives* owes its existence to a chance meeting that I had there in 2002. Earlier that year I had interviewed Richard Holt, a professor at the Centre and the doyen of British sports historians, for a radio documentary about Pierre de Coubertin, and he had kindly suggested that I present a paper about my broadcasting work at the De Montfort conference. While there, I was introduced to the archivist John Bromhead, who mentioned the National Centre for Athletics Literature at Birmingham University Library, which he had helped create and had catalogued. I have never been an athlete – a fast bowler's run-up is distance enough for me – and have never had any particular interest in athletics history. But I am always on the lookout for good sports-history stories, so when I found myself in Birmingham a year or so later I arranged to visit the University Library's Special Collections to see if anything in their athletics archive caught my eye. One catalogue entry for an oral-history tape immediately did: 'Peter Gavuzzi talks about running across America in 1928.' I had never heard of Gavuzzi, nor of such a run. But I was curious, and when I read the transcript of his conversation with John Jewell I knew immediately that I had chanced upon a remarkable story. So my first thanks go to John Bromhead, who quite unintentionally set me off on my long pursuit of Peter Gavuzzi and Arthur Newton.

The possibility of a book about them first came to me when I discovered that the Birmingham University archive also contained eight large boxes of the papers left by Arthur Newton at his death in 1959. They were still largely uncatalogued when I started going through them in the autumn of 2007, and discovering their contents was archival work at its best. I look back on many visits to Birmingham with great pleasure, and I am grateful to the staff of the library's Special Collections for their unfailing courtesy and helpfulness. That the gems housed in the Barber Institute of Fine Arts are but a minute's walk from the library was an added bonus.

Peter Gavuzzi's papers have no such imposing institutional home, but consulting them has been just as great a pleasure. They fill a large cardboard box at the home of his grandson, Guy, on the outskirts of Derby. He and his wife Susie have welcomed me there on innumerable occasions, and have plied me with tea and sandwiches while I have worked at their dining table in the cheerful company of their budgerigar. I am hugely grateful to them, and I hope Guy Gavuzzi feels that this book does justice to a grandfather I know he loved and revered.

My thanks also to the ultra-marathon expert Andy Milroy, in Trowbridge, for letting me spend a day going through Arthur Newton's fascinating letters to Len Dilks that are in his possession; to Alexander Stewart in Italy, for help with the genealogy of the Gavuzzi name in Piedmont; to the staff at the Imperial War Museum archives; and to that of the British Library, both in St Pancras and at the Newspaper Collection in Colindale. My brother Chris helped at a vital stage by offering me his apartment in Majorca as a place where I could write, knowing that I would not be interrupted.

I was able, fortunately, to track down a handful of people who got to know Peter Gavuzzi in his old age, and their memories of him feature in the final chapter of the book. My thanks to the Lancashire sports writer Harry Berry, to the champion middle-distance runner Bruce Tulloh, and to Andy Milroy. The sprinter and historian Peter Radford also helped me by assessing Newton and Gavuzzi in the context of the great pedestrians of the eighteenth and nineteenth centuries, about whom he has written so perceptively.

My agent Mark Stanton ('Stan') has been a constant source of encouragement, and I hope he thinks the book justifies the risk I know he felt he was taking when he added an unpublished middle-aged broadcaster to his stable of authors. At Yellow Jersey my thanks go to Tristan Jones, to Matt Phillips and especially to my editor Rowan Yapp. 'You'll be in good hands with Rowan,' Stan said. How right he was.

As I have been writing in my ground-floor study, my wife – the psycho-social studies academic Lynn Froggett – has been writing upstairs in hers. We don't often compare notes, but I cannot but be influenced by her tireless commitment to the task in hand. A sign of her doggedness and single-mindedness is that, despite all the years she has lived with me, she still refuses to see the slightest value in anything to do with sport. Will this book change her mind? I doubt it, but I'll still love her.

Index